Administration

Units 1, 2, 3 and 4

Level 1

Carol Carysforth
Mike Neild

www.heinemann.co.uk
✓ Free online support
✓ Useful weblinks
✓ 24 hour online ordering

01865 888058

Endorsed by OCR

Inspiring generations

Heinemann Educational Publishers
Halley Court, Jordan Hill, Oxford OX2 8EJ
Part of Harcourt Education

Heinemann is the registered trademark of
Harcourt Education Limited

© Carol Carysforth, Mike Neild 2003

First published 2003

07 06 05 04
10 9 8 7 6 5 4 3 2

British Library Cataloguing in Publication Data is available
from the British Library on request.

ISBN 0 435 46210 5

Designed by Kamae Design Ltd
Typeset and illustrated by J&L Composition

Original illustrations © Harcourt Education Limited, 2003

Cover design by Tony Richardson at the Wooden Ark Ltd

Printed in the UK by Bath Press Ltd

Every effort has been made to contact copyright holders of material reproduced in this book. Any omissions will be rectified in subsequent printings if notice is given to the publishers.

Websites
There are links to relevant websites in this book. In order to ensure that the links are up to date, that the links work, and that the sites are not inadvertently linked to sites that could be considered offensive, we have made the links available on the Heinemann website at www.heinemann.co.uk/hotlinks. When you access the site, the express code is 2105P.

Tel: 01865 888058 www.heinemann.co.uk

Contents

Acknowledgements   iv
Introduction   v

Unit 1 Preparing routine business documents   1
Unit 2 Working with colleagues and customers   39
Unit 3 Preparing for work in business organisations   81
Unit 4 Following routine office procedures   155

Blank documents for photocopying   209
Index   214

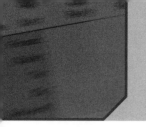

Acknowledgements

The authors would like to thank all friends and colleagues who have contributed to this book by, as ever, providing invaluable advice and information on a wide range of current administrative practices. Special thanks are also due to Linda Mellor, for her super editing, to Anna Fabrizio, our commissioning editor, for her consistently friendly approach and invaluable eye for detail and – as ever – to Margaret Berriman, our publishing director, for her constant support, invaluable friendship and useful ideas!

The authors and publishers would like to thank the following organisations for permission to reproduce copyright material:

BBC Photo Library, page 88
Investors in People, page 131
Stationery reproduced by kind permission of Macmillan Cancer Relief, registered charity number 261017, page 107.

Carol Carysforth and Mike Neild
July 2003

Introduction

This book has been written to introduce you to the skills you will need to work in administration and to help to prepare you for the OCR Level 1 Certificate in Administration.

Administrators today work in a wide variety of organisations and are responsible for carrying out a considerable number of tasks. To do these to a professional standard, they need to master a number of skills. All administrators regularly communicate with other people in writing, over the telephone or face to face. They use a wide range of equipment – from photocopiers and fax machines to their own computer. They need to understand and use office procedures that relate to routine tasks, such as opening and distributing the mail or filing. Probably even more importantly, they need to be able to work productively alongside their colleagues and to be trusted to deal with every customer to the best of their ability, no matter how they may be feeling at the time!

The book covers all these aspects of administration and will help you to learn and practise the basic skills you will need to work in an office. 'Real-life' examples are included in every unit to help you to understand *why* particular skills are important and how they apply in organisations today.

Some people have the misguided view that administrators only do routine tasks so the work can never be very interesting. Nothing could be further from the truth! Although all administrators must be able to do a range of routine tasks, if you continue to develop your skills you will quickly find that the work becomes far more varied. Administrators are highly valued by all organisations for the support they provide to busy managers and other staff, and they often have many opportunities to move onwards or upwards. A quick glance at any administrative job vacancies section on the Internet or in a newspaper will show you the range of tasks carried out by experienced administrators – and the salaries they are offered.

At level 1, you are at the start of your career. However, the skills and knowledge that you learn now are very important, as they are the 'foundation stones' of your future. It is hoped that this book will help you to develop both your abilities and your interest in administrative work, so that – even after you have completed your current course – you will be keen to learn more about the world of administration and able to move onwards in your own career.

Carol Carysforth and Mike Neild
July 2003

Dedication

To Margaret Drew, the tireless editor of *Focus on Business Education* magazine and stalwart of the STBE – with grateful thanks for her constant support and encouragement.

Preparing routine business documents

Introduction

This unit is about written business communications. It is important because you will have to communicate with other people in writing when you are at work. If you have a computer on your desk then you will be expected to compose and send your own emails. If you answer the telephone when someone is out of the office, you will often have to write down a message. These are just two examples of the business documents you will learn about in this unit.

Every time you send a written document, such as an email or message, your English skills are on display. The person receiving your document will know, immediately, whether you can write proper sentences, spell accurately and understand the words you use. In addition, everyone will expect your information to make sense, to be written in a business-like way and to be straightforward, clear and accurate.

This unit will help you to develop these skills.

▲ Written business communication is an essential part of administration work

Unit summary

In this unit you will learn how to prepare six different types of business document. These are listed below:

- ▶ **email** – an electronic message sent by computer.

- ▶ **memo** – this is the internal equivalent to a business letter. It is a document sent from one person in an organisation to another, about a business matter.

- ▶ **message** – this is written information obtained from a telephone call or a visitor which must be passed on to another person.

- ▶ **fax** – a document sent electronically using a fax machine.

- ▶ **business letter** – a letter sent from one business organisation to another about a business matter.

- ▶ **form** – you will not be expected to create a form, but must know how to complete one so that it is accurate. In addition, all the required information must be included. This can often mean you have to access and select information from different sources.

Once you can prepare these documents properly and professionally then you will practise these skills every day when you start work. As you progress in your career, and study at a higher level, you can build on your skills and apply them to other, more complex, documents.

In this unit, you will also learn how to identify, extract and use appropriate information contained in other types of documents, such as tables and leaflets. You will also practise choosing the right words, or vocabulary, and using these in a polite and business-like way, as well as improving your basic English skills, such as spelling and punctuation.

Assessment

Your assessment for this unit will consist of a written examination of two hours. You also have an additional 10 minutes to read the paper before you start writing. The first thing you will read is a brief description of the organisation you work for and your role. All the tasks you have to do will relate to this scenario and your own job role.

There will be four tasks on the examination paper which will test your ability to:

▶ prepare business documents

▶ extract and use relevant information for a specific purpose

▶ use appropriate style and tone, bearing in mind the scenario described in the examination paper

▶ use English accurately.

▼ Understanding emails

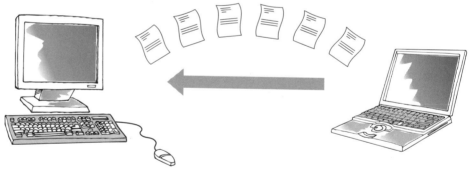

Emails are one of the simplest types of written communications – and also one of the most commonly used. At work, you might find yourself sending several emails every day to your colleagues. Your boss may also ask you to draft emails to send to people outside the organisation on his or her behalf.

You may send emails already – either to your friends if you have a Hotmail account – or to your tutor if you can use email at college. In this case, you can start to develop your email skills immediately!

Key facts about emails

▶ An email is a message, prepared on computer and sent electronically to another person.

▶ Both the sender and the receiver of the email must have a computer and email software.

▶ All email users have an email address. Your own work email address will be set up when you start work. You need a person's email address before you can send them an email. On an internal computer system, within a business organisation, all the email users will be listed in an electronic address book, with their email addresses alongside. You can usually key in a person's name and the system will automatically add the address and send it to the correct person.

▶ If you are sending an external email, then you will usually need to enter the full email address. This always has an '@' sign in the middle. For example, if you have a Hotmail account, your email address is probably: yourname@hotmail.com. Email software includes an address book, in which you can store addresses. Then you need only to enter the person's name and the address book will automatically link the name to the correct address.

▶ You can add attachments to an email. These are other documents held as files on your computer which can be sent with the email.

▶ You can send a copy of an email to another person at the same time as you send the original – or you can send an email to several people simultaneously. This is useful if you need to notify a number of people about something, such as the time and date of a meeting.

▶ You should *never* leave your email screen showing when you are away from your desk. Otherwise someone else can read your mail and may even be tempted to send a joke email in your name! This is a serious offence in most organisations – so never be tempted to do this yourself if someone leaves their email screen unattended. You can usually protect your emails by having your own password which you enter to access your email screen.

Preparing emails – the golden rules

▶ Start by completing the header. This is the top portion of the email. You will need to enter a response against each of the following words:

To: = the email address (or name) of the person to receive it

Cc: = the email address of anyone who has to receive a copy

Subject: = a short title which accurately summarises what the email is about.

▶ If you are sending an **external** email, then you may prefer to start with a short, standard greeting, such as 'Dear (name)' although this isn't essential. If you know the person well, you can use their first name, e.g. Dear Sally. If you do not, or if you are sending the email on behalf of your boss, then use the surname, e.g. Dear Mrs Young.

▶ If you are sending an **internal** email, then it is up to you whether you put a short greeting. However, this must be business-like if you are using email at work, especially when you are addressing people who are senior to you.

▶ Write the message, using normal punctuation. Don't be tempted to repeat question marks or exclamation marks in a business email, for example, 'are you going to the meeting???' *One* question mark is quite enough!

▶ Never type an email using all capital letters. This is called SHOUTING and is considered impolite.

▶ Don't include emotions, such as smiley faces (e.g. ☺).

▶ It is usual to close an external email with a simple statement such as 'Kind regards' or 'Best wishes'. At the end of an internal mail in which you have made a request, an obvious 'ending' is to say 'Thanks'.

▶ Many people prefer to add their name at the end. This is up to you. It isn't essential because your name is shown automatically on the header of your recipient's email. If you decide to put your name then you may put your full name on an external email but usually only your first name on an internal email.

OVER TO YOU!

Justine has prepared three emails this morning. One is an external email to a customer, which she has prepared on behalf of her boss. The second is to a manager in the company. The third is to a colleague who is a friend of Justine's. Note that although Justine's name does not show on these emails at the moment, it will be displayed at the top when they are received.

1 Identify which email is which – and give two reasons in each case for your decision.

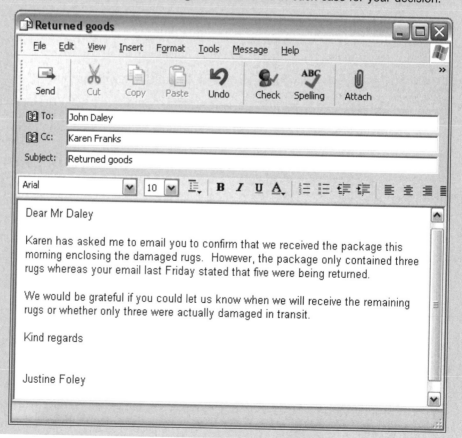

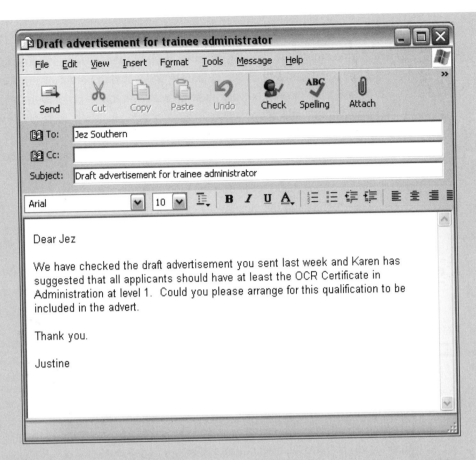

Draft advertisement for trainee administrator

File Edit View Insert Format Tools Message Help

Send Cut Copy Paste Undo Check Spelling Attach

To: Jez Southern
Cc:
Subject: Draft advertisement for trainee administrator

Arial 10

Dear Jez

We have checked the draft advertisement you sent last week and Karen has suggested that all applicants should have at least the OCR Certificate in Administration at level 1. Could you please arrange for this qualification to be included in the advert.

Thank you.

Justine

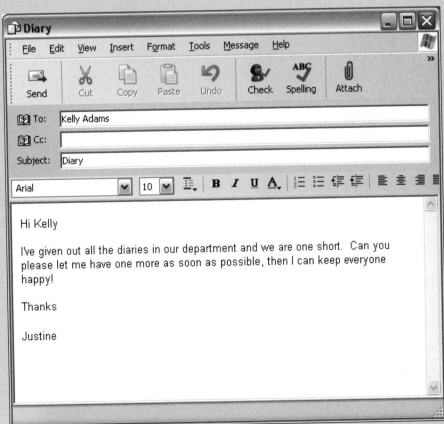

Diary

File Edit View Insert Format Tools Message Help

Send Cut Copy Paste Undo Check Spelling Attach

To: Kelly Adams
Cc:
Subject: Diary

Arial 10

Hi Kelly

I've given out all the diaries in our department and we are one short. Can you please let me have one more as soon as possible, then I can keep everyone happy!

Thanks

Justine

2 Suggest one reason why Justine sent Karen a copy of the email to Mr Daley.

3 Study the emails and then say whether each of the following statements is true or false.

   a) Contracted words (e.g. 'don't', 'we've' and 'couldn't') are allowed in internal emails.

   b) In an email, you can be very informal with everyone – no matter who they are.

   c) You can use well-known abbreviations in an email, such as 'phone' for 'telephone' and 'thanks' for 'thank you'.

   d) You can use text message abbreviations in an email and miss out the vowels, e.g. pse cfm u will b here b4 10.

   e) Emails should be short and to the point.

   f) The greeting and the close will vary, depending upon the recipient.

   g) All emails should have a short, appropriate, subject heading.

COMMUNICATION IN BUSINESS

All email software packages have spellcheckers. If you click on the spellchecker it will go through your email and highlight mis-spelt words. Despite this, however, surveys have shown that many people send very poor emails with terrible spelling and punctuation.

Why is this? Apart from the fact that some people cannot be bothered to use their spellchecker, the other problem is that spellcheckers are very limited. They can never identify words which are *real* words, but have been used wrongly. So if you write 'there' instead of 'their' or key in 'form' instead of 'from' then your spellchecker won't find your mistakes. This also applies if you are preparing any other documents on a computer. So be wary of your spellchecker. Remember to use it, but remember also that it is no substitute for your own checking!

Using English correctly

Your English skills will be seen by everyone who receives your emails. As a first step, make sure you always write in complete sentences and use basic punctuation properly.

▶ A complete sentence must have a subject and a verb. Therefore 'Sarah left' is a short, but complete sentence. 'Sarah' is the subject of the sentence and 'left' is the verb. Unless the other person knows what you are talking about, it is sensible to extend the sentence. You could say 'Sarah left the firm' or 'Sarah left her purse behind' to give your sentence more meaning.

▶ All sentences should start with a capital letter. Normally your sentences will end with a full stop. However, you must remember to put a question mark if you ask a direct question, such as 'Have you received it yet?'

▶ You should remember to put capital letters for:

– names of people and places, e.g. Prince William, New York

– standard abbreviations, e.g. BT, UN, AA

– specific job titles, e.g. Sales Director

– specific organisations, e.g. British Home Stores.

Do *not* put a capital for:

– the seasons of the year

– general directions, e.g. north, south, east and west

– general job titles, e.g. the manager, a tutor

– general organisations, e.g. the college.

▶ If you write 'thank you' in full, remember that it is *two* words. So is 'all right' – there is no such word as 'alright' in the English language!

OVER TO YOU!

1 Two of the following are not complete sentences. Identify them and change them into proper sentences.
a) Thank you for replying so quickly.
b) With reference to your email.
c) Looking forward to it.
d) I'm expecting him to call today.

2 Punctuate each of the following sentences correctly.
a) martin is going to paris in spring
b) the purchasing manager of cooper and fawkes phoned yesterday
c) rebecca worked at the bbc and then moved to the north of england and trained as a teacher
d) will ashraf will be attending college each wednesday from september

3 Maxine is worried because her English skills are poor. She has drafted the following email, which she has to send to all the staff, and has asked you to check it.
a) Identify all the spelling mistakes
b) Identify all the mistakes which would *not* be spotted by Maxine's spellchecker.
c) Identify the words where Maxine should have included an initial capital.
d) Correct all the errors and rewrite the email so that Maxine can send it without any problems.

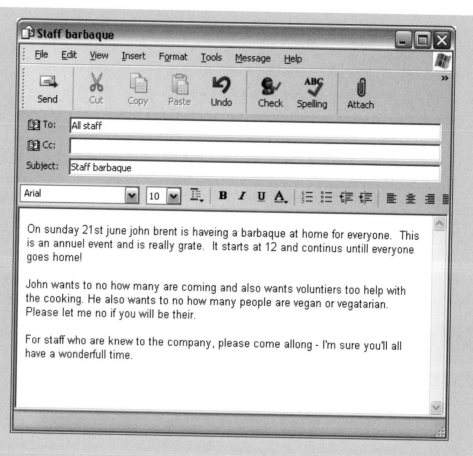

On sunday 21st june john brent is haveing a barbaque at home for everyone. This is an annuel event and is really grate. It starts at 12 and continus untill everyone goes home!

John wants to no how many are coming and also wants voluntiers too help with the cooking. He also wants to no how many people are vegan or vegatarian. Please let me no if you will be their.

For staff who are knew to the company, please come allong - I'm sure you'll all have a wonderfull time.

Check all your answers with your tutor.

▼ Understanding memos

Memos are written documents which are sent only *within* an organisation. Before email became commonplace, memos were the main method of sending written information from one person or department in an organisation to another.

Today, memos are less frequently used – but you must still know how to write them. This is because they are still used when the information is too long or complex for an email or when a written record needs to be added to the file for future reference. You are also wise to send a memo rather than an email to a colleague who rarely uses a computer – otherwise it may be several days before your recipient actually reads it.

Key facts about memos

▶ You send a memo only to a colleague who works for the same organisation as you – never to an external person.

▶ A memo is usually sent about only one topic. This is to help the person who will have to file the document.

▶ All organisations used to have printed forms for memos, with a special header. This is a printed area at the top of the memo, which you can see below. Today, you are often expected to create the header yourself on a computer.

▶ If you need to send multiple copies of a memo (for example, 10 or more), it is usual to print one copy and photocopy the remainder – unless you have a very fast printer.

▶ A memo may be initialled by the sender, rather than signed in full. This proves the sender has read and checked the memo and is quicker than signing an internal document in full.

Preparing memos – the golden rules

▶ The following is an example of a memo header. The order of the items may vary from one business to another, but each item needs completing. You should miss out the 'cc' option if no one is to receive a copy.

MEMO

TO: Jamie Kenyon   CC: Jacqui Barnes

FROM: Sophia Butt

DATE: 23 November 2003

SUBJECT: VENDING MACHINES

▶ There is no greeting or salutation in a memo. After the subject you simply start to write the information.

▶ The style of language in a memo is often quite informal. In this case you could use well-known abbreviations, such as 'thanks' or 'phoned'. However, this is not always the case. A memo about a very serious matter would be written far more formally and such abbrieviations would not be used.

▶ Being informal does *not* mean you should use slang or colloquial expressions! For example, you would write, 'The machine broke again yesterday. It hasn't worked properly for several weeks.' and *not* 'The machine packed up again yesterday. It hasn't worked properly for yonks.'

▲ 'The machine packed up again yesterday . . .'

Use English correctly

▶ A long memo may consist of several paragraphs. If you are writing a lengthy memo, remember to divide up your information into:

- an opening paragraph, which introduces the reader to the topic

- one (or more) middle paragraphs, which provide more information

- a closing paragraph, which says what you expect to happen next.

Sometimes you may have to group your information into a logical order before you can start to write. In this case, simply decide how to introduce the topic, which information will extend the reader's knowledge and what action will be taken next. These should link to your paragraphs.

▶ There are many common words used in memos which you should know how to spell correctly. They include the following:

colleague	acknowledge	receipt	received
grateful	transferred	believe	definitely
separate	responsible	difference	proceed
procedure	desperate	feasible	until
paid	unfortunately	liaise	fulfil

▶ Learn the 'I/we' and 'me/us' rule. If you are writing about yourself and someone else, remember that you always put yourself *last*. Read both names and if you can substitute the word 'we' then you call yourself 'I'. If you would have to substitute the names with the word 'us', then call yourself 'me'. For example:

Jack and I are going to be there = *we* are going to be there

The people with the highest scores were *Jack and me* = The people with the highest scores were *us*.

COMMUNICATION IN BUSINESS

Many problems at work can be caused by confusing dates and days. You can see this by reading the following extract from a company memo which was posted on the Internet.

> It may be me, but I'm finding the recent 'meeting is Wednesday, no Thursday, no Wednesday' sequence of memos very confusing. It seems that five people arrived on Wednesday, 12 January – when fifteen were expected! The remaining ten appeared on Thursday, 13 January.
>
> Is our next meeting on WEDNESDAY, 26 January? Could both the day and date be confirmed this time, please?

Arriving for a meeting *within* the company on the wrong day is bad enough, but imagine the problems caused if the meeting is being held 200 miles away – and the waste of people's time and money.

You never want to be the cause of such problems, so always check days and dates very carefully in *all* business communications you write – and include **both**. That way, at least if you do make a mistake, it will be glaringly obvious to anyone who checks a calendar!

1 Decide which of the two words shown should be included in each of the sentences below. Then look up the meaning of the word you have rejected in each case.

a) Please note that smoking is not aloud/allowed in this building.

b) Can you make sure that envelopes are included in the stationery/stationary order.

c) I am enclosing the draught/draft advertisement for the receptionist.

d) All job applications must be sent to the Personnel/Personal department.

e) He sent us a cheque/check for £250 last month.

f) Greg has decided to except/accept the invitation.

2 Read the memo that Kate has written about photocopying problems. Unfortunately, Kate has used one or two slang expressions and her spelling isn't very good. She has also missed out a question mark.

Identify all the errors and rewrite the memo.

MEMO

TO: Amelia Larabey

FROM: Kate Simpson

DATE: (today)

SUBJECT: Photocopying problems

We are haveing problems copeing with all the requests for photocopying and deliverying the documents on time. This is mainly becourse we have to prepare so many documents for the health and safety training coarse which Jim is holding next weak.

At the moment people just put documents to be copied in the tray in the admin office. It would help if we had a better system so that we could identify urgent documents immediatly and do these first or if we had a more modern photocopyer which we could control from our computers.

Please could I see you to talk about this problem. At present we are getting a lot of grief from staff who are throwing a wobbly when there work isn't ready on time.

KS

---

3 Your boss, Amelia Larabey, has just started writing a memo to the catering manager, Jason Woodbridge, to confirm her request for tea/coffee and sandwiches for 8 people at a working lunch to be held in her office next Tuesday. She would like the food and drinks delivered at 12 noon and for some of the sandwiches to be suitable for the two vegetarian members of staff who will be attending the meeting.

She is interrupted and asks you to complete the memo. Do this by:

a) Copying out the start of the first paragraph she has written and completing it with the basic information. Give the date of the meeting as well as the day.

b) Writing a second paragraph to give the additional details.

MEMO

TO: Jason Woodbridge

FROM: Amelia Larabey

DATE: (today)

SUBJECT: Working lunch requirements

Further to our telephone conversation yesterday, I would like to
confirm my request for tea/coffee and sandwiches for 8 people for next

---

4 When Amelia is free, she asks you to prepare a memo for her in response to the one she has now received from Kate about photocopying. Amelia says to you:

'I fully understand Kate's problem and I know they are very busy. Between you and me, we must do something. At the moment, though, a new machine isn't possible because we have already overspent on this year's budget. A new system would seem the best idea, although we'll have to find some way of making sure that the staff keep to it and don't simply put 'urgent' on everything. I agree it would be better if Kate and I discussed it and suggest we meet next Monday at 3 pm in my office.

'Can you send Kate a reply, please? You'd better put this information in a sensible order and start by thanking Kate for her memo.'

a) Decide which order you will write the information. Remember that you don't need to include all the comments Amelia made to you – you should repeat only those which she wants you to pass on to Kate.

b) Draft out your memo in three short paragraphs for Amelia's approval.

Check all your answers with your tutor.

▼ Understanding messages

Everyone has passed on a message at some time or other. You may take a phone call on behalf of a member of your family – or pass on a message from one of your friends to another. You may do this verbally or send a text message on your phone. At work it is normal to write down messages you receive, so that you won't forget the details or forget to pass on the information because you are busy.

You may receive a message from a visitor to your office – or because you answer the telephone and the caller wants to speak to someone who is away from the office or is too busy to speak at that moment.

Key facts about messages

▶ Most organisations have printed **message pads**. These are useful because the headings on the pad are specially designed to help you remember all the key facts to include. Most also enable you to make an automatic copy of the message for reference and are designed to be used for both telephone calls and visitors.

Message Form ☐URGENT ☐NON-URGENT

TO: _____ **DEPT:** _____

DATE: _____ **TIME:** _____

CALLER'S NAME _____

ORGANISATION _____

TEL No: _____ EXT No: _____

☐ Telephoned   ☐ Please return call

☐ Returned your call   ☐ Please arrange appointment

☐ Called to see you   ☐ Left a message

Message:

_____

_____

_____

_____

_____

_____

_____

_____

Taken by: _____

▶ Urgent messages must be marked clearly and passed on immediately. If the person who should receive it is away, pass it on to someone else who can deal with it. *Never* leave a message on an empty desk. It could easily be covered up as other papers are placed there or, if the person is away, ignored for quite some time!

▶ If you write your messages, rather than type them, make sure your writing is neat and clear. It is helpful to print any names which may be difficult to read.

Preparing messages – the golden rules

▶ Always pick up a telephone receiver with your non-writing hand and have a pen and paper close by.

▶ Essential information you always need to include is:

  – the *full* name of the caller

  – his or her organisation (or private address)

  – the telephone number *and* the regional dialling code

- the date and time of the call

- the message

- the *full* name of the person to receive the message.

- your own name. Put your full name if you work in a large organisation or if other people in your office have the same first name as you.

▶ A caller may not volunteer all the key facts you need so you may have to ask questions to obtain these. For example, simply ask politely, 'May I have your telephone number, please?'

▶ Each message contains a number of key facts. You must listen for these so that you can separate them from general conversation – especially if the caller is talkative! Always check the key facts by reading them back to the caller. For example, numbers, places, times and dates are all key facts – you can't guess any of these!

▶ A caller may not give you the information in a logical order. For that reason, it is sensible to make notes as you listen, then check these with the caller, *then* write them out on a message form or type out the message on your computer.

Using English correctly

▶ In every message you write, use simple, straightforward words.

▶ Keep your sentences short but vary the length a little so that your message 'flows' properly.

▶ Be very specific about names and be careful with pronouns, such as 'he' and 'she'. If you are writing about two people or more, it is very easy to cause confusion, for example:

'Karen said that both she and Sarah will be going but she will have to leave at 4 pm.'

In this case, you cannot tell whether it is Karen who will have to leave at 4 pm, or Sarah.

▶ Several pronouns cause problems when you are referring to people. *Never* use 'which' and 'what' – and you are safer to avoid 'that'. Instead use the word 'who'. Therefore you should write, 'She is the customer *who* called in last week' *not*, 'She is the customer *that* called in last week.'

▶ Check you know the difference between:

- 'there' (a place'), 'their' (belonging to them) and 'they're' (they are)

- 'to' (used before a verb or pronoun, e.g. to go to them), 'too' (meaning as well) and 'two' (the number 2)!

▶ In a message you will be repeating what someone has already said, so you should use the past tense. For example; 'He told me he can go' *not* 'He tells me he can go.'

▶ If you are repeating a request to your boss, remember to phrase this as a request, not as a command! It is far more tactful to write 'Please phone him tomorrow' rather than 'You must phone him tomorrow'.

COMMUNICATION IN BUSINESS

Most offices have telephone answering machines on which callers can leave messages when the office is closed. Another automated messaging system is Voicemail. This enables both internal and external telephone callers to leave a message on a person's extension when he or she cannot take the call. Extension users simply press a key to retrieve all the waiting Voicemail messages on their return.

A recent American study has highlighted two problems with recorded messages. The first is that callers often give the information in the wrong order. They start with the reason for ringing and give their phone number – or their name – only at the end. The second is that people often speak far too quickly and, in the case of telephone numbers, may say up to 10 digits too rapidly for the listener to write them down immediately. This means that the message has to be replayed for the key facts to be extracted accurately. The researchers are hoping that, in the future, answering machines will include the facility to 'skip' backwards in short sections – to save listeners from having to replay the whole message just to check the final number.

OVER TO YOU!

1. Each of the following sentences includes either one (or more) spelling mistakes or a problem with a pronoun. Identify the errors and rewrite the sentences. In the case of one pronoun problem, use your common sense to decide what the writer really meant to say!

   a) William Cox asked if you could visit there offices next week.

   b) The price we quoted for paper was to dear but we can send them a new quote in the next to days.

   c) Jason asked me to tell you it was Mandy that saw Mrs Jackson when she visited us last week.

   d) Their concerned that there expenses won't be payed on time.

   e) Keith Jennings rang to say that Jon Hollings can solve the problem and he will tell him when he gets back from holiday.

2. Emma made several mistakes when she wrote the following message. There are **seven** mistakes in the heading, and the message itself is poor. Emma hasn't varied her sentences and has made other important errors. Can you identify them? When you have found all the errors, rewrite the message itself so that it is clear, easy to understand and 'flows' properly.

Message Form ☑ URGENT ☐ NON-URGENT

TO: _Tracey_ DEPT: _Personal_
DATE: _20 Febuary_ TIME: _4.15 pm_

CALLER'S NAME _John_
ORGANISATION _He didn't say_
TEL NO: _308998_ EXT NO: _____

☑ Telephoned ☐ Please return call
☐ Returned your call ☐ Please arrange appointment
☐ Called to see you ☑ Left a message

Message:
He rang about the first aid training.
He can't do it when you wanted. He can only
start it after Easter. He is on holiday before then.
He is going to Tenerife. He could start on the
Monday after he gets back. He said he gets back
on the Thursday after Easter Monday.
He wants you to ring him. Then you can say if he
can start it then.

Taken by: _Emma_

---

3 Bill Jennings has left a message for your boss on your answering machine. You are fortunate that Bill speaks clearly and states his information in the correct order. He also spells out difficult words. Write out a message for your boss, using a copy of the blank message form at the back of this book. Remember to identify whether the message is urgent or non-urgent.

Hi, it's Bill Jennings here from Johnson and Ridley. It's 8.45 am at the moment. Can you please pass this message to Peter Anderson in Purchasing as soon as possible. Please tell him that the samples he wanted are being sent by courier today. He should receive them by 3 pm latest. If there are any problems, please ring our office on 020 387 3880. I'm out of the office until 4 pm, but if you ask for Katy Ilett – that's I-L-E-T-T - our administrator, she will be able to answer any queries in my absence. Thanks. Bye.

4 You are less fortunate when you listen to the next message which was timed at 8.50 on your answering machine.

a) Start by identifying the key facts in the message.
b) Then put them in a logical order.
c) Now write out the message neatly and clearly on a pre-printed message form.
d) Finally, decide whether the message is urgent or non-urgent.

Oh, good morning. Er, I wanted to speak to someone about the invitation we received. We got it yesterday. You're having a demonstration evening at a local hotel. It says here that it starts at 6.30 but my husband doesn't finish work until 6 and I don't think we could be ready and get to the Claremont Hotel before 7.30, so really we want to know if it's going to be worthwhile going. We live at 15 Ridgeway Avenue, Redbridge so it would take us at least half an hour. We'd like to come, if we can, but there's no point if it finishes as we arrive, is there? It's next Wednesday, according to the invitation. Could someone let me know? My name is Sandra Kemp, but the invitation was addressed to my husband, Tom. The letter with the invite was signed by a Lucy Holden, if that's any help. Tom said he thinks she works in your marketing department. Oh, our phone number is 480989. Do you need the code? If you do, it's 01982. Thanks.

5 Working in pairs, draw up a list of 'rules' for people who leave messages on answering machines. Then check your ideas with other members of your group.

Check all your answers with your tutor.

▼ Understanding faxes

A fax message is a document sent electronically from one fax machine to another. Fax machines are useful because they enable text, graphics, drawings or photographs to be sent to someone quickly, easily and cheaply. The machines themselves are easy to use and you can send a fax to an office abroad in the same length of time as you can send one to someone in a nearby office. You will learn how to use a fax machine in Unit 4 (see page 191).

Key facts about fax messages

▶ All fax machines transmit in black and white – so a clear black and white document produces a clear fax. A coloured document should be photocopied first.

▶ Each page of a multi-page fax should be clearly numbered, so it is easy to check that all the pages have been sent or received.

▶ Fax machines automatically print the time, date, fax number, name of the sender and page number at the top in small print. Because this print is so small, most organisations prefer to use a **fax cover sheet** which summarises the key items more clearly for the receiver. An example is shown on page 18. Note that the telephone number shows the international dialling code for the UK, because many faxes are sent and received from abroad.

▶ A fax message can be typed or handwritten. The 'tone' of the message will depend upon the type of message being sent and the person who is receiving it.

```
 _____
|                                                        |
|  FAX COVER SHEET              Freeman                   |
|                               Electronics               |
|  TO: Cassidy Security                                  |
|                               Middleway Industrial Park |
|  FAX NO: 03829-890031                 REDBRIDGE         |
|                                           Berks         |
|  FOR THE ATTENTION OF: Ian Fagan, Sales Dept  RD3 9PS   |
|                                                        |
|  FROM: Naseem Mehrban          Tel: +44 118-390289     |
|                                Fax: +44 118-398200     |
|  DATE: 20 March 200-        email: admin@freemanelec.com|
|                                                        |
|  SUBJECT: Security Assessment visit                    |
|                                                        |
|  NO OF PAGES (including this page): 2                   |
|                                                        |
|                                                        |
|  Message:                                              |
|                                                        |
|  Following our telephone conversation, please find attached a map |
|  showing our location.                                 |
|                                                        |
|  We look forward to meeting you tomorrow at 11 am.     |
|                                                        |
|                                                        |
|  Signature of sender: Naseem Mehrban                   |
|_____|
```

▶ Fax machines are often used to transmit original documents or graphics which could not be sent by computer. In this case, the message may be very short and simply explain the document(s) being attached.

▶ Fax messages do not have a formal opening (such as Dear . . .), nor is there a formal close. However, they are often signed, to add a personal touch or to authorise an official fax, such as an urgent order for office stationery.

Preparing fax messages – the golden rules

▶ Make sure you know the name and title of the person who is to receive the fax – and the department if you are sending the message to a large organisation.

▶ Check you have both the fax number and the dialling code.

▶ Check carefully the number of pages you are sending, and enter this on the first page. Many organisations like you to write 'page 1 of 3', 'page 2 of 3', etc. on individual pages of a fax, as a double-check.

▶ If you are sending an original document, or a graphic, write a short covering message which explains this.

▶ If you are writing a longer message, remember to keep it as short and simple as possible. People expect fax messages to be clear and to get to the point quickly!

▶ Never write slang in a fax message and try to avoid phrases such as OK. Because most fax messages are sent outside the organisation, it is better to be rather more formal and to use standard business phrases.

▲ Fax messages should be kept short and simple!

COMMUNICATION IN BUSINESS

Fax machines are used in a variety of situations to communicate *within* an organisation as well as with outside businesses. Customer service staff at Barclays Bank communicate with their personal bankers by fax – even if the personal banker is in the next room! The reason? Personal bankers give advice to customers face-to-face and this saves them being constantly interrupted by the telephone ringing.

Faxes are also used to communicate reports of stolen or lost credit or debit cards by organisations that offer 'card safe' policies to customers – such as Marks and Spencer Card Safe. Immediately a customer reports a stolen or lost card, the information is faxed to the bank, so the card can be blocked on the computer system. Bank fax machines which receive this type of information are monitored 24 hours, 7 days a week, so that immediate action can be taken.

Using English correctly

▶ Fax messages may contain standard abbreviations such as FYI (for your information), FAO (for the attention of), AKA (also known as) and ASAP (as soon as possible). Make sure you know what these mean.

▶ One of the trickiest punctuation marks for most people is the apostrophe. Just remember four basic rules:

1 In a contracted word, you put an apostrophe *in place of* the missing letter(s), for example don't (do not), can't (cannot), o'clock (of the clock).

2 An apostrophe also indicates *possession*. So instead of writing 'the coat which belongs to Ben' we write 'Ben's coat'.

If there is **one** owner, add an apostrophe plus an 's', e.g. Michaela's room, Ashraf's car. You also do this if there are many owners but the word is a special plural which doesn't end in 's', such as children's ward, sheep's eyes. If the word already ends in 's', you can just add an apostrophe, e.g. Prince Charles' house.

If there are **several** owners, and the word ends in 's', just add an apostrophe, for instance the owners' club, the girls' changing room.

3 *Never* use an apostrophe in a normal plural word, for example 'We bought a kilo of potatoes and two computers' is correct, but *two computer's* is not.

4 Beware of one exception to the rule. It's *always means* it is. You never add an apostrophe to denote possession. So you would write 'It's raining' and 'It's Maria's umbrella' *but* 'Its catch has broken.'

▶ *Never* write 'should of' and 'would of'. The correct phrases are 'should have' and 'would have'. This is a common error made by many people. Another is to confuse the following words:

– 'lend' and 'borrow'. If you need my book, then I am the lender and you are the borrower!

– 'teach' and 'learn'. 'He taught me to do that' is correct. 'He learnt me' is rubbish!

– 'cancel' and 'postpone'. If you cancel an arrangement you stop it forever. If you are only putting it off for a short time, use 'postpone' instead.

OVER TO YOU!

1 Check your understanding of the fax message sheet shown on page 18 by answering the following questions:
   a) What is the fax number of Freeman Electronics?
   b) What is the fax number of Cassidy Security?
   c) What is the name of the person who is sending the fax?
   d) What is the recipient's name?
   e Where does the recipient work?
   f) What information is on the second page of the fax?
   g) Why is this information being sent?
   h) Why is this being sent by fax rather than by letter or telephone? Give **two** reasons.

2 Draft faxes have been prepared containing the following sentences. There are mistakes in each one. Identify the errors and correct each sentence.
   a We are attaching the diagram but havnt yet recieved Bills' drawing.
   b) Karens train should arrive at 5 pm but if its late, please weight for her.
   c) We may need to cancel this Tuesdays meeting and hold it next Tuesday instead.
   d) The representatives' annual conference is next month and we should of booked accomodation by now because we need rooms for 35 people.
   e) The dial has been chequed and is now working but it's needle is bent and needs replacing.
   f) We are attaching our offishul order for the stationary and need the presentation folder's delivering tomorrow.

3 You work for Freeman Electronics. Your boss is Adam Lewis. He has asked you to send a fax to one of your engineers, Liam Knox, who is working in Italy at Ponti Brothers and staying at the Andreola Hotel in Milan, fax no 00–39–398–299081. Liam urgently needs two wiring diagrams sent to him. Adam has given you one to send but needs more details before he can send the second. He has asked you to check with Liam whether the second is for the control panel or the cooling system.

Ask your tutor for a copy of the fax message sheet at the end of this book and prepare the message to be sent to Liam. Use today's date.

4 There is a crisis in Milan and Freeman Electronics could lose a large order unless the problems there are solved quickly. Adam Lewis has decided to fly out to join Liam at the Andreola Hotel. He has asked you to draft two faxes and said to you:

a) 'Send a fax today to Liam Knox at the Andreola – I suggest you use the heading 'Hotel reservation'. Ask him to reserve a single room with private bathroom for me for 3 nights, from the day after tomorrow. You have the number, haven't you? Make sure you state my arrival and departure dates clearly. Ask Liam to confirm that the reservation is OK immediately, please.'

b) 'I also want to send a fax today to our Italian agent, Luigi Penaroli at Penaroli Associates in Milan. His fax number is 00–39–398–179877. Tell him that I'm coming to Milan – give him the date, of course. Ask him if he can meet Liam and me that evening – suggest 7 pm – for a meal at the hotel to discuss the problem at Ponti Brothers. Tell him where I'm staying, of course. If he can't manage that, suggest a breakfast meeting the following morning at 8 am. Can you think of a suitable subject heading yourself, please?'

Again use copies of the fax message form at the back of this book and write the faxes required.

Check your work with your tutor.

▼ Understanding business letters

A business letter is the standard method used to communicate with people outside the organisation. A business letter is always written on an organisation's letter-headed paper. The layout, or format, of a letter may very slightly from one organisation to another. This is often known as the 'house style'. Despite this, the main components of a letter are always the same.

There are many reasons why business letters are written. The first types of letters you will learn are those which:

▶ make an enquiry

▶ respond to an enquiry

▶ confirm an arrangement

▶ acknowledge a letter or request which cannot be dealt with immediately.

If you continue your studies to level 2 or level 3, you will learn about other types, such as letters making or responding to a complaint. If you practise the basics now, it will be easier to develop your letter writing skills.

Business letters are a formal method of communication – and are different from the informal, friendly letter you would send to a friend. You will find it easier to write business letters if you know some of the business phrases which are often used in them. You will learn about these phrases on pages 26–27.

Key facts about business letters

▶ At work, you will usually find letter-headed paper referred to as 'headed paper' for short. Wherever you work, you should check the 'house style' you are expected to use – and follow this.

▶ Many organisations spend a considerable amount of money on the design and printing of their headed paper. They do this to impress their customers and clients and show that they provide a high-quality, professional service. This means that any letters you write must be the same high quality!

▶ A signed business letter, on headed paper, is an important document. It could be used, for example, in a court of law to prove what the organisation said. For that reason, you must never write and sign a letter on headed paper without your boss's agreement.

▶ The components of a business letter are those items which are always included. They are illustrated in the example below. This letter has been written in response to an enquiry.

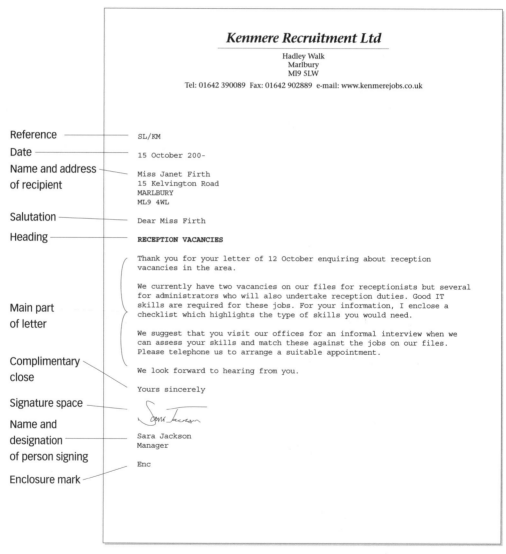

– The reference is usually the initials of the writer, followed by the person who typed the letter.

– The date is better written in full, e.g. 15 October 2003 and not 15/10/03.

- The name and address of the person who will receive the letter follows. There is usually no punctuation in the address and the town is typed in capitals. The postcode is better on a separate line and should *never* contain any punctuation.

- The salutation is the part that says 'Dear Miss Firth'. The title here must be the same as in the address line. *Never* include both the first name and the family name. You would either write 'Dear Janet' or Dear Miss Firth'. You should not write 'Dear Janet Firth'.

- A heading is often included, so that the person receiving the letter can see quickly what it is about.

- The 'body' or main part of the letter is divided into paragraphs.

- The complimentary close is the part that says 'Yours sincerely'. Variations are 'Yours truly' and 'Yours faithfully'.

- The signature space must be large enough for the writer to sign the letter.

- The name and designation of the person signing the letter is always included below the signature. The designation is that person's formal title in the organisation.

- An enclosure abbreviation is shown to indicate if any documents are being sent with the letter.

▶ In the example, you will see there is **no** punctuation except in the body of the letter, where full stops and commas are needed as usual. This is called open punctuation and is the most usual way of displaying business letters today.

▶ Traditionally, many letters were more formal and started 'Dear Sir' or 'Dear Madam'. This is rare today. However, if you do start a letter like this, you should always end it with 'Yours faithfully', not 'Yours sincerely'.

OVER TO YOU!

Obtain different examples of headed paper. Your college will use headed paper and may have a 'house style' which all administrators must use. Ask your tutor to explain what this is and to show you an example of the paper.

Then collect examples yourself from letters your family have received from organisations. See how they vary! Alternatively, your tutor may be able to show you examples of letter headings received at college from other organisations. You could have a vote to see which you think are the most attractive – and which ones appeal the least.

▲ Letterheads can come in many different styles

Writing a letter – the golden rules

▶ Check that you have all the information you need. This includes the name of the recipient, the address and postcode. Make sure you spell the person's name correctly. Many people feel very insulted if they receive a letter with their name spelt wrongly.

▶ Remember that a business letter is a formal document, so must never include contracted words, abbreviated words (e.g. photo for photograph) or slang expressions.

▶ **Keep it short and simple.** This is known as the KISS principle. This will also help to make the task of writing it more straightforward.

▶ *Never* use words or phrases you don't understand because they sound important.

▶ Learn some standard business phrases which are frequently used in letters (see page 27). This will often help you to avoid making grammatical errors.

▶ Use the first paragraph to explain the reason for writing the letter.

▶ In the second (and third) paragraph, give the details. If the matter is straightforward then this can normally be covered in one paragraph, otherwise divide it into two, so that it is clearer.

▶ In the final paragraph, conclude the letter. This may be just one sentence which tells the recipient what to do next or uses a standard expression such as 'We look forward to hearing from you.'

▶ Make sure you use the correct complimentary close to match your salutation:

Dear Sir *or* Dear Madam = Yours faithfully

Dear Mr Brown *or* Dear Mrs Brown = Yours sincerely

▶ After you have written the letter, read it through as if you were the recipient. Check whether:

- it is clear

- it is concise

- it is courteous

- all the information is in a logical order.

OVER TO YOU!

Kenmere Recruitment is an employment agency which interviews people who want to change jobs. First people must register with the company. At this stage, their qualifications are checked to make sure that these are as claimed. Then Kenmere will recommend them for interview with local companies in the area who have a suitable vacancy.

On page 22 you saw a reply that Kenmere sent to Janet Firth when she wrote to them. Imagine you are Janet, you have just moved to Marlbury and have heard that Kenmere has an excellent reputation. You decide to find out if they have any reception vacancies in the area. You have recently worked on reception in a small hotel, but would now prefer to work on reception in a larger business organisation. However, you are unsure of the skills you would need.

Your task is to write the original letter that Janet wrote to Kenmere Recruitment. Because this is a personal letter, you would not use headed paper. Instead you should type your home address at the top right hand side. Ideally, align it to the right margin on every line, put your town in capital letters and the postcode on a separate line. Your address is 15 Kelvington Road, MARLBURY, ML9 4WL.

Draft out your letter in three paragraphs. The first paragraph should state your reason for writing. You could start by saying 'I would like to enquire . . .'. The second paragraph should state your previous work history – and the fact you would like to know more about the skills you would need. The third paragraph should simply say 'I look forward to hearing from you.'

Check your draft letter with your tutor.

Using English correctly

▶ It is better if you can avoid starting a letter by saying 'I am writing', because that is obvious.

▶ Make sure that all your sentences are complete. 'Further to your letter of 23 April' or 'Following our telephone conversation 'are *not* sentences, because neither has a verb! In both cases you would have to extend the sentence for it to be complete, for instance, 'Following our telephone conversation, I am pleased to enclose your new membership card.' You can also avoid this by starting another way, such as, 'Thank you for your letter of 23 April'.

▲ Correct spelling is very important, especially for people's names and job titles

▶ Correct spelling is very important. Make sure you can spell all the following words without difficulty:

apparent	appointment	immediately	catalogue
regrettable	preferred	acceptance	truly
omission	faithfully	sincerely	accommodation
unnecessary	reference	permanent	privilege
commitment	confidential	application	temporary

▶ If you write a long sentence, use a comma where there would be a short break in the reading or speaking of the sentence. As a guide, look at how commas have been used in this sentence and the previous one. Commas should also be inserted:

- in a list of a items, e.g. We need paper, pens, notebooks and calculators.
- to separate a clause in the middle of a sentence. A clause is a short group of words. In this case you put a comma both before *and* after the clause. You can test for this because the sentence would make sense if the clause was removed, for example 'Mark Brown, the Sales Director, will be available on Friday'.
- to separate words such as 'therefore', 'however', 'unfortunately', 'interestingly' and 'consequently' from the rest of the sentence, e.g. 'We regret, therefore, that we cannot offer you a refund. We are, however, prepared to offer you a replacement.'

▶ Stick to simple words you know and understand. For example:

Write	Don't write
send	despatch
end	terminate
payment	remittance
try	endeavour
expect	anticipate

OVER TO YOU!

1 Each of the following sentences contains one error or more. Identify the error(s) and write out the sentence correctly.

a) Further to your letter of 16 May.

b) We are pleased to enclose our latest Spring catalog and price list.

c) Diana the new administrator starts work next week and will need a desk chair and computer.

d) We sincerly hope that you will be able to join us on this ocassion.

e) We regret we are unable to provide this information because all referances we receive are confidenshal.

f) Please book the acomodation for two nights as I have three meetings one on Tuesday and two on Wenesday.

g) As one of our prefered customers however we are prepared to make you a special offer on this three peace sweet.

2 From the list below, choose the simplest word or phrase which means exactly the same as the word on the left and which would be more appropriate in a modern business letter. Look up any words which you do not understand.

a) commence	end	start	initiate	get going
b) assist	facilitate	collaborate	help	hinder
c) peruse	inspect	consider	write	read
d) permit	allow	sanction	refuse	tolerate
e) concise	succinct	compact	short	lengthy
f) observed	recognised	watched	saw	spotted

3 Each of the phrases below is commonly used in business letters. Identify whether each would mainly be used:

i) at the beginning of a letter

ii) in the middle of a letter

iii) to close a letter.

a) We look forward to meeting you.

b) Thank you for your letter.

c) Please let us know if we can be of any further help.

d) We are pleased to inform you that . . .

e) We hope this information will be of use to you.

f) We are enclosing the information you requested.

g) We should be grateful if you could let us know . . .

h) We are pleased to confirm your appointment on . . .

i) Following our telephone conversation of yesterday, . . .

j) We look forward to hearing from you.

4 Jenny, the new member of staff at Kenmere Recruitment, was asked by her boss Sara Jackson to draft a letter to Janet Firth, confirming her appointment for an informal interview. This was agreed yesterday when Janet Firth telephoned Sara Jackson. However, Jenny has made several errors and doesn't seem to know what paragraphs are!

a) In pairs, study Jenny's letter and identify the all mistakes she has made. Compare your ideas with those of other members of your group.

b) Rewrite the letter, correcting the mistakes and dividing the information into three paragraphs. To help, use any of the standard business phrases you read in (3) above that would be appropriate.

Kenmere Recruitment Ltd

Hadley Walk
Marlbury
MI9 5LW

Tel: 01642 390089 Fax: 01642 902889 e-mail: www.kenmerejobs.co.uk

SL/JE

22 Oct

Miss Janet Firth
15 Kelvington Road
MARLBURY
ML9 4WL

Dear Miss J Firth

Following your phone call yesterday about the reception vacancies.
We'd like to confirm your apointment for an informal interview with
Mark Jarvis our recruitment consultant at 10 am next Thursday. Pleese
bring with you a copy of your CV as well as original certificates of the
qualficiations you've got. We're looking forward to seeing you.

Yours faithfully

Sara Jackson
Manager

5 Today is 27 November and Sarah Jackson has asked you to draft four letters which she will sign. Prepare your drafts on plain paper but set them out in the correct way.

a) Sarah has received a letter from Mark Openshaw of 14 Bagley Gardens, Moxbridge MB3 9WJ. Mark is a website designer who is getting married in January and will be moving to the area. He has enquired about suitable vacancies and has enclosed his CV. Sarah tells you: 'Start by thanking Mark for his enquiry. Then tell him that we have several in which he is likely to be interested. However, we do need to meet him before we can recommend him for any interviews. We are open every Saturday morning from 9 am to 1 pm, and he might find it easier to call in then, rather than during the week, as he is obviously still working in Moxbridge at the moment. Ask him to telephone us to arrange an appointment. If it helps, use the copy of the letter we sent to Janet Firth as an example.'

b) Sarah tells you that the next letter is related to an Open Evening which is being held by Kenmere Recruitment on Wednesday 21 January from 5 pm to 9 pm. Sarah tells you: 'Last time we had an open evening our flowers were done by Mrs Pippa West at Flower Occasions, 23 High Street, Marlbury. The postcode is ML9 5EL. I've tried to reach her by telephone but she must be on holiday – I can't get a reply. Can you please write to her. Tell her we are having another Open Evening and ask if she would be able to do the flowers for us again. We need a large display in reception and smaller displays in the office areas. We will need the displays to be delivered during the afternoon. Please say I'd be grateful if she could let me know as soon as possible if she can do this for us again.'

▲ Kenmere Recruitment Open Evening

c) Then Sarah says: 'Please write to Barry Hines. He's the manager of Bridgeview Printing Ltd, Canon Street, Marlbury ML9 8EA. Refer to my telephone call to him yesterday and confirm that we want him to provide 8,000 leaflets advertising the Open Evening and for him to arrange for these to be delivered as inserts in the local paper on Thursday 15 January. Please ask him to let me see a sample for checking once he has designed the leaflet. Tell him to telephone me if he wants any further information about the Open Evening.'

d) Finally, Sarah wants you to write a very short letter. She tells you: 'I've received a letter – dated yesterday – from a tutor at a local college asking if we could send someone to give a talk about the work of employment agencies next month. I'm away that week but Karen Shaw – our Recruitment Manager – might be able to do it. I won't know until Karen gets back from holiday a week on Monday. Write to the tutor, will you? It's Mrs Pam Barnes – her title is Senior Tutor – at Morton College, Bradley Road, Marlbury ML4 9PS. Just thank her and tell her we might be able to send Karen but can't confirm it until next week. Say Karen will write to her when she returns.'

▼ Understanding forms

Forms are completed on many occasions. You need to complete a form to enrol on a course at college, to apply for a driving licence or to obtain a passport. When you apply for a job, you are often asked to complete an application form. In all these cases you must complete the form accurately with your own personal details. You also need to write neatly and clearly – often using a black pen.

At work, you will often be expected to complete a form. Forms are used at work for a number of reasons, including:

▶ to record a customer enquiry

▶ to record an incident (such as reporting lost or stolen property)

▶ to request property maintenance or repair

▶ to make an insurance claim

▶ to apply for something (such as a place on a training course)

▶ to make a booking or reservation

▶ to ask people for their opinions.

You may need to obtain information from various sources, before you can complete the form. For that reason, in this section, you will also learn about extracting information. This means selecting *only* the information you need and inserting it in the correct place.

Key facts about forms

▶ All forms are issued for a specific purpose. You can normally identify the purpose by reading the heading.

▶ A good form is well-designed and asks you for information in a logical order.

▶ There are often sections on a form which you must *not* complete. These often have the heading: For official use only.

▶ At the top of the form there is usually a section which says how the form must be completed, e.g. in capital letters and in black ink.

▶ The spaces on a form should be large enough for you to enter the information – but some may be smaller than others. Watch for these so that you can adjust your writing size accordingly.

Completing forms – the golden rules

▶ Read the form through *first* – before you start.

▶ If the form is very important (such as a job application form), then take a photocopy and practise on this.

▶ Use block capitals when asked.

▶ Use black ink or ballpoint if this is specified.

▶ Write neatly.

- If you have to write your name, make sure you look carefully at where you complete your title (e.g. Mr/Mrs/Miss), your first name, and your family name (surname). Sometimes you are expected just to cross out the titles which don't apply – and only to write your first name and family name in full. Other times, you have to write all three.

- Check any address spaces. Often there is a separate space for the postcode.

- Check any spaces which you must *not* complete, for example where someone else has to sign the form.

- Identify options where you have to select one from two choices, e.g. 'Yes/No'. You may see a footnote at the bottom telling you to delete the one which doesn't apply.

- Complete all the sections which you can do easily. Then put a small pencil cross against any 'gaps' you have. Finally, go back and find the information you need to complete all the remaining gaps. Don't forget to rub out your pencil crosses at the end!

- If there are any sections which you *cannot* complete because they do not apply, you are better to put N/A (for 'not applicable') or a 'dash'. This makes it clear that you have not simply missed off the information. An example would be a space for an email address if you don't have email.

- If you have to include *your own* signature and the date at the end, don't forget to do this.

- Check the form carefully – to make sure you haven't left any blanks by accident.

▲ 'According to her application your grandmother was 272 years old last week!'

Using English correctly

- Remember that spelling is just as important on a form as it is on other written business documents! Check you can spell the following words:

receipt	enrolment	confidential	initial
questionnaire	advertisement	competent	consistent
definite	noticeable	reference	separate
omitted	cancelled	gauge	tomorrow

- Many forms include abbreviations, such as DOB (date of birth), P & P (postage and packing) or special terms, such as 'next of kin'. Always *ask* if you are unsure what an abbreviation or special term means – never guess the answer!

- Keep your information short and to the point. For example, if you were asked to 'describe damage to car' on a claim form, you could put, 'Front bumper slightly dented, broken wing mirror at right hand side.' You do not need to write 'The front bumper on my car is slightly dented and as well as that the wing mirror at the right hand side is broken.'

- Learn the difference between 'e.g.' and i.e'. 'E.g.' means 'for example'. You should use this when you are giving some examples of many things. Read the following sentence and instead of reading 'e.g.' read 'for example':

  The market sold many different types of fruit, e.g. papaya, mango and lychees.

  'i.e.' means 'that is' and is used only when you are giving a specific example. Read the following sentence and substitute the phrase 'that is' for the abbreviation.

  The restaurant is open later on Saturdays, i.e. until 1 am.

- Check you know the difference between:
  - 'where' (a place), 'wear' (to put on) and 'were' (the plural of 'was', e.g. they were here)
  - 'here' (the place where you are) and 'hear' (to listen)
  - 'formerly' (before or earlier) and 'formally' (in a formal manner)
  - 'loose' (not tight) and 'lose' (mislay).

COMMUNICATION IN BUSINESS

Today, many people complete forms on-line when they are using the Internet and want to register on a website or order goods. Some government sites also include application forms. For example, anyone who is working can complete a form on-line to find out how much state pension they will get when they retire.

People who design on-line forms build in safeguards to prevent problems. Unless all the key information has been entered in the correct way, the form is not accepted. Instead it reappears on the screen with an error message. For example, if you tried to type letters into a box for a number (such as date of birth) you would find these weren't accepted. This helps to prevent errors and is a useful safeguard. Unfortunately, the same doesn't apply when you are completing paper-based forms!

▲ If information is not entered correctly it will not be accepted by an on-line form

1 Correct the errors in the following sentences.

a) I decided to where my jacket so that I did'nt loose it.

b) I could'nt here him from were I was sitting.

c) Peters referance says he is a competant worker.

d) Two items were omited from the order, eg paper and envelopes.

e) The questionaire is issued every Summer.

f) She wants to greet them formerly tomorow morning.

g) It is important to get a seperate reciept for that.

2 Yesterday Rawinda had an accident at work and had to complete a form describing what happened. She has written quite a long account. Reduce this to no more than 30 words so that it will fit in the space on the accident form she has to complete. Do this by leaving out all the information which is not relevant to the accident.

> I came back from lunch at about 1.30 pm – I had been to the canteen with Jenny. We were talking as we walked down the corridor and opened our office door. There must have been a stationery delivery at lunchtime but instead of putting the box away, it had been put behind the door. The box was large and was in front of the filing cabinet. I walked in, still taking to Jenny and never saw the box, so I fell over it. I fell forwards and banged my head on the filing cabinet which was behind the box.

3 Obtain two forms such as a holiday booking form (found in the back of most holiday brochures), a shopping by post or mail order form from a catalogue, an application form to open a bank account or a college application form.

Then complete both of these neatly and accurately with your own personal details. Invent any other information required – you can choose a holiday, select which goods you want to order or decide which course you want to attend!

Check your answers and your completed forms with your tutor.

▼ Finding and extracting information

At work, you may need to obtain information from various sources when you are writing a business document or completing a form. For example, you may need to refer to a price list *and* a catalogue when you are completing an order form. You may also need to look in your office files to find out the reference number of your next order.

It is not difficult to find and extract information accurately. You need to be patient and to read the information calmly and carefully. It is helpful to highlight information, as you find it, using a highlighter pen. Don't do this, though, on important original documents at work – unless you are given permission to do so.

1 You may be asked to read a table, such as a price list, and extract information. Look at the table below and answer the questions that follow.

Office bookcases

Cat No	Description	Colour	Price £
839832	Bookcase, 750 mm high	Beech	79.99
839833	Bookcase, 750 mm high	Grey	79.99
839834	Bookcase, 1100 mm high	Beech	89.99
839835	Bookcase, 1100 mm high	Grey	89.99
839836	Bookcase, 1400 mm high	Beech	119.00
839837	Bookcase, 1400 mm high	Grey	119.00
839838	Bookcase, 1800 mm high	Beech	149.00
839839	Bookcase, 1800 mm high	Grey	149.00
839840	Extra shelf	Graphite	19.99

a) How many sizes of bookcases are sold?

b) How many colours of bookcases are there?

c) What does the abbreviation 'cat no' mean?

d) What does the abbreviation 'mm' mean?

e) What is the cat no for a beech bookcase, 1800 mm high?

f) How much would it cost to buy a grey bookcase 1100 mm high?

g) What is the cat no for a grey bookcase, 750 mm high?

h) How much would it cost to buy a beech bookcase, 1400 mm high with an extra shelf?

2 Kenmere Recruitment has produced a leaflet, advertising its Open Day. You have a copy on your desk when you answer the telephone to Petra Davies, a client who is enquiring about the evening. Use the leaflet to answer the questions she asks you.

FREE ADVICE FOR YOUR FUTURE!

OPEN EVENING AT
KENMERE RECRUITMENT

Looking for work? Want to change your job, but don't know where to start? Kenmere Recruitment has the answers!

Our database contains over 1,200 temporary and permanent vacancies in this area.

Key features of Kenmere's service:

- Free registration
- Personal consultation with trained consultants
- Privacy policy – we never disclose your personal details to any company without your permission
- Mobile phone alert – once you are registered, we will text message you to alert you to suitable jobs as we receive them
- Kenmere are specialists in local area recruitment. We don't hold national or overseas jobs – we concentrate on helping local companies to recruit wisely and well.

WANT TO KNOW MORE? CALL IN FOR AN INFORMAL CHAT

When?	Wednesday, 21 January 200-
What time?	5 pm – 9 pm
Where?	Hadley Walk, Marlbury – opposite Debenhams and 5 mins walk from the railway and bus station.
Can't make it?	Then telephone us on 01642-390089 to make an appointment to talk to one of our consultants. *There is no obligation to register.* Alternatively, email us at enquiry@kenmerejobs.co.uk.

---

a) What date is the Open Evening?

b) What time does it start?

c) How do I find your offices?

d) What does it cost to attend?

e) What does it cost to register with your company?

f) How do I know you won't tell my boss I've been to see you?

g) I'd be arriving by train. How far are you from the station?

h) How many vacancies do you have?

i) Are these only permanent vacancies?

j) Do you have overseas jobs, or jobs in London?

k) Can I email you? If so, what is the email address?

3 You have started work at Royton Estate Agency where you are told that all customer enquiries are recorded on a form.

This morning Mrs Roshani Baz telephoned. She and her husband already have a house in the area but want to sell it and buy a larger property.

Her address is 16 Cleveland Road, Hightown HG4 2JF and her home telephone number is 01829–393049.

Mrs Baz spoke to Bill Royton last week and he passes you the notes he made. He did not have time to complete a customer enquiry form and asks you to do this.

Telephone call notes

To: _Bill Royton_   Regarding: _Mrs Roshani Baz_

Contact: _Mobile no: 07367-309093_
Work no: 01829-592099

Notes: _Lives in terraced house – wants semi-detached or detached. Specifically wants house on new estate so her children will have friends to play with. Garage essential._

Prefers either Dinglewood estate or Blockbury area. Can afford up to £150,000.

Doesn't like idea of a bungalow. Has 4 children and doesn't think there would be enough room unless bungalow was very large.

Garden must be flat as her husband has a heart condition.

Can be contacted at home or work.

Signed: _Bill Royton_   Date: _24 Sept_

▲ Notes from telephone call to Bill Royton

Ask your tutor for a copy of the customer enquiry form at the back of this book and complete it carefully.

4 Kenmere Recruitment has a registration form for clients. You are asked to complete one for Petra Davies – who could not attend the Open Evening. Petra has sent an email and also spoken on the telephone to Karen Shaw, the Recruitment Manager.

Ask your tutor for a copy of the Kenmere recruitment form at the back of this book and use the information Karen has given you to complete all the **relevant** sections of the form.

Telephone call notes

To: _Karen Shaw_   Regarding: _Petra Davies_

Contact: _16 Wellington Drive, Middlemere MD5 4PP_
Home phone number is 01989-300084
and her mobile is 07383-599973.

Notes: _Rang her 24 Jan._
Wants to register with us. Explained must verify her qualifications and she must sign form.

Currently employed and happy, but 'open to offers' as wants to move on in the near future. Current earnings £12,000 a year. Only wants permanent job.

Unmarried but prefers title 'Ms' to 'Miss'.

Achieved OCR Admin Cert level 2 + NVQ 3 Customer Service whilst at work. Very interested in developing IT skills and wants to study for European Driving Licence (ECDL). Uses computer at work at present.
Is emailing details of current job.

Signed: _Karen Shaw_   Date: _24 Jan_

▲ Notes from telephone call to Karen Shaw

Registration

File　Edit　View　Insert　Format　Tools　Message　Help

Send　Cut　Copy　Paste　Undo　Check　Spelling　Attach

To: KarenS@Kenmerejobs.co.uk

Cc:

Subject: Registration

Arial　10　B　I　U　A

Dear Karen

Thanks for your phone call. I can call in to register with Kenmere next week.

In the meantime please can you note that I've been working at Telmere Stores for two years as Customer Service Administrator. I log all customer queries and complaints on computer and make sure these are answered promptly.

Please send any emails to me at petradav@hotmail.com.

Best wishes

Petra

Working with colleagues and customers

Introduction

This unit is about the two most important types of people you will meet at work – your work colleagues and your customers. Some of your colleagues will work alongside you, whereas others may be in different parts of the organisation. Some will be older, more experienced and more senior than you. Others will be your own age and may become your friends. However, regardless of who they are – or what they are like – you will be expected to cooperate with them and help them when they are busy. You will be expected to have a friendly and positive attitude, even when you are busy yourself. Learning these skills is important – and is a key focus of this unit.

You may see customers every day or talk to them mainly over the telephone. Customers are vital for every business because without them a business would cease to exist. Upsetting or losing a customer is therefore a serious matter, and yet customers vary considerably – in their attitudes, their needs and their moods. Learning how to deal with all types of customers effectively, so that they always feel good after dealing with you, is another important part of this unit.

This unit covers the basic skills you need to work effectively with both your colleagues and your customers.

Unit summary

This unit is divided into two separate elements.

▶ **Element 1 – Contribute to the work of a team.** This element focuses on working with your colleagues.

▶ **Element 2 – Communicating with customers.** This element covers different types of customers, whether you deal with them over the telephone or face-to-face.

The skills in this unit will help you to deal with other people thoughtfully, positively and effectively in a wide range of situations, so that people are pleased to deal with you and work with you.

Element 1

In this element you will learn how to:

▶ **Confirm your own responsibilities, including working arrangements.** This means you must make sure you understand what you have to do, why it must be done, how you should do it and by when. You will also learn what to do if a problem occurs that could make you miss the deadline.

▶ **Carry out allocated tasks.** To do this you need to understand your instructions, work safely, observe any security or confidentiality requirements and complete the work as required.

▶ **Work with others to complete tasks.** This involves cooperating with other people, asking for help if you have a problem and passing on information properly.

▶ **Assist other members of the team as needed.** In this section you will learn how to help other people and still manage to complete your own work on time.

▶ **Communicate appropriately with others.** Communications are very important in teams so you must know how to communicate appropriately both when you are speaking and writing to a colleague.

▶ **Maintain good working relationships.** How do you maintain good working relationships with other people and what do you do when something goes wrong?

▶ **Review own contribution to a team.** This section tells you how to assess your own contribution to a team. Was it good or could it be improved? How do you know?

Assessment

Your assessment for Element 1 will consist of practical activities. You will work as a member of a team on **two** separate occasions and will have to prove that you can work with them effectively and productively to do a task.

Your tutor will assess you in relation to *all* the aspects of teamwork you have learned. These are the items in bold, in the list above.

Element 2

In this element you will learn how to:

▶ **Present a positive image to customers.** You will learn why a positive image and effective customer service is important and how to give a positive image yourself.

▶ **Follow company procedures for greeting and addressing customers.** You will find examples of company procedures which tell you how to greet and address customers, both face-to-face and over the telephone.

▶ **Use appropriate tone and manner.** This section covers the tone and language you should use with customers.

▶ **Convey information clearly and accurately.** You will learn how to make sure you are clear and accurate, and also about the information you must not give.

▶ **Communicate effectively with customers.** To do this you need to listen carefully, understand what has been said and make yourself understood.

▶ **Refer any problems to the relevant person.** How do you identify a problem, whom do you ask for help and when?

Assessment

Your assessment for Element 2 will consist of practical activities. You will communicate with customers on **two** separate occasions. On one occasion this will be by telephone and on the other it will be face-to-face. On one occasion you will have to prove that you can deal with a problem which needs to be referred to another person.

On both occasions you will be assessed in relation to the first five aspects of customer service you learned. These are the first five items in bold, in the list above.

Element 1 – Contribute to the work of a team

In many businesses today, each person works as a member of a team for most of the time. What is a team and why is teamwork so important when you are at work?

A team is a group of people who are working together to achieve the same aim. There are many famous examples – such as sporting teams, yachting crews and well-known bands such as Coldplay or Blue. In many occupations, such as fire and ambulance crews, training people to work as a team is essential. In all these cases, the members of the team:

▶ are committed to the same goal

▶ work together cooperatively to achieve that goal

▶ help and support each other

▶ put the team goal *above* their personal goals.

Teams are always more effective if the members have different skills which, when put together, enable them to successfully complete a range of tasks. This means that good planning is needed by the team leader to take advantage of the skills of each person.

▲ Teams must pull together to achieve a common aim

Working as a member of a team

For some people, working in a team is easy and much more fun than working alone. Others find teamwork hard because they don't like having to rely on other people. They get upset or annoyed if anyone lets the team down or doesn't do a perfect job.

When you are working as a member of a team you sometimes have to change your behaviour. You cannot just say what you think, or simply please yourself. You have to think about the effect of your actions on the others in the team.

Check how easy you would find it to work in a team by doing the quiz below – then see how suited to teamwork you are.

Teamwork Quiz

1 You have promised to help your sister who is moving house on Saturday. On Friday, you receive an unexpected invitation to meet an old friend who will be in your area on Saturday just for the one day. You would:

a) Accept the invitation immediately. Your sister will have to manage without you.

b) Ring your sister and see if she can move another day.

c) Ring your friend to see if there is any possibility she could meet you at your sister's house – so you would have an excuse for leaving early.

d) Ring your friend and say sorry, but you can't possibly let your sister down.

2 You are working with a friend to produce a document on a computer. In two days you have completed ten pages but she has managed only two. You would:

a) Tell her she is useless.

b) Take the work off her, sigh heavily, and say you'll do it yourself.

c) Ask her to explain why she is having a problem – but stress she will have to work more quickly.

d) Ask her why there is a problem – and offer to help her.

3 You are hopeless at proof-reading your work – you just know it isn't one of your strengths. A colleague sees an important letter on your desk that you have just prepared and points out three errors. You would:

a) Tell him to mind his own business.

b) Thank him through gritted teeth, re-do the letter and keep the work on your desk covered up in future.

c) Correct the errors and then point out every mistake you see him making over the next few weeks, to get your own back.

d) Thank him, re-do the letter and vow to improve your proof-reading skills.

4 You have worked with three other members of your class to prepare the reception area for an open evening. The principal of the college arrives whilst the others are having a short break and praises your efforts. You would:

a) Stress how long it took you and how hard you worked.

b) Thank her – and make sure she knew your name. Then tell the others when they come back.

c) Thank her – say how nice she looked, briefly mention that a few of you had been involved but stress you had done most of the work.

d) Thank her on behalf of the team – and then rush to tell the others.

5 You have an important document to photocopy, collate and distribute before 3 pm. Two colleagues offer to help you, even though they are busy themselves. Would you:

a) Thank them, make sure they knew what to do and leave them to it.

b) Thank them, ask them which jobs they'd like to do and then watch them carefully to make sure that they were doing them properly.

c) Thank them and divide up the jobs among the three of you –making sure you were doing the jobs you like.

d) Thank them, work out with them the best way to do the job and then thank them again afterwards.

6 Yesterday, when you were working in the mailroom with three colleagues, everyone was told that two important parcels had to be despatched. Today you are all in trouble because the parcels are still sitting on the mailroom table. You would:

a) Tell your supervisor immediately that John was supposed to send them, not you.

b) Tell your supervisor you were busy franking envelopes all afternoon and the parcels weren't your job.

c) Smile at your supervisor and stress it was nothing to do with you and then stare hard at your colleagues to encourage them to 'own up.'

d) Apologise and explain that you were all very busy which was how the parcels were missed.

Key:

Mostly A's: You are a nightmare to work with and very likely to annoy everyone. You are unreliable and hurt people – so you can expect little help or cooperation in return.

Mostly B's: You make an effort to do the right thing, but can't bring yourself to go the full distance! Treating people exactly as you would like to be treated yourself is important.

Mostly C's: You are not a 'people' person – and are apt to be rather devious and underhand to try to get your own way. This won't impress anyone – least of all your boss!

Mostly D's: The right approach! You are thoughtful, helpful and take into account the feelings of other people with your words and actions. It's sometimes hard, but well worth it.

▼ Understanding your responsibilities

When you work in a team you have *two* sets of responsibilities. You have a responsibility to the team *and* an individual responsibility to do your own work properly.

Your responsibilities to the team are:

▶ to do your own job well

▶ to follow instructions

▶ to keep other people informed about progress and problems

▶ to help other people when necessary

▶ to stay cheerful and positive – even when things go wrong!

Your other responsibilities relate to the actual task(s) you have to do. Quite simply, unless you understand what you have to do, and how you have to do it, you are unlikely to do it very well!

Confirming your working arrangements

Your working arrangements relate to what you have to do, how you will do it and how long you have to do it. Because there are several items to check, it is helpful to have a checklist, so that nothing is forgotten. This is a list of essential items or questions. Before you start any job you should make sure that you know the answer to each one. It is sensible to write down the answers – so that you don't forget and have to repeat the question!

Your activity checklist should include:

1 a description of the overall task that needs to be done.

2 the purpose of the task (i.e. why it needs to be done). This helps you to plan and understand the work better.

3 a list of all the separate tasks or actions which must be done. You must highlight those which are your individual responsibility.

4 a note of all those tasks which are being done by other people because you will need to know who is doing each one. This is important in case you have to ask another team member about a particular matter or pass on information about it.

5 the resources that are required and that you can use, such as access to a photocopier or printer or the type of paper you should use.

6 the deadlines – both for the whole task and for your own jobs.

7 what you must do if there is a delay or problem.

Gemma's tutor is sending out information about the course and the college to businesses in the area who may be willing to offer work experience placements to students. She has asked Gemma, Shahida and Kelly to help her.

Anna Shaw is the tutor. She has prepared a checklist for them. Read it carefully and answer the questions below.

TEAM ACTIVITY CHECKLIST

Overall task: Prepare and send out a letter together with a course leaflet and a college booklet to 30 business organisations in the area.

Purpose of task: To obtain work experience placements for students, so good impression is very important.

Tasks to be completed and by whom:

Word-process and check letter	Shahida
Print 30 copies	Shahida
Give copies to Anna Shaw to sign	Shahida
Photocopy 30 copies of course leaflet	Gemma
Obtain 30 copies of college booklet from admin office	Kelly
Print 30 address labels from computer database	Kelly
Stick address labels on envelopes	Gemma and Kelly
Collate insertions – letter, leaflet and booklet	All
Insert in envelopes and seal	All
Take envelopes to mailroom	All

Resources:
A4 letter-headed paper
A4 brown envelopes
Course leaflet
Computer
Photocopier

Deadline: All envelopes must be posted no later than this Friday, 7 October.

Delays or problems: Please inform Anna Shaw immediately.

1 In your own words, describe the task the students have to do.

2 Identify **all** the jobs Gemma has to do.

3 Identify the person whom Gemma should see if:
   a) she wants to know when the letter will be word-processed
   b) she is waiting for the address labels
   c) she has a problem because the photocopier has broken down.

4 Three of the college booklets are crumpled. Can these be sent out? Give a reason for your answer which directly refers to the *purpose* of the job.

5 Shahida is very quick and accurate at word-processing whereas Kelly is the only one who really understands databases. How has Anna Shaw, the tutor, used this information when she prepared her checklist?

6 By mistake, Gemma sticks her set of address labels on A5 envelopes, which are too small for the booklets.

    a) What should she do? Give a reason for your answer.

    b) How could the checklist have helped her avoid this problem?

7 Suggest **two** reasons why Anna Shaw wants to know immediately if there is a problem.

PEOPLE IN BUSINESS

You might think that the worst person to have in a team is someone who makes a drama out of a crisis. But in some offices, teams are being trained by those people most familiar with dramas – the actors themselves. The author of a leading book on teams, Michael Maynard, has recommended that there is no better way to learn teamwork.

The reason is quite simple. Actors have to learn to work as a team very quickly to put on a professional performance in a theatre. They can therefore teach other people how to do this. In addition, acting out roles can give people confidence and help them to express themselves in ways that won't offend or upset their colleagues.

Many famous organisations are now involved in this type of learning, including Marks and Spencer, Halifax and NTL. You can find out more about Arts and Business at www.heinemann.co.uk/hotlinks

"To be or not to be; that is the question..."

▲ Actors are part of a team on stage

▼ Carrying out your allocated tasks

Some tasks are easy to do whereas others are harder. A lot depends upon the task you have been allocated to do and the skills you have.

A task which worries you is one which is outside your 'comfort zone'. This is because you think you haven't the ability or skills to cope – or because you don't understand your instructions. If you take a deep breath, and approach the problem in the right way, then you will often feel a greater sense of achievement afterwards than if the task was simply routine. Tackling something new and challenging is often the best way to learn!

The actions to take when you are given a task are similar – but there are certain *additional aspects* to take into account if you are worried in any way.

Instructions for known and familiar tasks

Everyone can make a list of tasks they can do well. If you are asked to do a routine job then don't think of it as boring. Rather, take it as a challenge to produce your best work *ever*, working both quickly and efficiently. Even stamps look better when they are stuck on straight rather than upside down or crooked!

In this case:

▶ Write down the task (so you don't forget)

▶ Listen *carefully* to the instructions

▶ Make a note of any *special* instructions

▶ Ask for an explanation if there are any instructions or terms you don't understand

▶ Check that you are certain you can follow the instructions and carry out the task properly without any problems. If you have any worries, look at the section below.

Instructions for tasks outside your 'comfort zone'

If you are asked to do a completely new task then you need to listen extremely carefully to the instructions and write *everything* down. Ask questions afterwards to check anything you are unsure about.

If you are still concerned, then do the following.

▶ Decide *why* you are so worried. Is it because you dread new things? Is it because you have been asked to do something for the first time? Is it because you don't understand exactly what is required?

▶ Decide what help or additional skills you would need to do the job. Do you need more practice? Do you need someone to give you a demonstration? Would it help if another member of the team worked with you? Do you just want another explanation, but in more detail this time?

▶ Speak privately to the person who gave you the job. Explain your worries and what help you think you need. The key point is to stay positive. Don't refuse to do it – it could be a great chance to learn something new.

▶ When you are given help or shown a demonstration then remember to 'listen → watch → practise'. Make notes of each stage if you are worried you might forget your instructions.

▶ Agree to report back on your progress at regular intervals. This will give you more confidence because you know where to go if you feel you can't cope.

Safety issues

Working safely is very important. Accidents can easily happen through carelessness, thoughtlessness or just plain stupidity! Many of the routine items used in an office every day may look harmless but can be quite lethal if they are not used properly. For example:

▶ Paper can cut your finger or tongue. When a piece of paper is lying on carpet, it is the same as a banana skin – so pick it up!

▶ Stapling your finger instead of the paper is an experience you will never forget – if you are using an electric stapler the result is even more horrific.

▶ Electricity is a key feature of all offices, which means there are plugs and wires around. Treat all electrical equipment with respect and *never* poke around inside, for any reason.

- Stationery is heavy. Carrying too much or not lifting it properly can cause serious back injuries.

- Files are large and bulky. Carrying too many will restrict your vision, piling too many on a shelf is very high risk! They could easily fall down on you.

- Filing drawers should *never* be left open – neither should desk drawers. It's all too easy to walk into them.

- If you spill something, clean it up immediately; if you break glass or china then wrap it in paper before you put it into the wastebin; if you pass someone the scissors do so with the *handles* pointing towards them.

- Never place boxes, bags or anything else on the floor where someone may fall over them.

You will learn more about health and safety in Units 3 and 4 – this is only a basic list. If you have any concerns about safety issues with any jobs you are asked to do, then talk to your tutor or team leader immediately.

▲ Carrying heavy items incorrectly can cause serious back injuries

Security and confidentiality issues

If you cannot be trusted, then there is a limit to the number and type of jobs you can be asked to do. 'Trust' doesn't just mean being honest, because you are being asked to handle money; it also means being reliable, thinking for yourself and being discreet.

Reliability is important when there are security issues. If you are asked to lock the door to a room when you have finished, do you remember – and put the key back safely where it belongs? Or would you forget? Would you also think to close the window – especially of a ground-floor room – if no one had actually told to you to do? This is an example of thinking for yourself.

Discretion is extremely important for all administrators who, as part of their work, see many items of information which are confidential to the business or its customers. You may never be tempted to discuss the names and addresses of everyone in your group, but how would you react if you were doing some filing for your tutor and spotted a confidential report on someone you knew? Could you be relied upon to keep quiet and not even tell your best friend in confidence? Remember, confidentiality means *never* sharing any secrets, with anyone!

Completing work as required

You can truthfully say you have completed work as required when:

- You have done everything that you were asked to do. This means you have followed your instructions and nothing is missing or still needs to be done.

▶ There are no mistakes or problems which must be solved before your work can be used. For example, if you have photocopied a document the text should be aligned properly so that the image is absolutely straight and not crooked.

▶ You have done it to the deadline. Of course, sometimes you may have a deadline problem which cannot be avoided. In this case, as long as you have notified your team leader immediately and done what you were then asked to do, you have still completed the work as required.

▶ You have tidied up the working area afterwards! This is the boring bit that many people prefer to forget – but it isn't nice for the next person to work there if you leave everything in a mess. Tidying up means leaving the area as you found it *and* putting away properly any spare stationery or equipment.

OVER TO YOU!

Tarzeem and Emily are working together to prepare and print some letters for their tutor. As a group, read how they go about this and then spot all the mistakes they make. Then discuss what they *should* have done – each step of the way – with your tutor.

Tarzeem (*waving a disk in the air*): 'Did she say all the letters were all on this disk?'

Emily: 'No! Don't you ever listen? The letters are on the disk she gave *me*. I've to update them with this year's information and then put in the names and addresses from another file. (*Proudly*) I learned how to do that last week. *You've* got the disk with the document which has to be enclosed with the letters. That's also to be updated. There's a lot of numbers in that, so we'll have to check it carefully when you've finished.'

(*Both open the file folders they've been given and spread out the papers.*)

Tarzeem (*a little while later*): 'I can't find which document it is. There's loads on here.'

Emily: 'I thought she gave you the file name?'

Tarzeem: 'Hey, look at this. This is a letter she wrote to Mark's parents last week about his behaviour. And *this* one is a memo to another tutor about an end of term trip for both our groups. Did you know about that? I must tell Tahira, she's in that group.'

Emily (*irritably*): 'I wish you'd just get on. I'm going to be finished before you at this rate.'

(*Both work quietly for a while.*)

Emily: 'Right, that's it, I think. I'll print out the first one and see what it looks like. Typical, there's no paper in the printer.' (*She finds a packet of paper in the drawer and puts it on the desk. She opens it, and puts some sheets in the printer.*)

Emily (*a few minutes later*): I don't believe it, it's all smudgy. It's this printer. I think it needs cleaning.' (*She opens the lid and peers inside, then walks across the room to get a cloth.*) 'This is useless, the cloth is bone dry. I'm going to the cloakroom to get some water.'

(*Emily returns with a wet cloth and washes inside the printer.*)

Tarzeem: 'You'll have to hurry up, I said I'd meet Tahira at lunch time. I'll have to leave in five minutes.'

Emily: 'You're joking, we haven't printed anything yet. Have you finished keying in all those figures?'

Tarzeem: (*working furiously*) 'Just two minutes. Is that printer working now?'

Emily: 'No, something's gone funny. I don't know what to do.'

Tarzeem: 'Just say the printer wasn't working. It's not our fault, is it? If we save the documents then we've done what we were asked. Now come on, let's get out of here.'

(Tarzeem quickly logs off, grabs her bag and goes out of the door.)

(Emily looks round the room and notices Tarzeem has left the disk in the computer and her papers on the desk. She shouts after her but it's too late. She quickly stuffs the papers she has in the file, picks up her bag and leaves the room.)

▼ Working with others to complete tasks

A major benefit of working in a team is that there is always someone to help you. Equally, everyone else should be able to rely upon you for help, too!

Asking for help

This is a skill in itself! If you can't ask properly – or if you expect other people to drop what they are doing immediately to come to your aid – then you are likely to be disappointed. The key points to remember are:

▶ Identify the best person to assist you. This should be someone who has the skills to help you. Preferably, it shouldn't be the busiest person!

▶ Choose your moment. Don't interrupt if someone is in the middle of a difficult job. Wait until they have finished.

▶ Ask politely – even if this person is a friend or colleague of yours, rather than your tutor! You might start with an apology, such as 'I'm really sorry to bother you but I'm stuck with this. Can you spare me five minutes?'

▶ Hopefully the response will be positive. If it isn't, *don't* get annoyed or start an argument! Ask someone else instead.

▶ Remember to say 'thank you' afterwards. Remember, too, that you now owe this person a favour in return!

Cooperating with others

In a team, the team goal comes before individual goals. You might remember this from the start of this chapter. This means that, even though it may be annoying, there are times when you have to stop what you are doing and become involved in something else. Or you may have to work in a different way than you normally would because it suits everyone else.

Reporting back as necessary

The person who gave you the job will expect you to report back from time to time. This person is likely to be your team leader, your immediate boss or, at college, your tutor. You will find that reporting back becomes particularly important when you are given more complex work to do which will take you quite a long time. At a basic level it is simple courtesy to report back because it stops people wondering how you are going on! At other times, it is essential. You should report back:

▶ On a routine basis, to give a progress report on the job.

▶ Immediately, if there are any problems or difficulties, such as:

   – a member of the team is ill

   – there is a resource problem, for example, you run out of paper or envelopes

- someone makes a mistake which will affect the deadline

- the work is taking longer than expected

- anyone has an accident or has made a serious error

- you receive conflicting instructions or information and need to find out what to do.

If you inform your team leader quickly about a problem, this means that action can be taken to solve it. The longer you delay, the more critical the situation is likely to become!

▲ You should report back immediately if someone is ill

Communicating information

There are two types of information you must be able to communicate in a team:

▶ information which must be passed on to other people, because it affects the way they will do their own tasks

▶ very important or essential information which they need – often immediately.

When you work in a team, people can make the assumption that if they tell *you* something, then they have told the rest of the team as well! This isn't true if you keep what you have learned to yourself. If you have any doubts, remember that you are always better to tell your team members too much, rather than too little.

You may receive information from your team leader, someone outside the team or find out something yourself. For example, if you look out of the window and see it is snowing heavily, then you may think it is important to communicate this quite quickly – especially if some of your team live quite a distance away. Or you might read a message on your computer from the IT department saying that the network will be closing down for maintenance in half an hour. If you are the first person to read this, you should pass it on immediately as it will significantly affect everyone else.

Whenever you receive information that affects *any* of the tasks being done by the team as a whole, or the whole job, then you must tell everyone else.

Very important, or essential information, must be passed on accurately and immediately. This means stating the facts clearly and not exaggerating!

OVER TO YOU!

You are on work experience in the college office. You are working with three members of full-time staff: Susan, Hamida and Sam. Susan is in charge of the office. All three are helpful and welcoming when you arrive.

The first day is quite eventful. Explain exactly what you would do in each of the following situations.

1 At 10 am the telephone rings. Susan has disappeared, Hamida is helping a student at reception and Sam is on his break. You have never answered the office telephone before and don't know what to do or say, so you let it ring. Hamida has to leave the student and rush to answer it.

2 Susan asks you to find out some train times using the Internet. She says she will explain what to do but you are worried you will forget her instructions or make a mess of it.

3 You are asked to put some documents in a file which Susan needs to take to a meeting in 20 minutes. After working for 10 minutes you realise that you will not finish the job in time. You ask Hamida for help but she is too busy finishing an urgent report that Susan must also take to the meeting.

4 The telephone rings. This time, you answer it. It is Susan's boss who says that the meeting has been delayed and won't now start until 4 pm that day.

5 You are helping Sam to prepare the outgoing mail before he takes it to the mailroom in another building. On your way to the stationery cupboard to collect some more envelopes, Susan asks you to make sure that the mail doesn't go yet because she must finish packing an urgent parcel.

6 Susan has gone to the meeting and Sam has taken the mail. Susan told you that if you had nothing to do you could find out more about researching on the Internet and you have just logged on. Hamida is in the next office. She is unpacking, checking and storing a large stationery order which has just been delivered and is working hard to get the job finished before she leaves tonight.

▼ Assisting other members of the team

You can assist other members of your team in three ways:

▶ by helping them if you are asked

▶ by providing information

▶ by sharing resources with them.

When a job is straightforward and everything is going well, then assisting other people is easy. Life becomes more difficult if you are busy yourself or if things keep going wrong. To cope with this you need to learn how to balance everything – some people call this 'keeping all the balls in the air' because it becomes something of a juggling act!

Giving help

Hopefully, your answer to the last question in the Over to You! section above was that you would log off your computer and go and help Hamida! *Offering* to help is always better than waiting to be asked – providing you are not jeopardising your own work.

You should always help other people when:

▶ you can spare the time

▶ you are willing to 'make time' (for example by staying late to help in a crisis or giving up part of your lunch break)

▶ you know how to do a job (or want to learn)

- the job is one for which your team is responsible

- another team member is worried or upset and you know you can be of practical assistance.

However, this does not mean you will always be in a position to give help. You should apologise and refuse if:

- you are so busy yourself that you would miss your own deadlines if you stopped

- you have no idea what to do and showing you would take too long

- the other team member is doing something which your boss wouldn't approve of

- you would be giving away confidential information

- you have a personal commitment which really does mean you cannot stay to help that day.

If you have to refuse, then you should suggest that your team member has a word with someone else – or your team leader – to find out what to do.

Another method which often works is to change your routine – as you will see on page 53.

Sharing information

You have already seen that it is important to pass on information you receive. Sometimes, however, you may discover this information yourself. You may discover (or already know) a quicker or easier way of doing something or spot something that is going wrong and need to point it out.

Sharing information is very useful – that is one way in which teams maximise the skills of each member. However, pointing out to someone that they are not doing a job properly can be tricky and needs tact! For example, *never* say 'You're making a mess of that' or 'There's an easier way of doing that.' Both these statements are very critical and are likely to cause annoyance. Instead make a positive suggestion, such as 'That's really good, but I think there's a quicker way. Do you want me to show you?'

Sharing resources

Resources are something many people don't like to share! Perhaps you can remember someone from school who wouldn't let you borrow a ruler, their liquid paper or a pencil – even when you were desperate? These types of people work in offices, too! *They* would argue that you should make sure you have everything of your own that you need but when you are working as a team you often have to use communal resources.

There is usually no problem when there is plenty for everyone. It is when resources are scarce that there are problems. In this situation, you may be tempted to grab all the folders or headed paper you need first, to make sure that you are fine even if the rest of the group is not! Or (even worse) to hide the resources you need so that no one else can use them!

▲ Sharing is all part of team work

The key point to remember is that you are in a *team*! This means that the needs of other people in your team are as important as your own. Only when you truly think this way can you claim to be a good teamworker!

The balancing act

Many people have very fixed ideas that their own way of doing something is best. Added to this, some people dislike change. They prefer a fixed routine which they follow, come what may.

The problem with this approach is that it doesn't allow for flexibility – which is essential in most offices. Work pressures fluctuate – one day you may be frantically busy; the next day, less so. Even if you are already busy, this doesn't stop urgent jobs appearing or crises occurring. So, how do you cope if you are extremely busy and then have to do even more? And bear in mind that on days like that, if anything can go wrong, it probably will!

The key is to **prioritise**. This means concentrating on what is both important and urgent. You may have to change your priorities if you are asked to do something even more important or more urgent – or if things go wrong. However, at all times you should be able to identify the **most critical task** which must be finished first. If you can help to complete this, then do so – because your own jobs are less important. If you are the person doing the critical task, then meeting the deadline is very important and you may need to ask for help yourself.

If you cannot identify the critical task, then talk to your team leader. This is one time when 'reporting back' helps you. If you are really stuck how to solve a problem and you tell no one, then it is still your problem! If you tell the team, it is everyone's problem. If you tell your team leader then you again share the problem. This is another reason why communicating with other people is so important as you will see below!

PEOPLE IN BUSINESS

Recruitment agencies, stationery producers and magazines often carry out surveys of their staff or workers to find out what annoys them the most about other people in an office.

Recent surveys have identified all the following habits as being extremely irritating. Which do you think would annoy you the most – and, even more importantly, which ones do you think you might be guilty of?

▶ General untidiness in and around the office

▶ Borrowing stationery or small items of equipment (like staplers) from other people's desks without asking

▶ Failing to say 'good morning' or 'hello' first thing

▶ Being noisy and shouting across an office

▶ Making a cup of tea or coffee (or getting one from the machine) and not offering to do the same for anyone else.

▶ Leaving the kitchen area in an office in a complete mess

▶ Hoarding stationery and labelling all your possessions with your name in liquid paper (such as your ruler and stapler).

▼ Communicating appropriately with others

In this chapter so far, you have learned about the importance of communicating with other members in your team and your team leader, how to ask for help and how to make suggestions to other people.

Communicating with your colleagues is so vital that this section covers other things you must know. This is because you can cause more offence in five minutes by the way you communicate than, possibly, anything else you do! On the other hand, if you are a good communicator, life becomes much simpler and far more pleasant!

Identifying the correct person

Many people who have a problem whinge and moan to a colleague who cannot do much to help apart, perhaps, from listening and sympathising. If you are asked to photocopy 50 urgent documents and can't get near the photocopier because someone else is doing a massive copying job then it is useless stomping back and complaining to your friend. So, what should you do in this situation?

You could go and find your team leader and explain the problem. That would be better than moaning and groaning. At least your team leader would tell you what to do next. But a better way is to try to solve the problem yourself first. Then you still have your team leader 'in reserve' in case you need additional help.

Start by explaining the problem to the person at the copier. Do this in a friendly and positive way; for example, 'I'm sorry but I have a problem. I have to do 50 copies of this document urgently for Dan Baker. He's waiting for them. Can you tell me when you will be finished?' What you haven't *explicitly* said is, 'Will you stop for a minute because I think my job is more important than yours.' However, you have given that impression! If you are lucky, the person will let you 'interrupt' their job to do yours. This is easy on most photocopiers.

If you are unlucky, the other person will be less positive. You may get the response of 'I'll be finished in an hour' or (even worse) 'I haven't a clue, come back later.' Before you get annoyed, remember that you may be the tenth person in 15 minutes to arrive with the same request – and the person already at the copier will have a deadline, too!

▲ How long could you wait?

The critical point here is whether you can wait an hour. If so, there's no problem. If you can't, then you could try a second time by saying: 'I'm sorry, but he needs it within the next 10 minutes.' This might work. If it doesn't, then you will have to see your team leader for help.

The main point of this example is that you identify the correct person to ask each time. Basically:

▶ ask a colleague *only* if he or she can be of practical assistance

▶ always ask someone who has the skills and/or ability to help you

▶ leave your team leader or boss until last, when everything you have tried on your own has failed. The exception is when the problem is critical and you need help immediately.

Use a suitable method of communication

You can communicate with a colleague in writing or by speaking to them. Your options are:

▶ **written**: message, email or memo

▶ **spoken**: face-to-face (when you speak to someone in person) or telephone.

Your choice should be based on the **reason** for the communication and should take into account the following factors.

▶ who the other person is

▶ where they are situated

▶ the urgency of the situation

▶ the complexity of the information

▶ whether or not both of you have access to email.

Use the table below to help you to decide which is best in different situations.

Choosing the best method of communication

Spoken			Written	
Face-to-face	**Telephone**	**Message**	**Email**	**Memo**
Use when:	*Use when:*	*Use when:*	*Use when:*	*Use when:*
You want to see the other person's reaction or check their understanding.	You want to discuss something and obtain a quick response.	You need to give basic information to someone.	You need to contact someone quickly.	You want to provide a paper record which can be filed for future reference.
You need to explain something in detail.	The other person is not near to you.	The other person is not available at the moment.	The other person isn't at their desk right now.	You need to provide detailed information.
You want an immediate answer.	You need to check or find out something quickly.	The other person works near to you.	Information is detailed and is better written down.	The situation isn't urgent.
The topic is personal or confidential.	You want to hear someone's reaction to a suggestion.	The other person doesn't have email.	You need to inform several people.	The person doesn't have email.

Styles and manner of address

Today people are far less formal than in the past. You probably call your tutor by his or her first name. But would you do that with the college principal or a visitor? And how do you address people you know well in a work situation?

The basic rules are as follows:

▶ With people older or more senior than yourself, use their surname unless you are told otherwise, e.g. 'Good morning Mrs Kent' or 'To: Mrs Kent' if you are writing a message.

▶ With your own colleagues, use their first name. Don't ever use derogatory terms or nicknames at work and shouting 'Hey you' across an office is certainly not appropriate!

▶ If a stranger or visitor is present, be more formal with your colleagues, speak more quietly and never say anything indiscreet which would embarrass anyone.

▶ Never forget that 'please' and 'thank you' are two of the most valuable words in the English language!

▶ If you have to interrupt a person who is doing something, apologise or say 'Excuse me.'

Language and tone

The language you use – both when you are writing and speaking – can be formal or informal. Very informal language is the way you speak to your close friends. You probably use many words and expressions that even your parents don't use or even understand.

Formal language is the way you should speak at an interview. Hopefully you would try to use 'standard' English, which everyone can understand, and avoid the use of any slang expressions. On other occasions you may operate somewhere between formal and very informal – such as when you are talking to your family.

At work, you should use more formal language with older and more senior colleagues – and you shouldn't use very informal language with anyone.

You should also be aware of your tone. This doesn't just mean your tone of voice but the words you choose. 'Tone' creates an emotional response in the other person. It can make them sympathetic to you – or even angry. This depends upon whether your tone is polite, friendly or apologetic – or whether it comes across as rude, abrupt or insolent. If it is the latter, you are unlikely to get a very positive response from anyone! If you are speaking to someone, rather than writing to them, then your attitude will also be obvious from the way you look and stand. We all respond better to someone who looks at us properly and smiles, rather than someone who looks sulky or bored.

Remember that you can read more about language and tone in written communications in Unit 1.

OVER TO YOU!

1 Which method of communication would you use in each of the following situations? Choose from face-to-face, telephone, message, email and memo. In each case give a reason for your answer.

a) The office administrator has asked you to tell your tutor that the assessment papers she wants to post must be in the office no later than 2 pm this afternoon. You know your tutor is in class at the moment and wouldn't want to be disturbed.

b) You have to let your tutor know the names, addresses and telephone numbers of six local coach companies which you have looked up in *Yellow Pages*. She regularly organises student visits and will probably refer to this information regularly in the future.

c) You have been asked to contact the student support office at the other side of the college to find out the dates of Ramadan next year.

d) You are asked to communicate the dates of Ramadan urgently to all the tutors in the building.

e) You want to ask your tutor if you can leave early tonight because you have a doctor's appointment.

2 All these phrases you may use to your friends – but how would you translate them for a work colleague?

a) 'Oliver said you've wangled tomorrow off!'

b) 'He works loads. How scary is that?'

c) 'She hangs out with Ken at lot – she thinks he's dead sweet.'

d) 'If someone is always in my face, I blank them.'

3 Below are four ways of asking someone to wait. Put these in order with the *least polite* one first. It's easy if you think about which would annoy you the most!

a) I'm sorry, but would you mind waiting a moment?

b) Can you wait a minute, please.

c) Wait, will you!

d) Will you wait a moment.

4 Read the following and answer the questions that follow.

The administrator in the college office is very strict about the amount of stationery she will allow students to use. She has issued your team of three with 100 sheets of printer paper for a task you are doing for your tutor. This should be plenty because you have each to prepare a one-page document and print 25 copies. Sara doesn't proof-read her document and discovers there are two errors only after she has printed it. Sadia forgets to check the paper guides so her copies are crooked. You haven't started to print out your document yet.

a) Would you agree to Sara and Sadia reprinting their documents before you did your first print-out? Give a reason for your answer.

b) What, exactly, would you say to Sara and Sadia at this point?

c) If you, too, made a mess of your first print-out, how would this affect the situation?

d) If you needed more paper, who would you ask? Give a reason for your answer. You can choose from:

   i) one of your team members

   ii) the administrator in the office

   iii) your tutor

e) What, exactly, would you say to the person you asked?

f) What would you do if the first person you asked said 'no'?

▼ Maintaining good working relationships

It is in your own interests to have good working relationships with all your colleagues at work – and especially with your own team members. If you don't get on with each other, then this will prevent the team operating effectively. You could even end up spending more time squabbling than working!

It is important to remember that we all notice irritating faults and habits in other people – but rarely spot our own! If you think you are always right then this will immediately cause problems – especially if someone else thinks the same. Equally, you shouldn't think you are always wrong. Give and take is essential in any team.

OVER TO YOU!

Study the table opposite which lists those personal qualities that can help to develop and maintain good working relationships in a team – and those which can destroy a good team. Then try a simple test.

1 Identify all the good qualities you have – and see if you can spot any faults you have.

2 Then think about another person you often work with in a team. Identify that person's good qualities and faults.

3 Now study the result and, depending upon your result, do either option a) or b) below.

a) If you have identified *more* faults for this person than for yourself, try the test again, this time thinking about someone else. If you get the same result, be aware that this might indicate that you are more critical of other people than you are of yourself.

b) If you have identified more faults in yourself, then again try the test thinking about someone else. If you regularly have this result, think about what you can do to improve your own opinion of yourself.

At the end of the day, always remember that no one is always right, and no one is always wrong!

Personal qualities of team members

Qualities which help the team to be more effective

- A positive attitude – you focus on what *can* be done, not what can't
- A positive image – you give a positive impression of your team by the way you talk, act and look.
- Loyalty to other members of the team – you would never gossip or talk about someone behind their back.
- A commitment to the team – you put its needs above your own even if this causes you minor problems at times
- Respect for other members of the team and their right to have different views or opinions from yours.
- Tact and courtesy – because you also respect their feelings
- Listening skills – to help you understand what other people mean and how they feel.
- A helpful and supportive attitude.
- Patience, tolerance and the ability to count to 'ten' if you feel you are getting stressed.

- Sensitivity – so you don't upset people with unnecessary or inappropriate remarks.
- Dependability – so you can always be relied upon to do your share of the work to the best of your ability.
- Generosity – you are happy to praise people who do a good job and thank people who help you.

Qualities which can destroy team effectiveness

- Childish behaviour to get your own way – such as sulking, being moody or sighing heavily if you are asked to do something you don't like.
- Selfishness – you always want your own way.
- Jealousy or resentment if someone else is praised or achieves something.
- Carelessness – so that most of your work has to be redone.
- Lack of responsibility – you blame other people (or life in general) for your problems and mistakes.
- Deviousness – you will be economical with the truth if it suits you (in other words, you will tell lies!).
- Impatience and irritability the minute you are put under pressure.
- Moaning or complaining about the job, the task you are given or the people you have to work with.
- Negativity – so that you always see the problems but never the solutions.
- Tactlessness, discourtesy or insensitivity to other people's feelings.
- Disloyalty – you will gossip or tell tales if it suits you.

▼ Procedures for reporting conflict

No matter how hard you try, there will be times when you do not agree with another member of the team. If this person is the team leader, or is senior to or older than yourself, then you might just have to back down and accept the situation. Try to do this gracefully because it makes life much easier afterwards! If you create a huge fuss, then you might have a problem when you next have to work with this person, especially if you feel you have been humiliated.

If this person is your own age, and working at the same level as you, then you could end up having an argument. So, what should you do if you disagree with someone or if you feel another team member is almost impossible to work with?

Step one – try to solve the problem yourself

As a first step, decide whether the matter is worth arguing about! If you are all having a bad day, then you might find that you fall out with someone about something really silly. You can recognise this quickly; the main sign is that if you told someone about it later then the tale would sound quite ridiculous.

If the matter is serious and the outcome really matters to you – or would affect you a lot – then you are less likely to be willing to back down completely. In this case:

▶ Listen carefully to the views of the other person. Then think about a compromise that you could live with. This won't be what you wanted originally, but is somewhere between their idea and your own. Now suggest the compromise. If you are *both* willing to compromise then you are likely to find a solution which you can both accept.

▶ Remember your communication skills. Don't accuse someone of being unfair or – even worse – stupid. Hurling insults at someone is more likely to make them insist that they are right! Instead, simply state how you feel and say why you are concerned, rather than criticising the other person. For example: 'I've tried to suggest two ideas but each time you've turned them down. I know I can't be right all the time but this makes me feel that I can't suggest anything that suits you. Could you spend a few minutes explaining why every suggestion I make is rejected?'

If you think about it, it is quite difficult to answer this question without starting a discussion – which is often the first step to solving the problem. If it doesn't – and the argument gets worse – you are better to walk away (and calm down) rather than to continue.

Step two – reporting problems to your team leader (or tutor)

Unfortunately, there may be times when you have no alternative but to admit defeat. These include situations when:

▶ you have a difficult or ongoing problem with an older or more senior team member

▶ you have a problem which is causing you distress or embarrassment

▶ you have tried your best to resolve the problem but have failed

▶ you are being bullied or threatened by someone else.

You should ask to see your team leader in private. It helps if you can remain calm and state the facts clearly – although this may be hard. If you are worried about seeing the team leader on your own, then ask if someone you trust can accompany you. If the situation is really serious and you honestly feel you cannot approach your team leader, then talk to someone else with whom you feel you have a better relationship.

You will help your team leader if you do the following.

▶ Start with a clear description of the problem, when it started and how long it has been going on.

▶ Provide specific examples – and don't make wild accusations.

▶ State what you have done to try to solve the problem.

▶ Explain how the situation is making you feel.

▶ Focus on facts, not the people involved and their personalities.

Your team leader will take this seriously and will probably take notes. He or she may make useful suggestions as to how you could change the way you are handling the situation. You should listen carefully. Ask for time to think about these ideas rather than reject them. If you feel that any are completely unworkable then say why.

You should expect your team leader to want to talk to the other person as the next step. This is essential if the problem is to be solved. Your team leader is likely to try to negotiate a compromise which you can both accept – or even insist on one! Much depends upon the seriousness of the situation and whether the problem has occurred before.

If you are unhappy with the outcome – or if the problem continues – then you should identify someone else who you can talk to. If you are at college, you will find there is a stated procedure all students can follow in this situation – which you were given during your induction. All workplaces have similar procedures, as you will see below.

PEOPLE IN BUSINESS

All organisations have **grievance procedures** for solving employee problems officially – and all employees have a legal right to see a copy of these when they start work. Grievance procedures cover any situation where there is a problem which cannot be resolved quickly and informally by a manager. In most organisations they are normally used only as a last resort because most disagreements are solved as quickly as possible.

They are, however, essential as all employees must, by law, be protected from serious threats – such as bullying, harassment and discrimination.

▶ **Bullying** is when you are threatened, taunted or mocked by someone. This is usually someone who is more powerful than you.

▶ **Harassment** is behaviour which embarrasses you, such as suggestive or racist remarks or intimate questions about your personal life. Both sexual and racial harassment are illegal and should be reported immediately.

▶ **Discrimination** is when you are treated differently because of your gender, race or because you have a disability of some kind. You can read more about discrimination in Unit 3, page 147.

OVER TO YOU!

Discuss – as a group and with your tutor:

a) What has 'gone wrong' in each of the following situations.

b) What the 'victim' in each situation could do to try to put things right.

Then identify the one situation which should be reported immediately, and say why.

1 Alana frequently works with Carly and thinks she is good fun. Lately, however, she has noticed that whenever there is a difficult (or boring) job to do, Carly finds some way to get out of it. Yesterday, when they were clearing out a stationery cupboard, Alana found she was carrying and moving everything – and dusting the shelves – whilst Carly just tidied a few folders and papers. Alana accused her of being lazy, which resulted in a row and now they aren't speaking to each other.

2 Joanna is older than Shahira – and always thinks she knows best. She is always criticising Shahira's work and saying she is sloppy and needs to take more care. Shahira has retorted that it is nothing to do with her and she is too picky. Yesterday, when they were trying to complete an urgent job, Shahira made a few mistakes, Joanna told her she was useless and Shahira told her to get lost. Joanna has now said she is going to report Shahira to the tutor.

3 Martin is a whiz at IT and frequently helps Chloe when she is stuck. He hates filing and the 'trade-off' has been that Chloe will help him to file his course handouts. This has worked well for some time but Chloe's IT skills have improved considerably over the last few months, yet he still thinks she should file all his handouts for him! Chloe thinks this is unfair and the situation will have to change.

4 Amelia has been friends with Jon since the course began and they started working in a team together. Recently, he has become very resentful if she works with anyone else or helps them. Last week he sent her two emails saying he couldn't cope if she wasn't friends with him. The last two nights, she is certain he has been following her home and watching her house from his car. When she mentioned this to him, he went into a rage and said she had caused the problem.

▼ Reviewing your own contribution to a team

We all learn in many ways – such as reading, listening and watching other people. One excellent way to learn is to try something yourself and then constantly practise to improve your skills. This is how you learn to ride a bike as a child, use a computer or drive a car. It is also a very valuable way of learning how to work as a member of a team.

You learn by experience, however, only if you think back over it afterwards to check you understand:

▶ what you did very well – so that you can repeat it in future

▶ what you didn't do very well – and why. This may be because of something outside your control or because of something you didn't know at the time but understand now. If the problem occurred because of something you *still* don't know, now is the time to concentrate on finding the answer so you don't have the same problem next time.

When you are working in a team, ideally the team *as a whole* should look back at what happened and identify how it can improve. This prevents one team member claiming everything was great whilst another says it was a disaster. In this case, you can see immediately that something is wrong with their teamwork, given they can't even agree on the outcome!

Reviewing the team activities

For your OCR award, you have to carry out two activities and, in each case, you have to complete a candidate evidence sheet to review what you did. You are likely to find this easier if you review promptly, immediately after you have completed the activity, or in stages if the work goes on over several sessions. Ten minutes after each session is likely to be easier than an hour at the very end!

On your evidence sheet you must describe:

▶ **The purpose of the team's activities**. If you created a checklist of the activity (see page 43) then you can use this to refresh your memory for this section.

▶ **The tasks you performed yourself**. Again, you can obtain this information from your checklist. Sometimes you may have been asked to do additional tasks after you wrote the checklist. Make sure you record everything you did.

▶ **How you contributed to the work of the team**. This should include how you communicated with other people, how you shared resources, how you helped and supported other team members – as well as how you checked your own work and did everything you could to meet the deadlines.

▶ **The roles of two other team members and how each of them contributed**. You now have to describe what *each person* did. Their tasks, too, should be shown on your checklist. You need to say how they communicated with you, how they shared their resources, how they helped and supported you and how they tried to meet their own deadlines.

▶ **Whether or not the team was successful**. This will normally be the case if you can say 'yes' to the following:

– the work was produced to the deadline

– the finished work was of the required quality

– team working relationships are still intact.

▶ **A description of two factors which contributed to success or failure**. This is more difficult. You need to provide evidence to support the claim you made above and say *why* you are claiming success or failure. If the work was of good quality, produced to time and you still get on well as a team then this is good evidence. Or you may have received special praise for your efforts by your team leader.

If the team was less successful, then try to think about why *without* blaming anyone else!

▶ **How the attitude and behaviour of the team members affected the team's performance**. This is the most difficult question of all – unless you happily worked together as a united team the whole time. No team is perfect, so there could easily have been times when there were problems and yet you still could have had a successful result. It is how the team coped with problems and difficulties that matters the most.

If you have encountered serious problems working with a member of your team and overcame this, then focus on how you solved the problem rather than go into great detail about how this other person let you down. You are then stating the positive points about the experience, rather than the negative. It also shows that you have learned what to do in this type of situation.

OVER TO YOU!

Razia, Mark and Sara have worked as a team to do a task for their tutor. Read what happened and then, working in a team of two or three yourself, answer the questions below.

1. Identify the tasks and roles which were undertaken by each person.
2. Was the team successful? Give **two** reasons for your decision.
3. Decide how the attitude and behaviour of *each* team member affected their overall performance.
4. If the team worked together again, what do you think they should do differently – and why?

Now compare your answers with those of other groups in your class.

The information booklet

Razia, Mark and Sara have been asked to prepare an information booklet on their course for next year's students. This will contain:

- A welcome message (to be written by the them) and then a brief description of the course (which their tutor has written).
- A list of college facilities that new students will find useful.
- A description of the type of work the students will do.

When they have prepared each page their tutor will check it. When the printout is approved, they must then make 40 photocopies and staple these neatly.

They divide up the tasks between them. Sara agrees to do the welcome message, Mark will do the list and Razia opts for describing the work.

Sara is good at English and finds the welcome message quite easy. Her short, friendly message is quickly approved. She then keys in the description of the course.

Mark has been given a College booklet which lists the college facilities. He and Sara discuss which would be best to include and finalise their list. This, too, is approved.

Razia finds describing the work more difficult. She asks the others for help but they are too busy. They suggest she contacts their tutor to ask for more guidance.

The following day, Mark says their pages look boring because there are no graphics. He decides to insert some clipart. He makes an excellent job of his own page, but doesn't make the same effort with Sara's page, which annoys her.

Razia is still struggling – her page still hasn't been approved. Sara suggests they all work together to get this page finished. Sara helps with the English and Mark adds a few graphics. After one or two minor corrections, Razia's page is approved.

The next day, there is a problem. The main photocopier has broken down and the only one they can use is smaller with no automatic collator and stapler. They agree to photocopy each page separately and collate and staple the booklets themselves.

Razia carefully positions each original correctly so that all the copies are straight. She takes a 'test copy' of each page to check it. Soon she has a neat pile of copies and places these on the table, face down. The others start collating. When they have finished Sara flicks through a booklet. To her horror, pages 2 and 3 have been reversed. She blames Razia who starts to get upset until Mark says there is no point arguing. They will have to start collating all over again at some stage, so it might as well be now. The team works in silence for a while.

Mark starts stapling the booklets. He does the first few very quickly – until Sara points out he is making a mess of it. The staples aren't positioned neatly down the left, but are all over the place. Removing the staples spoils those he has done, so he starts photocopying enough pages to replace these booklets whilst Razia and Sara take over the stapling.

By lunchtime, the job is complete. The team check they have the right quantity and take them triumphantly to their tutor. 'Great', she says, 'Now, what have you learned from the experience?'

Element 2 – Communicating with customers

Every business needs customers otherwise it would go out of business. 'Your' customers are all those people who contact you because they want something. They may telephone the company and you just happen to answer the phone or they may call in when you are working in a reception area. At this point, to that customer, you *are* the same as the business in their eyes. If you are efficient then you will give a good impression of the business. If you are unhelpful and inefficient, you could help to convince that customer that he or she would be better going somewhere else next time. This is the power you have in relation to customers – and why it is so important that you learn to communicate with them and help them as much as you can. In any business, customer satisfaction is everyone's responsibility, including yours.

▼ Present a positive image to customers

Your range of customers

As an administrator, you will have *two* types of customers – external and internal.

▶ **External customers** are all those businesses or individuals who contact or visit your organisation because they want to buy a product or service or to make an enquiry.

▲ You need to support internal customers
in order to give good service to external customers

▶ **Internal customers** are all those people who work in the same organisation as you, but not in your team, and who want you to provide a service for them. A typical example is someone who works in another department who telephones you for information or asks for a copy of a document you have filed. Often they need this to help *them* to assist an external customer.

The importance of effective customer service

You can judge effective customer service yourself every time you visit a shop or restaurant. How quickly are you served? Is the service given with a smile or are you virtually ignored? What happens if you want extra help or advice? How knowledgeable and helpful is the person who is serving you? More importantly, how do you *feel* at the end of the encounter – delighted, neither pleased nor displeased or so annoyed that you'll never go near the place again?

All staff who deal with customers have a huge responsibility. With external customers, they can undo months of advertising in a second by being surly or unhelpful. Equally, they can actively convince customers to return again and again – just because of their attitude. Your internal customers may have less choice about where to go but they can certainly choose who to ask! You can be certain the word will quickly spread if you gain a reputation for being unhelpful or forgetful.

Successful businesses have proved, over and over again, that a key factor in their success is the fact that all their staff work hard to keep customers happy. It costs far more to attract a new customer than it does to keep an existing customer, so it is very sensible to hang on to those you have already got. In addition, if customers have a bad experience, they tell all their friends and colleagues and this gives the business a poor reputation – which influences other people to go elsewhere.

It is therefore in your own interests to provide effective customer service, so that you not only gain an excellent reputation yourself for looking after customers but you also help your employer to go from strength to strength.

Think back to the experiences you have had as a customer. Try to identify:

a) one occasion when the customer service was good

b) one occasion when it was exceptional

c) one occasion when it was terrible.

Then compare your experiences with other people in your group. Finally, list 3 aspects of customer service which have impressed everyone and 3 which have really annoyed you all.

The importance of a positive image

A positive image is so powerful that it leaves a customer with a good impression, even if the person they contacted couldn't actually help them very much at the time.

This is important because, with the best will in the world, you won't be able to meet the needs of all of your customers on the spot. You may not know the answer to a query or you may not have access to the information they want. However, if you project a positive image then you will convince each customer that you have done your best and can be relied upon to provide the answer as soon as possible. So, how do you do this?

A positive image depends upon:

▶ your appearance – which should be smart and tidy

▶ your voice – speak clearly and don't mutter or shout

▶ your facial expression – which should show interest or concern, not irritation or boredom

▶ the words you use – which must be appropriate to the situation

▶ your attitude – which shows you realise how important each customer is.

The overall impression you give must be 'You are my customer, you are important to me, I have time for you and want to help you to the best of my ability.'

The importance of personal presentation

Next time you are in a supermarket or a shop, try a simple test. Look at all the checkouts or assistants and decide which person you would prefer to approach if they were all free *and* if you had a minor problem you wanted to mention. Then think about why you made that choice. The answer is likely to be because of the *appearance* of each person. This is because it is your only 'clue' as to how efficient and helpful each one is likely to be.

Most organisations are very aware of this and expect staff who deal with external customers:

▶ to have squeaky clean and tidy hair

▶ not to wear too much make-up or inappropriate jewellery

▶ not to have eaten garlic or curry recently

▶ to wear clean and well-pressed clothes (or uniform)

▶ to have clean hands and nails

▶ to wear clean shoes.

Most businesses have a full-length mirror in the cloakroom so that all staff can check their appearance before going on the sales floor.

As an administrator you may not have quite the same pressures from your employer as sales staff, but you will still expected to wear clothes that are appropriate for an office and to be clean and tidy at all times. Today people wear less formal clothes in an office – but this doesn't mean they should look scruffy!

PEOPLE IN BUSINESS

Many employers have dress code guidelines for their employees. These obviously vary depending upon the type of work being done and whether the employee regularly comes into contact with customers or not. Providing the dress code is fair to everyone and does not discriminate on grounds of sex or race, then it is quite legal to state what employees should wear.

Male employees who regularly deal with customers may be told that they cannot grow facial hair. Female employees may not be allowed to wear too much make-up. Both may be forbidden from wearing nose-studs or any other type of facial jewellery and not allowed to wear jeans and trainers at work. Female employees are not normally allowed to wear revealing clothes – such as crop tops or strappy tops, even in summer when the weather is hot.

If an employee deliberately ignores the dress code then this is can be a valid reason for dismissal.

OVER TO YOU!

Work in teams of two or three for this activity.

The receptionists in your college have been arguing that they would prefer a uniform. The college is now deciding what this should be and also wants to write dress code guidelines to cover other aspects of their appearance. Your student group has been asked to help by suggesting answers to the following questions.

When you have done this, compare your answers with other groups in your class.

1. What do you think the 'image' of the receptionists should be to *all* the customers of the college? Start by writing a list of all the different types of customers, of all ages, before you answer.

2. Why do you think the receptionists would like a uniform? Do you think this is a good idea? Give a reason for your answer.

3. What do you think the uniform should consist of? Remember that you must not discriminate between male and female receptionists (such as by saying all female receptionists must wear a skirt) and you may want to consider whether saris, tabards or other types of dress should be included as options.

4. What colours would you choose – and why?

5. How many items of each type of clothing do you think should be issued to each receptionist? Bear in mind that you want them to wear clean clothing all the time but there will be a limit to the amount of money the college can afford.

6. What other aspects of their appearance do you think should be considered? Make a list and be prepared to justify your answers.

▼ Greeting and addressing customers

Whenever you greet or address a customer you should follow the procedures which your employer has specified. These will depend upon the type of business you work for – some are more formal than others. During your first few days at work you will be normally told how to greet customers you meet and how to respond when you answer the telephone.

Styles of address

Whenever you **telephone** a business organisation, listen to the way you are greeted.

▶ Many organisations still use a formal greeting, such as 'Good morning, Watson's Solicitors, may I help you?'

▶ People working in individual departments may just give the name of the department and who they are, for example, 'Marketing department, Martine Cole speaking'

▶ Customer service and sales staff may be instructed to give their names to all callers, 'Hello, Tariq speaking, how may I help you?'

When you greet someone **face-to-face**, your style of address will vary, depending upon whether the customer is external or internal and whether you have met the customer before.

▶ You are unlikely to know the name of most external customers you have to deal with. In this case, a smile and 'Good morning' or 'Good afternoon' then, 'Can I help you?' is usually enough. If you work in an organisation where all customers call by appointment, then you could also add, 'Could I have your name, please?'

▶ If you *do* know the name of an external visitor, then use it! This makes that person feel special. So this time you could say, 'Good morning, Mr Briggs. What can I do for you?'

▶ You can be less formal with internal customers, but do be aware that some may be senior managers in the organisation, so be careful! If the person is unknown to you, a smile and 'Hello, can I help you?' should be fine, no matter who it is.

▶ Obviously, again if you know the person's name, it is better to use it – either 'Hello, Mrs Jenkins, what can I do for you?' or 'Hi, Jenny, can I help you?' It depends upon who the person is, how well you know them and the usual way in which people are greeted in that organisation. If you are in doubt, just be polite!

Your organisation's image and presentation

All organisations are different in many ways – but alike in one. They all want to give a good impression to their customers. The way they do this may vary, but the aim is the same.

You can check this yourself, as a customer. Banks, for example, work hard to give an impression of efficiency and security. The atmosphere is quiet. No one speaks very loudly and customers often queue in silence. Staff are quite formal with the customers even when they are giving help and assistance.

Compare this to a hairdresser you use regularly, or a shop which sells CDs and DVDs. The organisation may have a far more modern and informal image. Music is playing and people are chatting and laughing. Your hairdresser may call you by your first name if he or she knows you well, but in most shops the staff will have been trained never to do this unless a regular customer specifically tells them to do so.

In an administrative job you represent your organisation every time you deal with a customer. You will be expected to reflect the overall image that the business is trying to achieve in the way you greet people, how you talk to them, your behaviour in general and the speed at which you deal with their query – as you will see below.

▲ Do you reflect the image of your organisation?

PEOPLE IN BUSINESS

Staff who regularly deal with customers usually have to undergo specific customer service training which includes greeting and talking to strangers. Even some very informal organisations insist that their staff use the terms 'Sir' or 'Madam' whenever they are talking to a customer. Although you may think this is very formal, research has shown that most people – including young people – like this approach because it makes them feel important.

Interestingly, organisations also commonly issue name badges to their employees which often only show the first name. So the assistant is saying 'Sir' to the customer, whilst the customer can respond by using the assistant's first name. Again, there is a good reason for this. If the customer has a query later, then he or she knows the person to contact.

If you think you would be embarrassed calling people 'Sir' or 'Madam' then you may be interested to know that this is almost a peculiarly British feeling! In America, male customers are routinely addressed as 'Sir' and female customers as 'Ma'am'. On the Continent, people use these terms in their own language without any problem.

From now on, you may find it interesting to listen to people working in stores, hotels and on customer service counters to see how the staff address their customers. And if you go on holiday, keep listening – but this time for terms such as Monsieur, Madame or Mam'selle in France or Señor, Señora or Señorita in Spain.

Prompt service

Many organisations have specific customer service standards or targets. These may state, for example, that the telephone must be answered before it has rung four times, that no visitor must be kept waiting for more than ten minutes in reception and that all customer letters must be answered within five working days.

The reason for these targets is to ensure that all customers receive a prompt response. Customers are often busy people themselves, who rapidly become impatient if they have to wait for long, and then decide to go somewhere else next time.

The key test, however, is not just how quickly you acknowledge someone or answer the telephone, but what you do next! Basic queries are always easy to answer promptly, but what is your reaction if you are faced with a query you cannot answer or are asked for something which could take you ages to find or to do a job you dislike? The following points should help.

▶ Your likes and dislikes should have nothing to do with your choice of job or your efficiency! A useful tip is to do jobs you don't like quickly, then you can move on – otherwise the mere thought of them can depress you all day.

▶ If you cannot assist a customer immediately yourself, either ask a colleague for help or apologise to the customer and explain why there is a delay. This does not then mean that you can keep that customer waiting for ages. Focus all your efforts on finding either the information the customer needs or someone else to help. Until someone else has taken over, that customer is still your responsibility!

▶ If it will be impossible to help the customer at that time then you have to agree what will happen next. This must suit the customer as well as you! For example, you may need to make a specific appointment for the customer to return or agree a time when someone can telephone with the information. Make sure you note down the telephone number carefully and correctly together with any dialling code. If you agree to send information by post then make sure you have the correct address and postcode. If you say you will email someone, make sure you know their email address. Then remember to put this job on your 'to do' list, so you don't forget it.

▶ Finally, don't panic if a customer arrives and the telephone rings at the same time. Simply stop what you are doing, greet the customer and say 'I'm sorry, but would you mind if I just took this call?' Then greet the telephone caller and try to keep the conversation relatively short. Agree to ring back if necessary – and certainly do this if the call is internal. Then turn back to your customer and say, 'I'm sorry to have kept you waiting.' The reason for doing it this way round is because the customer in front of you can see your problem, and so should be more understanding, whereas the person on the telephone would have no idea why you weren't answering promptly.

▼ Using an appropriate tone and manner

You have already read about the importance of tone with colleagues in your team, on page 56. If you have forgotten what this is, look back now and refresh your memory.

You should always speak politely to all your customers – no matter who they are or what they look like – and try to help them. You already know that you should use a customer's surname unless you are specifically told to use their first name and that you should be more formal with senior staff at work and external customers than with your own team. It also helps if you remember these tips, too.

▶ Think before you speak – even if you are taken by surprise. This means you are less likely to be tactless or thoughtless.

▶ Watch other people who are good at dealing with customers. Listen to the way they talk to a customer – and model your behaviour on someone who particularly impresses you.

▶ Think about the way *you* like to be treated. Then set this as your minimum standard!

▶ Think carefully if you need to ask a personal question, such as, 'How old are you?' If you must obtain personal information from a customer then put it diplomatically, e.g. 'Would you mind telling me your date of birth – I need it for your application form.' Often simply telling someone *why* you need the information makes all the difference!

▶ Practise dealing with customers so that you gain more confidence. This is the only way you will develop and improve your communication skills so that you can cope in a variety of situations.

▼ Conveying information clearly and accurately

An essential part of any administrator's job is to be able to pass on information to other people – including customers. However, it is no use passing it on if the information is incorrect or the other person cannot understand you! You also need to be aware of information which may be confidential or which you are not allowed to provide.

Clarity of information

There are three aspects relating to clarity of information. It depends upon your ability to check your facts and understanding, choose the right words and speak clearly.

▶ **Checking your facts and understanding**. You will be able to provide clear information only if you understand what you are saying. Any information you pass on must also be accurate. Whether you have looked up information yourself, or received a message from someone else, you should always write down and double-check all the key items – especially any dates, times, names or places. *Never* be tempted to guess a fact just because you don't like asking someone to repeat something. If you are worried about how to take a message properly, you can read how to do this in Unit 1, page 12.

▶ **Choosing the right words**. This means using only words that you understand yourself and being precise. Refer to people properly by name and, if necessary, by their job title so that there is no doubt who you mean. Always use both the day *and* date if you are confirming when something will be done or will take place. Speak in proper sentences. Don't use slang or any words a customer would not easily understand. Remember that if you say 'OK', this will normally be taken as an agreement that you have understood and will do something; so don't use 'OK' just to confirm you have heard someone properly!

▶ **Speaking clearly.** It is no use having accurate facts and saying the right words if you mutter, speak at high speed or don't look at someone you are speaking to! If you are talking face-to-face with a customer then *always* make eye contact and don't talk too quickly. If you have to leave a verbal message on a telephone answering machine or use Voicemail, don't gabble at high speed so that you can hang up as quickly as possible. If you do, your information will often be totally incomprehensible. Again, for tips, look back at Unit 1, page 15.

The need for confidentiality

All organisations deal with a large amount of information which they would never divulge to their external customers. There may be written rules on this which state the information you can provide and that which you cannot but you will also be expected to use your common sense. You can safely assume that any information which directly relates to staff or customer personal details, or to the financial aspects of the business, is always confidential.

Generally, confidentiality is less of a problem with internal customers, because most of them will have access to the same information as you. However, the type of information they are allowed will depend upon their job role and seniority in the company. Whilst a senior manager or director will have access to all types of information, a junior member of staff will not, so you still need to be careful.

When you first start work, you can avoid any problems by erring on the safe side. If you are asked for any type of information which you haven't seen your colleagues provide regularly, then simply explain that you must check with your supervisor or team leader first. This is far wiser than taking a chance and causing a serious problem by your actions.

OVER TO YOU!

1 You are on duty in your college reception area for an Open Evening and are expected to greet people as they enter the building. Suggest how you would greet *each* of the following.
   a) Two parents and their son – none of whom you know.
   b) The mother of your friend
   c) Your younger sister
   d) A member of the college staff you don't know very well.

2 During the evening, your tutor tells you she has run out of leaflets for a course and asks you to go to the office to get some more. When you return, she asks you to give one to two parents who are talking to another member of staff in the corner.

   Explain exactly what you would say to the parents when you approached them.

3 You are alone in an office and are in the middle of a tricky job, sorting out some files. A manager from another office calls in and starts to speak to you, the telephone rings and you suddenly see a delivery man standing at the reception window.

   Decide what you would do and say to each person in this situation – and in what order – and then compare your answers with other members of your group.

4 Rephrase each of the following sentences so they are said in a more tactful way.
   a) 'I can't do it now, you'll have to wait a bit.'
   b) 'I didn't hear you. What did you say?'
   c) 'I haven't a clue.'
   d) 'Yes? What do you want?'
   e) 'What's your name?'

5 You are working for a photographer, John Parker, on work experience. He is rushing out when he suddenly asks you to phone a customer, Joanne Davis, who enquired about

wedding photographs yesterday. He wants to know if he can call to see her at 7 pm on Thursday. Her number is 809709.

a) Which 'checks' should you quickly make with John Parker to ensure that you have the correct facts?

b) Assuming that there is no answer when you ring, so that you have to leave a message on the answerphone, write down exactly what you would say.

c) Later that day, Joanne Davis rings back. She asks if you could let her have the name and address of someone else for whom John Parker has taken wedding photographs, so that she can check what his work is like. What would you say in reply, and why?

d) Joanne Davis will be out on Thursday evening and over the weekend but could meet John Parker the following Monday at 7 pm. You do not know whether John Parker is free or not that evening. What would you do in this situation?

▼ Communicating effectively with customers

It is one thing just to say a few words to a customer and quite another having a conversation or asking a series of questions. Yet this may be essential if you going to help a customer properly. Good communication is not just about saying things properly, but also about making sure that the other person has understood you.

In this situation, you will communicate effectively only if you:

▶ listen carefully

▶ check the customer understands you

▶ ask appropriate questions to check understanding or to obtain the information you need.

If the person is standing in front of you, then you can use their (and your) body language to help you and, in this section, you will see how to cope when you are on the telephone and so cannot do this.

You also need to know how to spot potential problems and to learn how to deal with them.

Listening skills

Most people are very poor listeners. In any conversation they impatiently wait for the other person to finish speaking so they can say the next thing they have just thought of. In some cases they even interrupt the speaker, to have their own say.

You can tell how well someone listens by the amount of information they can remember afterwards. If they can remember only their own contribution to the conversation, then this proves they haven't been listening at all!

You will be a good listener only if you concentrate on what someone else is saying at the time they are saying it. It helps to make notes – especially if you are on the telephone or the information is quite detailed. However, this isn't always possible. If you meet an internal customer in a corridor who gives you a message for someone, then you may have to repeat it to yourself over and over so that you don't forget it before you can write it down.

Try hard to develop your listening skills whenever you can, such as when you are listening to the radio or television or are in class. See if you can spot when you are 'switching off' and try to prevent it. Test yourself by seeing if you can repeat back *accurately* what someone else has said to you a few minutes before.

Understanding each other

There are several reasons why a customer may not understand you – or you might not understand the customer. These include the following:

▶ Either, or both of you, are bad listeners.

▶ The customer doesn't speak English very well – such as a foreign visitor.

▶ The customer is not speaking clearly because of a speech impairment or a very strong accent.

▶ The customer is using technical terms or jargon you don't understand.

You have already learned about the importance of developing your own listening skills – but you can hardly insist that your customers do the same! A good plan is never to try to speak when your customer is speaking. Listen to what the customer says, repeat it back to reassure the customer that you have understood what was said, then say what you need to say and listen carefully to the response.

If your customer doesn't speak English well or doesn't speak clearly – or is using terms you don't understand, try not to be embarrassed. Instead, deal with the problem as practically and positively as you can. Use the table below to guide you.

Solving problems with customer understanding

Reason for problem	What to do
A foreign visitor cannot speak English very well	• Speak relatively slowly and *very* clearly so that all your words are distinct. • Use simple words in short sentences. • Avoid slang or local expressions. • Rephrase your sentence if the visitor looks puzzled. • Listen carefully when they repeat something back to you. • Provide dates, numbers and other essential information in writing.
A customer has a speech impediment	• Listen carefully and concentrate on what is being said to you. • Repeat back what you have heard. • Don't confuse a speech problem with a lack of intelligence. Your customer may just have had several teeth removed by the dentist! • As a last resort, ask the customer to write down a word you really cannot understand.
A customer with a very strong accent	• Concentrate on what is being said. • Ask the customer to speak more slowly or repeat the sentence. • Repeat back what you have heard. • Again, as a last resort, ask the customer to write down any words you cannot understand.
A customer using technical	• Never be tempted to pretend you know

terms or jargon	something you don't.
	• Explain that you are not a technical expert so you need their help in understanding the information.
	• Write down a specialist term or abbreviation and check the spelling.
	• Ask a team member for help if you get desperate.
	• Ask either your team member – or the customer – to explain the term, so that you'll know it next time!

Sometimes you may be uncertain whether a customer has understood you or not. There are two main ways in which you can check this. You can ask questions and you can assess body language. You can read about both of these below.

Asking appropriate questions

There is a difference between asking appropriate questions and interrogating someone! There is also a difference between the questions you should ask if you are obtaining information and if you are providing it – and just want to check the other person understands you.

▶ **Obtaining information**. If you know you have to contact a customer to obtain information, make a list of questions first. Remember not to ask any unnecessary personal questions and to phrase your queries tactfully. Explain why you need the information and don't rush through the list. Repeat the information back at each point to make sure that you have understood what was said.

▶ **Providing information**. Never give people a list of facts too quickly. Think of your conversation as having an introduction, a middle part and an ending. An appropriate introduction means you explain what you are talking about so the customer quickly realises what the conversation is all about. At key points, ask appropriate questions to check the other person's understanding. This doesn't mean being patronising! Never say, for example, 'Do you understand me?' or 'Am I making myself clear?' or you imply the other person is simply being dim! Instead ask, 'Is that what you wanted to know?' or 'Do you need me to explain this in more detail?'

Interpreting body language

Body language relates to the way we use facial expressions, posture and other gestures to say how we feel. Someone who is puzzled will frown, whereas someone who understands you will often nod in agreement. People who are interested in what you are saying look at you and lean forward. Someone who is bored looks away and may even start to move away from you. People who are impatient and in a rush may tap their feet or check their watch. There are dozens of signs and signals you can spot to see how customers are reacting to what you say.

You should also note that your customers are watching *your* body language! If you yawn, look away or check your watch when you are speaking then you are giving all the signals of boredom or disinterest – regardless of what you are actually saying.

If you are to communicate effectively then your body language should be in harmony with the words you use and you should react to any signs of bewilderment you see. At that point you should stop and say, 'I can see you're looking worried, do you want me to repeat that part?'

▲ Positive body language means positive communication

▲ Negative body language means negative communication

On the telephone, remember that you cannot see bewilderment – but you can hear silence and you can often spot when someone *sounds* baffled. So if the other person says very little, or if his or her voice has changed, stop and check that there are no misunderstandings. In addition, listen carefully to the replies you receive, because this might be the first sign you get that you are not communicating effectively.

Despite all your efforts, however, there will be occasions when you have a problem. How to identify and cope with these is covered in the next section.

PEOPLE IN BUSINESS

The WOW! Awards are awarded to UK organisations which not only have high customer service standards but who also manage to uphold these and WOW their customers through their professionalism and service.

The WOW awards are sponsored by a business called Stephens & Co. Their managing director, Derek Williams, talks to companies about customer service. The company provides a range of training courses and has worked with organisations such as the BBC, Barclays Bank and Interflora.

You can read about the service given by companies who have won an award by clicking onto the WOW website at www.heinemann.co.uk/hotlinks and can find out about the type of service which impresses customers. You can also read useful business tips such as 'Who has the most power when a customer telephones your business? The managing director or the receptionist?'

What is *your* answer to this question?

▼ Identifying and coping with problem situations

There are several reasons why you may have a problem when you deal with a customer but the main ones are likely to be because:

▶ you do not know enough to help them

▶ the customer is agitated, nervous, shy or upset

▶ the customer is annoyed or angry and has a serious complaint.

In many cases, you may think there could be a problem, yet by handling the situation positively, you cope well on your own. If you feel you are out of your depth, or the situation is becoming worse, then it is important that you get help. That way, the encounter can eventually be ended to the customer's satisfaction.

Use the information below to help you identify potential problems, when to ask for help – and who to ask.

▶ **You do not know enough to help them**. This problem will fade with time and as you become more experienced. Remember that it is quite possible to be helpful and to give a positive impression without knowing the answer to a question. If you have forgotten how to do this, then look back at page 66. If someone else – such as a colleague or your team leader – is nearby, then always ask for assistance. If not, or if your colleague cannot help, then explain that you will have to refer the request to your supervisor or team leader and will then telephone the customer yourself with the answer later, get someone else to do so, or send the information by post. Then check you have every single detail correct so that there can be no misunderstandings about the request. Finally, make sure you pass on the information accurately to your supervisor or team leader as soon as you can and obtain clear guidance on what you should do next.

▶ **Customers who are agitated, nervous, shy or upset**. Our feelings affect the way we speak and behave. They are also reflected in our body language. Someone who is agitated may speak quickly or find it difficult to speak at all. A shy or nervous person will be hesitant and try to avoid eye contact. People who are upset may have trouble speaking and controlling their emotions.

You can encourage someone who is shy or nervous by taking your time, smiling and making sure you don't rush them. If someone is agitated and is speaking too quickly, you may have to ask them to slow down a little. Try to say this tactfully! If someone is genuinely distressed and upset then try to arrange for any conversation to take place in a private office or in a screened-off area and – whilst you accompany them to this area – ask someone else to notify your team leader.

▶ **Customers who are annoyed, angry or have a serious complaint**. If someone is annoyed or angry, you can usually spot this very quickly. They may be slightly flushed and will probably speak more loudly than usual. This is because they have something bottled up which they want to tell you about, such as a serious complaint about something. In this case:

– let them have their say without interrupting

– apologise for the problem they have experienced (This is not the same as accepting the blame. You are apologising on behalf of your organisation.)

- take down all the details, so the customer can see you are taking the matter seriously

- assure the customer you will refer the problem to someone who can deal with it straightaway – and do so

- try not to get upset. The customer is annoyed with the organisation – not you, personally. However, this does not mean you should have to tolerate personal insults. If an angry customer is being verbally abusive in any way, ask your team leader or a colleague for help immediately.

OVER TO YOU!

Answer questions 1 to 3 first on your own and then compare your answers with other members of your group. Then work in pairs for the final activity.

1 Maria is asked by a senior manager to do what appears to be quite a complicated photocopying job. At the end of the conversation she can remember only the words '50 pages', 'urgent', 'tomorrow'. She goes to see her supervisor, who immediately asks who gave her the job. Maria doesn't know. She also doesn't know whether she is holding 50 pages or if 50 pages are required of each document.

a) The supervisor is annoyed, can you say why?

b) What is the *first* thing that Maria should have found out?

c) What questions should Maria have asked to check her understanding?

d) Suggest *two* things Maria could do to try to solve the problem.

2 Look at the following illustration of a reception area. Can you identify:

a) Which person is in a rush and is becoming annoyed at waiting?

b) Which person is very nervous?

c) Which two people have arrived together?

d) Which person is quite relaxed about waiting?

e) The attitude of the receptionist on the left?

f) The attitude of the receptionist on the right?

Give a reason for your answers.

3 Kim is working at a local newspaper office on work experience and has been asked to help out on reception. In each of the following situations, explain what you would do if you were Kim.

a) She is approached by a woman who keeps showing her last night's paper and pointing to a photograph. Unfortunately, the woman speaks English very poorly and although Kim tries hard she cannot understand what the woman is saying.

b) A man arrives and says he has come to collect a package which has been left for him. His name is Tom Bryant. Kim searches the area but cannot find anything with his name on it.

c) A woman arrives, says her name is Julia Kent and she has an appointment with Kim's boss, Lynda Bell. Kim telephones her boss to inform her but there is no reply.

d) A young man approaches the desk. He says he is Masoud from IT services and he needs to check one of the motherboards. Kim hasn't the faintest idea what he is talking about.

e) An older man comes to her and waves a folded paper in the air. He says that he advertised his car in the paper last night but the phone number given was wrong so he wants his money back. He is quite angry and claims all the staff are totally inefficient because this is the second time this has happened to him.

4 You want to talk to a travel agent about going on holiday, but when you call in during your lunchtime it is very busy. An assistant comes over to you, apologises for the delay and asks if she can help.

You tell her you want information about a planned trip to a specific place, you state the dates and how long you want to stay, and explain the type of hotel you want and how you want to travel. You ask if someone can ring you and give her your name and telephone number, which she writes down.

Now role play this situation with a colleague. One of you should decide exactly where and when you want to go and other details related to the trip. The other plays the part of the assistant – who during the conversation can write down only the telephone number.

The aim of this activity is to test your listening skills. After the conversation has ended, the assistant should write down as much as he or she can remember. Then check if the details are correct and reverse roles.

If you are both very good at this, you can make your information a little more detailed to see if you still do well!

Preparing for work in business organisations

Introduction

One of the best things about learning administration is that it gives you the skills to work in a wide variety of organisations. Just about every business needs administrators! This provides great opportunities, but it also means that when you start work you might not understand why that particular business operates as it does and how it is organised.

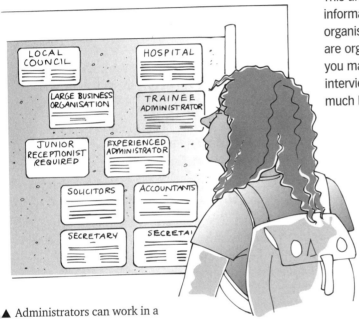

This unit prepares you for work by giving you basic information about different types of business organisations as well as examples of how activities are organised and the type of administration tasks you may be asked to do. When you go to an interview, or start work, you should then have a much better idea of what to expect.

Wherever you work it is expected that you will be well organised and work safely. You will also have certain legal rights and responsibilities to your employer. It is important that you know about these because there can be serious consequences if you fail to meet them.

The aim of this unit is to provide you with the knowledge you need to enable you to contribute effectively to the work of the organisation from the very start.

▲ Administrators can work in a wide range of organisations

Unit summary

This unit is divided into four sections.

▶ **Describe business organisations.** Here you will learn about the different types of business organisations that exist and how they are organised in relation to their activities.

▶ **Describe administration activities.** This section covers the range of administration tasks which are carried out in most business organisations, as well as the equipment and documents which are used.

▶ **Describe ways to be organised in order to improve work.** Here you will find out how to be well organised, so that you work efficiently and tidily, as well as how you can improve your own work and performance.

▶ **Identify rights and responsibilities at work.** Finally, you will learn how to work safely as an administrator and your legal rights and responsibilities as an employee.

Assessment

Your assessment for this unit will consist of a written examination of two hours. You also have an additional 10 minutes to read the paper before you start writing.

There will be four questions on the examination paper, one for each main section of the paper. Each question will have a number of sub-sections and you will be expected to answer all of these.

Some of the questions in the *Over to You!* sections of this chapter are practical activities to help you to understand more about various topics. Others are similar to the type of questions you will find on the examination paper. Answering these will give you practice in how to think and respond to gain good marks.

▼ Describe business organisations

As an administrator you may start work in a very small firm, with only a few employees – or your first job may be in a large organisation, with many different departments. If you change jobs later, you may find your next company is organised in a different way – even if it is roughly the same size!

These differences occur because all organisations organise their activities in the best way for their own needs. This will depend upon the type of work carried out, the size of the business, who owns it and what the organisation is trying to achieve.

However, some aspects are common to all business organisations – such as needing to make a profit and wanting to please their customers. There are also common activities carried out by all businesses – such as answering customer queries and keeping financial records. Once you realise what these are, and the most usual ways of organising them, it will help you to adapt if you later work somewhere different. You can also understand the reason for the differences and settle in more quickly.

Organisations in the private sector

Most businesses in Britain are in the **private sector**. This means that they are **owned by private individuals**. There are four types of privately owned business and these can be divided into two categories – those which have unlimited liability for their debts, and those which have limited liability.

▲ You can see different private sector businesses in the high street

Unlimited liability

Unlimited liability means that the owners are responsible for all the debts. If the business struggles, then the owners may have to sell their personal possessions to pay them. If they cannot do this, they are declared bankrupt. For this reason, businesses which have unlimited liability usually operate on a small scale.

There are two types of organisations which have unlimited liability.

1 **Sole traders**   This type of business is owned and run by *one person*. Examples include many greengrocers, newsagents and market traders. This person makes all the decisions about the business. He or she may employ other people as assistants, but there is only one owner.

The advantages of being a sole trader include:

▶ being independent and not having a boss

▶ being able to make quick decisions

▶ the owner can keep all the profit

▶ a personal service can be given to customers.

However, there are also some disadvantages:

▶ unlimited liability for all the debts

▶ working hours may be very long

▶ illness and sickness create problems – and so do holidays. A sole trader does not have paid holidays

▶ success is completely dependent upon the owner's skills

▶ it can be difficult to raise money to expand or modernise the business

▶ the owner is responsible for all aspects of the business, including the routine paperwork.

2 **Partnerships**   A partnership is owned and run by *two or more people*. Examples include many doctors, vets, solicitors and accountants. The partners must agree about all major decisions affecting the business.

There are several advantages to being a partner:

▶ any problems or worries can be shared and discussed.

▶ it is easier to raise money if all the partners contribute.

▶ between them, the partners will have a greater range of skills than one person and may be able to **specialise** in what they are good at.

▶ there is always someone to cover during holidays or if someone is off sick.

There are also disadvantages, for example:

▶ the partners have unlimited liability for the debts

▶ the partners may not always agree, so there may be arguments

▶ the profits must be shared

▶ all the partners must be consulted before a decision is made

▶ If a partner leaves, the others must buy out that partner's share, otherwise the partnership may have to be dissolved.

Limited liability

Some business organisations have **limited liability**. In this case the owners are liable to pay debts only up to the limit of their investment. They would not have to sell their personal possessions if the business was in trouble. For this reason, large organisations prefer the protection of limited liability. So do smaller businesses which need to invest in expensive equipment or stock.

There are two types of business organisations which have limited liability.

1 **Private limited companies**   This is the name given to businesses which are run privately, often by a family. All these companies have 'Ltd' at the end of their name, such as many local garages and retailers.

Private limited companies have certain advantages:

▶ the main one is the protection of limited liability. If the owners (who are usually the directors) have invested £500 each, this is the maximum they can lose, no matter how much the business owes

▶ the business can remain small and its affairs are still private

▶ because the owners work in the business they know it well and will work hard to help it succeed

▶ banks are more willing to lend money to limited companies.

There are, however, some disadvantages.

▶ a limited company has to comply with more regulations and laws than sole traders or partnerships.

▶ all the owners have shares in the company and are called shareholders. One share equals one vote, so the owners with the most shares are always the most powerful.

2 **Public limited companies**   These are organisations whose shares are traded on the Stock Exchange. All these companies have 'plc' at the end of their name. They include famous businesses such as Tesco, Marks and Spencer, and Debenhams.

There are advantages to operating as a public limited company:

▶ because shares can now be sold to members of the public, it is much easier to raise money for expansion and development

▶ a very large company often has an advantage over its smaller competitors because it can buy or produce goods in bulk and sell them more cheaply.

However, again there are some disadvantages:

▶ Public limited companies have to comply with many laws and regulations

▶ All their business affairs can be made public and problems may be reported in the press.

▶ If the company does not make a good profit many shareholders may sell their shares. This can cause financial problems.

The objectives of private sector businesses

All businesses in the private sector have **one** common objective: they all aim to make a profit. If they did not, then they could not pay their bills and would have to close.

Some businesses also want to increase their sales and to grow larger – but not all. Your local grocery store may be run by a husband and wife team who have no desire to run a large business or a chain of shops.

Large businesses may increase their sales by selling goods more cheaply than their competitors and all businesses can aim to sell more by providing a better service to their customers than their rivals.

Working in the private sector

All businesses in the private sector check their business performance regularly. The business would aim to be competitive, retain its customers and attract new ones. It would want to keep its costs down and increase sales because then it would make more profit.

In a small firm, you would probably find you were expected to do a wide variety of jobs and to be very flexible. This might mean working late, if the company is busy – but you might not always be paid for this! You would be expected to work hard and cooperate to help to make the business successful.

In a large company, your work may be specialised because you would be more likely to work in a particular department – as you will see on page 90. Your hours would be fixed and overtime may be paid.

As an employee in any company you would receive a regular wage and have the right to paid holidays and statutory sick pay if you were ill (see page 148.)

ORGANISATIONS IN BUSINESS

When Charles Dunstone left school his first intention was to do a business degree at Liverpool University. That was until he worked as a computer salesman at NEC during his year off and liked it so much he decided to stay there. He then transferred to NEC's mobile phone division, which sold phones to large businesses. He soon discovered that there were no organisations to help small businesses or individuals who wanted to buy mobiles. This gave him the idea of starting his own business.

In 1989, when he was 25 years old, he started his business using £6,000 he had in the bank, and called it Carphone Warehouse. A year later, his friend and partner David Ross joined him. Today their business is Europe's largest retailer of mobile phones.

Although Charles Dunstone could have started his business as a sole trader – or gone into partnership with David Ross – he decided that Carphone Warehouse should be a private limited company. This is because they would have limited liability – which is a safer option for a business buying and selling mobile phones. In July 2000 the company floated on the London Stock Exchange. It is now a public limited company with over 8,000 employees and more than 4,000 shops in the UK alone.

You can find out much more about Carphone Warehouse at its website at www.heinemann.co.uk/hotlinks.

OVER TO YOU!

1 Identify the type of organisation which each of the following businesses is most likely to be. Give a reason for your answer in each case and then compare your ideas with other members of your group.

a) A plumber who works for himself.

b) B & Q – the large chain of DIY superstores.

c) A jewellery shop which is owned by a local family.

d) Three brothers who own a local firm of estate agents.

2 Martin and his brother opened a car repair workshop two years ago. They run it as a partnership but are thinking of converting their business to a private limited company.

a) Identify the main reason why they might want to do this.

b) Describe 2 further advantages they will gain.

c) Describe 1 disadvantage of their plan.

3 Shahida is fantastic at making her own dresses. Her sister, Parveen, is not as good at sewing, but has an eye for design and is good at choosing fabrics. Shahida cannot decide whether to run her own business or to go into partnership with Parveen and has asked you for help.

List the advantages and disadvantages for Shahida of both her ideas, then say what you would suggest she does – and give a reason for your decision.

4 The chart below summarises some of the main aspects of private business organisations, but some of these are missing.

Copy out the chart and complete it yourself from the notes you have read in this section. Then keep it safely to help you when you are revising for the examination.

The main aspects of private business organisations

Type of organisation	Owner(s)	Control	Objectives	Liability
Sole trader	One individual			The owner is personally liable for all debts.
		The partners must all agree about major decisions.	To make a profit. May want to expand or to improve customer service.	
Private limited company	The directors/ shareholders (often family members)		To make a profit. To increase sales or beat their competitors. May want to expand.	The owners could lose the money they have invested in the business but are not personally responsible for debts. They have limited liability.
	The owners and shareholders – who can be members of the public	The directors run the business every day but the shareholders can vote at important meetings.	To make a profit. To expand. To be more competitive. To increase sales.	

Organisations in the public sector

All public sector organisations are **owned by the state** – or government – on behalf of all of us. There are three types.

1 **Public corporations**   There are only a few public corporations in Britain. The main ones are the Bank of England, the BBC, the Royal Mail Group and British Nuclear Fuels. These are all large businesses which continue to be owned by the state because they provide services which everyone needs (such as the Royal Mail) or are expected to operate in the public interest (such as the Bank of England). There are no shareholders. Instead the government states how the business should operate and can be involved in the choice of the most senior people to run it – such as the Chairperson and Board of Directors. The money to run the business comes mainly from taxes collected by the government and a government minister is responsible for the overall performance of the business.

▲ Different public sector organisations

2 **Local authorities**   There are local authorities in every area in Britain. Their aim is to provide services for the local community according to the needs of the area. For that reason, the services provided in a rural community are different from those provided to an inner city area.

If you worked in your local town hall (or county hall) or for a district council, you would be employed by the local authority. Their actions are controlled by local councils – and the councillors are chosen in local elections.

The money to provide local services, such as refuse collection and road maintenance, comes from three main sources. The government gives local authorities money each year, called the Revenue Support Grant; all householders in the area pay council tax and all businesses have to pay a business rate. The council, and the local authority, has to account for its spending to the government and to the local people.

3 **Government departments**   There are many government departments, all of which deal with different matters at a national level. They oversee public services which are provided across the nation, such as education, the National Health Service, social security benefits, defence and the armed forces, the police and prison service and motorway building and maintenance.

Each department has its own government minister who is responsible to parliament for the performance of his or her department. This is because the money to run the department comes from general taxation, such as income tax and VAT, which is paid by everyone.

Working in the public sector

Most public sector organisations operate on a large scale – such as hospitals, police forces, government departments and local authorities. The main focus is on providing a service. Because these organisations are accountable to the government and use public money for their operations, they are very careful about their spending.

If you had a job in the public sector you would probably work in a department which is responsible for one particular aspect of the whole organisation. For example, in a local authority there are separate departments for housing, environmental health and social services.

ORGANISATIONS IN BUSINESS

The BBC is in the public sector. It is a public corporation and is responsible to the government for its television programmes. It obtains the money to make these through the TV licence fee which all television viewers must pay. This fee is collected by the BBC, which is the licensing authority, on behalf of the government.

In contrast, ITV is in the private sector. It is a public limited company and is owned by its shareholders and run by its directors. It raises the money to make programmes by charging advertisers. This is why you see adverts on ITV but not when you are watching the BBC.

Some people think this difference is unfair. They argue that some viewers may not like BBC programmes but still have to pay the licence fee. They also say it makes life easier for the BBC because it doesn't have to do anything to obtain its money – and knows in advance how much it will get.

Others disagree – including the BBC. They argue that the BBC cannot just please itself what programmes to produce. It has to produce more programmes 'in the public interest' – such as news programmes, whereas ITV could show soaps all day if it wanted. If the BBC did that, then MPs could criticise this in the House of Commons and the Minister of Culture, Media and Sport would have to respond to their questions.

▲ Frankie Dettori, Sue Barker and Ally McCoist on the BBC programme *Question of Sport*.

Ben has just completed an IT course at his local college and is looking for a job. He has seen three interesting advertisements in the local paper.

▶ An IT technician is required by a large hospital in the area.

▶ A small company which produces games software wants an IT trainee.

▶ A large computer superstore in the area is taking on IT specialists.

Ben's other option would be to set up in business himself. He is particularly good at designing websites and thinks he could interest local businesses if he can keep his price low.

Work in groups to do the following activities.

1 Decide whether each job advertised is in the private sector or the public sector.

2 Identify the *differences* Ben is likely to find between the three jobs on offer, bearing in mind the type of organisations he could work for.

3 Decide the main differences Ben would find between being an employee (in any of the firms) and being self-employed in his own business.

4 Decide which job you would advise Ben to take if:

a) he wants the least risky job of all

b) he wants the most exciting and fast-moving job but doesn't want to work alone

c) he wants to make all his own decisions

d) he likes dealing with a wide range of people, every day.

Compare your ideas with other members of your group.

The activities of business organisations

All organisations carry out a range of activities to achieve the aims of the business. In a small firm, these activities may be shared amongst a small number of people who are overseen by one or two managers. In a larger firm, the activities will be carried out in departments. Each department will have a manager and these managers will be responsible to a more senior person – usually a director.

Roles and responsibilities in business

Employees in a business usually operate at different levels. This is good because it enables people who work hard to move up in an organisation. In a very small business there may only be two or three levels. In a large business there may be up to seven levels – or even more! This is known as a **hierarchy** and is often shown in the shape of a pyramid.

▲ A business hierarchy

The pyramid shape occurs because, in a hierarchy, there are always fewer people in the top jobs (maybe only one person) and more people lower down. All the people in the hierarchy have specific titles and certain responsibilities related to these titles.

- **Directors** operate at the most senior level. They are responsible for the long term planning of the business, its financial performance and often oversee the work of several managers or a very large department. The chief director often has the title of Managing Director or Chief Executive.

- **Managers** are responsible for the work of specific departments or parts of a very large department. They must make sure that all the activities in their department are carried out to the required standard, that deadlines are met and that any problems are sorted out quickly. A manager is often responsible for the work of quite a large number of staff.

- **Supervisors** assist managers who are responsible for quite a large department or area of work. They are responsible for fewer staff than a manager but must make sure their own section runs smoothly and safely and that all the jobs are done to the deadline. They have to solve basic problems but would discuss a serious problem with their manager.

Below supervisors in the pyramid are all the remaining workers in the organisation.

Departmental functions and activities

All large businesses are divided into departments. Each department is responsible for specific activities which need to be done within the business. Even if you work in only one department in a large organisation, you will do your job better if you understand what is happening in other parts of the business.

The table below gives you the names of the main departments you will find and the key activities they carry out.

Departments in business

Department	Main activities carried out
Finance	Paying all the bills received by the business, paying staff wages, sending out invoices for goods or services provided, recording all the money received and paid out to calculate the company accounts which show the profit (or loss) made by the business.
Personnel	Looking after all welfare of all the human resources (the existing staff) in the organisation; recruiting all new staff (including placing job adverts, reading applications and interviewing applicants); organising training activities.
Research and development	Designing new products or services; testing these to make sure they work and meet customer expectations
Production	Making all the goods sold by the organisation, maintaining all the production equipment, checking the quality of all goods produced.
Buying	Buying all the raw materials required by the company (such as denim if the company makes jeans); buying all the other supplies used by the business; checking prices to make sure the company is not paying too much
Marketing	Finding out customer opinions and views, linking these to the way the product or service is sold, promoting the company and its products.

Sales	Advertising the product or service, dealing with customer queries, visiting customers.
Administration	Providing office services, such as document production, collecting and distributing mail, filing and photocopying; supporting other departments by undertaking these services; working with customers by responding to queries and providing information.

The titles of departments – and the number of departments – varies from one business to another.

▶ An organisation which produces goods must have a production department where the goods are made. If the business provides a service then this department may be called Operations. For example, in an airport, the Operations Manager is responsible for the flight schedules.

▶ A small company may not need a separate personnel or 'human resources' department because there may be only a few staff employed.

▶ Another variation is that the buying department is called the purchasing department.

▶ A business which buys and sells goods, such as Dixons, would not need a research and development department, and neither would most businesses which provide a service. R & D departments are normally found in companies which produce goods and need to constantly develop their products eg Apple computers.

▶ Sales and Marketing are often combined into one department and you will also often find that there is no separate Administration department. Instead, administrators are employed within each of the departments.

▶ Many businesses today also have a separate IT department – or this may be linked to Administration.

You therefore need to be able to think about the size of the business and what it does, before you decide which departments it would be likely to have.

Key activities in *all* businesses, however, include finance, purchasing (if goods are made or bought for resale), production (if goods are made) and sales.

OVER TO YOU!

Four people have given you information about their jobs at Scientronic plc. Their job titles are: Finance Director, Sales Manager, Personnel Manager and Quality Control Supervisor. Read their comments and then answer the following questions.

1 Identify the title of each person who made a statement.

2 Which person is the most senior?

3 Which person is the most junior?

4 To which four departments do they belong?

5 Suggest 3 other departments at Scientronic and describe 2 activities which would be carried out in each of them.

a) 'It costs a lot of money to recruit new staff so I am very keen to make sure that we look after our existing employees. If anyone has a family emergency we immediately talk to them about taking time off work. We send flowers if anyone has a new baby, an accident or is in hospital, and can arrange company loans or advances if they have a serious financial problem.'

b) 'Because we deal direct with business organisations we employ representatives who visit our customers every month. This helps us to keep in touch with what customers want and to answer their queries in person.'

c) 'We make scientific equipment for industry. It is important that our Production Department is well organised so that all the items are produced on time to meet our customer's orders. However, even more important is the fact that all the equipment we make is checked carefully to make sure it works accurately and it is my job to make sure this is done.'

d) 'I am responsible for a large team of accountants. Some of these monitor our revenue and spending on a daily basis. This is vital because we must always make sure we have enough money in the bank to pay our immediate bills. Every year we publish our annual accounts. This is a legal requirement for public limited companies. An important document for our shareholders is our profit and loss account, which states how much profit we have made that year.'

▼ Describe administration activities

All administrators carry out a variety of activities every day. This is one reason why the job can be so interesting. They also use a range of different equipment, from large expensive items, such as photocopiers, to small ones such as hole punches and staplers. This helps them to do their work quickly and easily.

Administrators also deal with a wide variety of paperwork every day. These documents often vary from one department to another. For example, a sales department will make out customer orders and, after the order has been delivered, finance will issue an invoice stating that payment is due.

You will do your job much more effectively if you understand the activities that you will be expected to carry out, the equipment you will have to use and the routine paperwork you will find in any office.

Administration tasks carried out by business organisations

Administration activities are carried out in every department in a business. Many activities, such as filing and document production, are carried out in all departments. Others are more likely to be done in certain departments than others. For example, you would be more likely to be working with customers regularly if you were in sales than if you were in personnel, because personnel only deals with current and prospective employees.

The following table identifies which departments are most likely to carry out certain activities – and also identifies those activities which are carried out by all departments.

Departmental admin activities

Administration activity	Department(s)
Making and receiving telephone calls	All
Reception work	Administration department Sales department (if customers have direct access) Some Personnel departments (if there is a separate reception area there for greeting job applicants)
Preparing documents	All
Filing	All
Opening and sorting mail	Administration department may do on this on behalf all the company or may be responsible only for delivering mail items to individual departments, who then open and sort their own post.
Preparing and mailing items	All departments will send items for despatch to the mail room. Administration department will be responsible for making sure these are prepared for despatch and mailed.
Using the photocopier and fax machines	Today all departments usually have their own photocopier and fax machines. A larger photocopier may be available in Administration.
Updating records (written and electronic)	Personnel will update staff records Sales will update customer records Buying will update stock records Finance will update financial records Administration may also update general records
Using a computer to carry out tasks	All
Working with customers	Mainly sales department, though finance may have to contact customers who query invoices.
Stock control	Buying department for raw materials Administration department for stationery

Equipment used by administrators

As an administrator you will have access to a variety of equipment to help you to do your job. At work, you will need to understand the main purpose of each type of equipment as well as how to use it. To achieve Unit 4 of this award, you will have to *demonstrate* that you can use specific items of equipment, such as a photocopier, fax or mailroom equipment. For this unit you need to know the reasons why certain items of equipment are used by specific departments.

▲ All administrators use a variety of equipment

Photocopiers

Photocopying is a routine activity in most organisations. A variety of documents may need to be copied every day by all departments.

Photocopiers range from large-scale models which can produce up to 100 documents a minute to much smaller versions. In addition, they have many different features.

▶ Some will print only black and white copies, others will print in black and white *and* colour.

▶ Some will only print copies, others will collate as well. Collating means that the pages in a multi-page document are automatically put in the correct order.

▶ Many will staple – either down the side, across the top or in the top left-hand corner. The position and number of staples is set by the operator.

▶ Virtually all will enlarge or reduce text or graphics.

▶ Most will print out on either A4 or A3 paper or address labels. (Note: A3 paper is twice as big as A4).

▶ Some will not only reproduce paper copies but can also receive copying instructions direct from a computer.

▲ Photocopiers come in many different sizes

If an organisation invests in a very large and expensive photocopier, then this will have to be shared by several departments. It may be placed in a separate room, near the Administration office.

Other organisations prefer to buy several smaller photocopiers and provide one for each department. This is more sensible if the departments are in different buildings on a large site. No one wants to have to walk for five minutes through pouring rain to copy three pages!

Fax machines

Fax machines are used to transmit documents to someone immediately. You can also talk to the other person, either before or after you have sent the fax, because every fax machine has a telephone attached and is linked to a telephone line. This is because fax machines work by scanning the document and then sending the image down a telephone line as digital pulses. The receiving machine then converts these back into the same image.

Like photocopiers, fax machines vary in size, from small machines that sit on a desktop to quite large ones which take up more space,

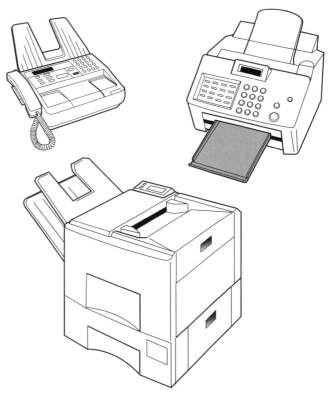

▲ There are different sizes and types of fax machine

have more features and may transmit and receive documents more rapidly. Large organisations often have several fax machines, such as one in every department, and perhaps a larger machine in administration as well. Even very small firms often have a fax machine, although it may be able to do other things, such as operate as an answering machine or computer printer. These types of 'combined' machines are called 'multi-function' devices – because they have several functions or uses.

Remember that fax machines are always used to send and receive urgent documents. It is therefore important that incoming faxes are passed on as quickly as possible to the right person, and not left on the machine!

Telephones and switchboard

On almost every office desk you will find a telephone, although it is likely to be different from the one you have at home, with more facilities and more options. It will also be connected to the main telephone system and will be just one telephone extension out of many. It will have a unique extension number, such as 2154. Callers who ring the company telephone number will have their calls answered by a switchboard operator who can put calls through to any of the extensions on the system. Some very large organisations have more than one switchboard and hundreds of extensions!

▲ Telephones in business today

Large switchboards often look more like a computer and keyboard than a telephone. The VDU can display which calls are waiting to be answered and how many callers are holding on (and for how long). This helps the switchboard operator to manage the calls efficiently. In some smaller companies, the switchboard operator may also work as the receptionist, greeting both telephone callers and visitors to the organisation. In a large business, with a very busy switchboard, this would be impractical. In this case the switchboard operator(s) will work in a separate area.

Modern telephone systems enable extension users to be dialled direct by regular outside contacts and customers. The caller just adds another two digits in front of the extension number. This reduces the number of calls which have to be handled by the switchboard.

Other facilities available for extension users include:

- dialling out direct, without having to go through the switchboard
- transferring callers to another extension. This is essential if a caller is put through to the wrong extension by mistake
- rerouting callers back to the switchboard
- automatically recalling another extension which is currently engaged
- redirecting calls to another extension. This is useful if someone will be away from their desk for some time
- an interrupt feature. In this cases the line 'bleeps' if a caller is waiting. This encourages the user to speed up their current call, so that people aren't kept waiting
- last number redial. This automatically redials the last number you called
- on hold. This allows an incoming call to be held whilst the correct person is found to deal with the call. Some modern systems will also keep reminding you that the caller is still waiting!

Finally, if you are very lucky, you will have a system which identifies the number of each caller and shows this on a display screen – so you know who is calling before you pick up the handset. Or you may have a cordless handset, so that if you have to walk across the room to check a file, you can still continue speaking to the caller.

ORGANISATIONS IN BUSINESS

Today everyone has got used to 'music on hold' – even if they don't like it very much. When you telephone most business organisations and are asked to hold on, you hear piped music whilst you wait.

Modern technology has changed the way incoming calls are dealt with over the last few years – and taken a huge burden away from many switchboard operators.

Many organisations have pre-recorded messages which give information about their services – such as cinemas which pre-record the times of performances. This saves the switchboard having to answer basic enquiries. Virtually all call centres and ticket agencies have queueing systems, so that callers are greeted with a pre-recorded message and then queued automatically. Further messages are given at regular intervals to customers who are still waiting.

The most sophisticated systems ask the caller to press specific numbers on the handset to choose the option they want. The caller may then be given another 'menu' of choices – and so on. This can be useful if the caller knows which department he or she wants, but exasperating if the caller simply wants to talk to another human being as quickly as possible!

Computers, printers and software

Today, one of the most commonly found pieces of equipment on any desk is a computer. Most administrators use a desktop PC but many managers may also use a laptop, especially if they frequently travel away from the office.

A desktop computer consists of a monitor, keyboard, processing unit and a mouse. Today most processing units (the 'brains' of the machine) are housed in a 'tower' unit, which also includes a floppy disk drive and a CD drive.

Desktop computers can be linked together over a computer network –

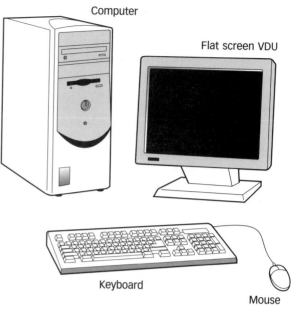

▲ The main components of a computer system

which means files and messages can be sent easily from one computer to another. Important information which is needed by everyone – such as customer details – is held on the network and can be accessed by all staff. Nearly all organisations today operate on a network system and so too will your college. Ask your tutor if you are not certain how this type of system works.

Computer users in an office may have their own individual printer. The most popular are inkjet printers, which work by spraying ink onto the paper. Inkjet printouts need to be dry before they are handled or they smudge, but this usually only takes a few seconds. Modern inkjet printers are inexpensive and provide good-quality copies in colour or black and white.

Alternatively, the company may have purchased laser printers, which are more expensive but operate much faster. The quality is also better. Because these printers are more expensive, one

▲ An office may have a laser or inkjet printer

may be shared by a small group of computer users. When the printer is busy, further print jobs are automatically 'queued' and dealt with in turn.

Computers are essential items in all offices because of all the different types of jobs which can be done on them, from writing letters and sending emails to preparing company accounts. The right software must be installed for this – and it will vary from one area of the business to another.

The table below shows some of the most commonly used software in business and the departments which are most likely to use it.

Computer software in business

Type of software	Main use	Departments
Word processing e.g. Word	To produce and edit documents	All – but mainly administration
Spreadsheet e.g. Excel	To carry out calculations and analyse figures	Mainly finance
Database e.g. Access	To create records which can be searched and analysed for information	Sales – for customer records Buying – for supplier records and stock control Personnel – for staff records
Presentation graphics e.g. PowerPoint	To produce presentations which can be shown on a computer or on a screen when linked to a data projector	Sales – for presentations to customers Personnel – for training events for staff Administration – for special presentations to the Board of Directors
Graphics e.g. Photoshop	To produce special graphics or insert photographs into documents	Marketing – for marketing and sales materials, such as catalogues
Accounts e.g. Sage	To input financial data and create company accounts	Finance
Payroll e.g. Sage	To calculate wages and salaries	Finance
Communications and Internet software e.g. Outlook Express and Internet Explorer	To create and send emails and to access the Internet	All

OVER TO YOU!

You are preparing to attend an interview for the job of junior administrator in the sales department of a large company. You are trying to think of answers to questions you might be asked.

How would you respond to each of the following questions in an interview? Answer these yourself and then compare your ideas with the rest of your group. If you wish, you could then try to repeat questions 1, 2, 3 and 5, this time choosing a different department in the company.

1 Can you suggest 3 administration activities you may be asked to carry out in this department?

2 Can you think of 1 administration activity you might have to do in this department more than in any other?

3 We have our own photocopier in this department and our own fax machine. Can you suggest 1 reason for using each of these machines?

4 You will obviously have to answer the telephone and we have a modern system installed. What facility on your extension would you use in each of the following situations?
   a) A caller was put through to you by mistake and really wanted the finance department.
   b) You were going on a staff training day and would be away from your desk all day.
   c) You were talking to someone in another office and heard a 'bleep' on your line.

5 You will use a computer as part of your work. Suggest 3 different types of software you would need on your system and say what you would use them for.

Franking machines

Franking machines are found in only one place in an organisation – the mailroom. They are used to print the exact mount of postage on an envelope, or on a label which can be attached to a package or parcel. This is much quicker than sticking on stamps and much less hassle! In addition to the postage amount, adverts and slogans can also be added.

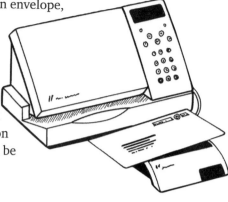

Postage units are stored in the machine. The total number of units is the amount that can be spent on postage. When the units are running out they can be topped up electronically by telephoning the manufacturer who transfers the units into the machine and then sends a bill for the value of the units to the organisation. Only authorised staff are allowed to contact the manufacturer.

▲ A franking machine is much faster than sticking on stamps

Filing equipment

Filing equipment consists of the cabinets (and the items inside them) in which files of documents are stored. There are four main types of cabinets.

▶ **Vertical cabinets** are the most common. These have a number of large drawers one above the other. Cabinets are available with two, three, four and five drawers – but four drawers is the most popular.

▶ **Lateral cabinets** are like a large cupboard. When you open the door or cover you see rows upon rows of files inside, placed side by side. Some cabinets are designed to be multi-purpose, with files at the top and shelves for other supplies lower down.

▶ **Horizontal cabinets** consist of small drawers, each of which will hold a small amount of paper. They are useful for documents which are very large or must not be hole-punched, such as drawings and photographs. They are therefore more common in design and marketing offices than in administration.

▶ **Rotary cabinets** are really a stand, rather than a cabinet, on which files can be placed in a circle. They rotate – just like the stands you see in some shops for books or postcards.

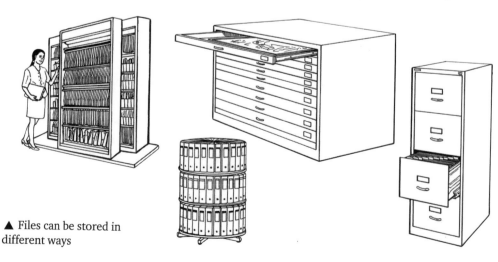

▲ Files can be stored in different ways

Within the cabinets all the documents must be grouped and labelled so that they are easy to find. This is done by using the following items.

▶ **File folders** in which the documents are placed. It is normally better to fasten the documents into the folder so that they are secure. The folder may be plain brown (the cheapest variety) or coloured. Some filing systems are 'colour coded' to help users find the files they want more easily. Many folders have a 'tab' at the top on which you can write the name of the file.

▶ **Document** (or **envelope**) **wallets** are often used to store papers on a temporary basis, especially if the file may be frequently borrowed to be taken out of the office or to meetings.

▶ **Suspension files** are 'pockets' which hold files. These hang down inside a cabinet drawer or along a lateral cabinet. The best type are linked together to prevent any folders or documents being lost between the pockets. All suspension files are designed so that a label can be attached. Some have a clear plastic fastening in which you slide the name of the file. On others, you insert the name first and then 'clip' the plastic fastening on to the file.

▶ **Lever arch files** and **box files** are seen in all offices. Lever arch files are like a very large ring binder and are used for specific documents which can be hole-punched. Box files are the same size but are used for brochures and booklets which cannot (or must not) be punched.

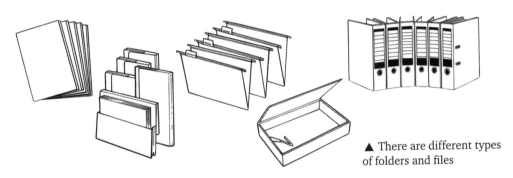

▲ There are different types of folders and files

Additional items

Other frequently seen items of equipment you will find in most offices are listed below, together with their main use(s).

▶ **Calculators** will mainly be used in finance but are useful for anyone who has to work with figures. You probably have a small one yourself. In an office, calculators often have a print roll attached. These are very useful as it is then possible to check that all the numbers in a calculation have been entered correctly against the printed record.

▶ **Guillotines** are used to cut thick batches of paper accurately and precisely. The paper is placed carefully against the guide marks and a sharp blade cuts the paper. The blade is always positioned within a guard, for safety, and the guard must *never* be removed. It is important to use a guillotine carefully. If you make a cut in the wrong place, you can waste a large amount of paper very quickly! To prevent this problem, in many offices you will find **rotary trimmers** instead. These hold less paper but are more precise. The blade is much smaller and is rolled across the paper. It is much easier to make a precise cut with a trimmer than with a guillotine.

Guillotines are used by departments which produce documents on a large scale – such as marketing and sales which may produce customer leaflets or catalogues. Trimmers are a useful accessory near a photocopier.

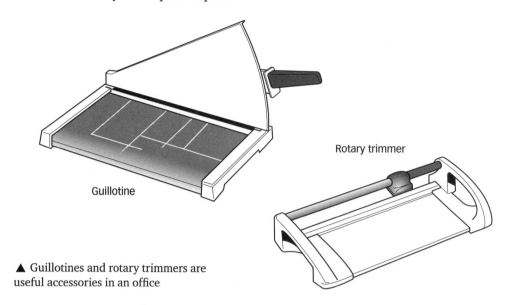

Rotary trimmer

Guillotine

▲ Guillotines and rotary trimmers are useful accessories in an office

▶ **Hole punches** are another item you probably have yourself, especially if you need to punch holes in class notes to store them in a ring binder. All but the smallest versions have a ruler, or guide. The small ones have a notch which identifies the centre point. If you ignore the ruler (or the notch) then you will find that the papers you punch all have their holes in a slightly different place – and look a mess in a file.

The trick, with a small punch, is to fold the paper in half and make a *gentle* crease. Then line up the crease with the notch on your punch. If you do this every time, then all your holes will be correctly aligned and your filed papers will look much neater.

▲ Always put papers neatly in a file

The other common fault is to try to punch too much paper, so that it tears. In an office, bulky documents should always be punched using a heavy-duty punch. This has a longer handle and is far more powerful.

▶ **Staplers** are found on everyone's desk. There are small ones, 'heavy-duty' versions (which will staple far more pages together) and electric staplers. Always check where the staples must be positioned before you start – and watch what you are doing. This is particularly important if you are using a heavy-duty or electric stapler. *Never* staple a document so that the text is obscured, and never try to use a small stapler to staple a lot of pages. This will make the staple 'buckle' and the back pages won't be fastened properly and will fall off. In this case you will need another small item of equipment – a **staple remover** – to take them all out again!

You can adjust the setting on most staplers so that the prongs point outwards on documents which need to be fastened only on a temporary basis. This makes the staples much easier to remove.

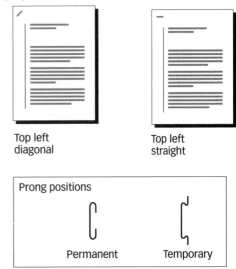

▲ Staple and prong positions

▶ **Flip charts** are used for presentations. They consist of very large (A1) sheets of paper, which are fastened at the top. The chart itself is fastened at the top to a frame or easel and the presenter can write on the paper and 'flip' over each page after use. Your tutor may use flip charts in class. In organisations they are mainly used by sales staff for presentations to customers and by personnel staff at training events.

▶ **Overhead projectors** (**OHPs**) are used to display overhead transparencies (OHTs) to a group of people. Your college probably has one in most of the classrooms. They consist of a lamp, to illuminate the image on the OHT, a glass screen on which the OHT is placed and a lens which projects the enlarged image onto a screen. To work properly both the glass and the lens must be scrupulously clean.

The presenter can prepare OHTs in different ways. The most basic method is to write on them with a special pen. Alternatively OHTs can be produced on a computer printer or on a photocopier. These methods are often preferred because printed OHTs are much clearer. However, different types of OHT are used in each case, so it is important to check the instructions on any box to see which you need for a particular job.

In a business, you may find OHPs in sales and marketing or in personnel for training events because they are normally used to make a presentation to a large number of people. Today, however, most organisations prefer to prepare computer presentations using packages such as PowerPoint.

The activities below will help you understand more about office equipment and why it is used, so that you will answer questions on the examination paper more easily.

1 Either in your classroom or in a training or administration office at your college, find one example of *each* of the following items of equipment. Look at it carefully to see how it works and, if possible, use it yourself.

▶ a filing cabinet – either horizontal or lateral – and preferably both

▶ a heavy-duty punch and a heavy-duty (or electric) stapler

▶ a guillotine or a trimmer

▶ a flip chart and an OHP

▶ a calculator which takes a printout on a tally roll

▶ a fax machine.

2 Your college will have a switchboard, a franking machine (probably in a general office or mail room) and several large photocopiers. Check with your tutor if you can see at least one of these in operation (probably in small groups) and talk to the person who uses it regularly. You will find it more valuable if you prepare a few questions to ask. For example, you could ask the switchboard operator which are the busiest times of the day for calls and how she or he copes when it is hectic. You could find out what supplies are required for the franking machine and photocopier, and what happens if something goes wrong.

3 All offices use paper and envelopes and these are available in several different sizes. It is sensible to understand these. Look at the chart opposite and then look in a stationery catalogue to find an example of each one – and how much they cost.

Then practise folding A4 paper so it fits into a DL envelope. It may take you a few attempts before you can do it properly. Finally, try folding a printed letter carefully so that each line of the address shows through properly in a window envelope. Ask your tutor for help if you are struggling.

Paper and envelopes

Item	Information
Paper	Sizes – A4 (most popular), A5 (half of A4), A3 (double A4), A1 (the largest size and found in flip charts) Quantities – a pack of paper contains 500 sheets (sometimes called a ream). Colours – various but the most popular is white for general office use. Types – lined paper for writing can be bought loose or in A4 pads. Unlined paper is used in computer printers, fax machines and photocopiers. Always check the packet to make sure the paper is suitable for the machine you are using, as paper quality and type varies.

Envelopes   Sizes – C4 takes A4 paper flat or A3 folded once, C5 is half this size and C6 is smaller still. DL is the main size used for letter and takes A4 paper folded twice across the centre.

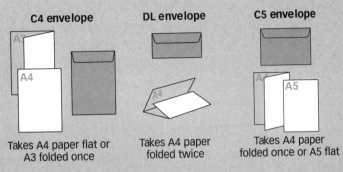

C4 envelope

Takes A4 paper flat or
A3 folded once

DL envelope

Takes A4 paper
folded twice

C5 envelope

Takes A4 paper
folded once or A5 flat

▲ Envelopes come in different sizes

Colours – mainly white for correspondence and brown for invoices and other items.

Types – can have gummed flap, self-seal or peel and seal. Wallet-style envelopes open on the longer side and pocket-style open on the shorter side. Window envelopes have a transparent panel where the address shows through – these are popular because it saves having to print an envelope. However, the address *must* be positioned precisely in the window.

DL window envelope

Takes A4 paper folded
twice according to
guidelines so address
shows **clearly** in window

Other varieties include heavy-duty envelopes, cardboard-backed envelopes (for photographs), airmail (made out of very light paper) and padded Jiffy bags to protect fragile items.

4 Your brother has worked as an estate agent for several years and has now decided to set up his own small business. He has asked you to advise him on what equipment and software he will need.

Work in a small group of two or three to decide the key items of equipment he should buy. Use a stationery catalogue to help you, or visit a stationery store in your area, such as Staples, or surf the Internet.

To help you with ideas, you will find suggestions of useful websites at www.heinemann.co.uk/hotlinks. The various websites cover: equipment, stationery and general office products; computers and software; photocopiers; fax machines; franking machines; telephone handsets and systems.

For each item you select, suggest why your brother would need it and what he would use it for.

Then compare your ideas with other groups in your class.

The documents used in business

Paper is a common feature of all offices, but some paper has a specific purpose. Another term you may hear for this is **office documentation**. This simply means the pre-printed documents which are often used in offices.

Some types of documents will be more commonly used by some departments than others. Many have their own name or title. It is important that you know what these mean, otherwise – if you are asked for something – you are unlikely to have much of a clue what is meant!

Internal and external mail documents

▶ **Letter-headed paper**   All business letters are produced on letter-headed paper. The letter heading gives key information about the organisation, such as the name, address, telephone and fax numbers and website. The directors may also be listed and the logo of any awards the company has won.

▶ **Fax message sheet**   Most modern fax machines use plain paper but a special 'fax message sheet' may be sent first. This is similar to a letter heading because it gives key information about the company but it also contains other information the recipient needs – such as who sent the message. You can see an illustration in Unit 1, page 18.

▶ **Emails**   These are normally printed out on plain A4 paper. If the company wishes all emails to have a specific heading or notes at the bottom then this information will be programmed into the computer system so that it will be printed automatically on all printed emails.

▶ **Leaflets**   Leaflets and catalogues may be sent out by the company. These always look more eye-catching and effective if they are printed in colour.

All departments will produce business letters, faxes and emails but leaflets will be produced and sent mainly by the sales department.

▲ Different types of business stationery

Routine stationery

▶ **Compliment slips** These are small pieces of paper which contain the key information about the organisation. There is room for a short message to be written on the paper. A compliment slip would be sent with a set of leaflets or a catalogue rather than a business letter. It is a quick and courteous way of identifying the sender.

▶ **Business cards** These are essential items for staff such as sales representatives who regularly meet external customers. They provide the main contact details for that person and are often exchanged with a new contact so that both people have each other's details.

▶ **Appointment cards** You may be offered one of these yourself when you make an appointment at the hairdresser or the dentist. They are small printed cards on which is recorded the date and time of the next appointment.

▶ **Address labels** These are purchased in bulk and can be used in a photocopier or a computer printer. The number of labels per sheet of paper varies, but the more labels there are, the smaller is the space for the address. Address labels save typing envelopes for large mail-shots. Instead, they can be photocopied from a master list or printed out from a computer database. They are invaluable for departments which contact a large number of people at the same time, for example if sales is writing to all customers, personnel is sending a letter to every member of staff or the buying department has to contact several suppliers at the same time.

ORGANISATIONS IN BUSINESS

Knowing the correct terms for commonly used office documents saves you from being the target of practical jokes! One manager in an organisation regularly asked new staff to obtain for him a 'verbal agreement form' from the Post Office. (Think about this for a minute!) He took great delight in the problems this caused – both for the staff who actually asked for it and for the Post Office. There is no such thing, of course, because a verbal agreement is oral, not written, but too many new staff felt that they didn't know enough about business documents to argue with their boss!

Purchase and sales documents

All organisations need to buy goods, such as stationery for administrators, food supplies for the canteen or refectory, and cleaning materials. Manufacturers, who produce goods, also need to buy raw materials.

All businesses sell the goods they make or the services they provide. This results in sales documents which are sent to the buyer.

▶ **Requisition**   This is an internal document which is completed when goods are required. If you needed more paper, you might need to complete a stationery requisition to obtain the paper from a central store. You would need to have the requisition approved by your manager, who would sign it to confirm your request was authorised.

▶ **Order** or **purchase order**   This is the main official purchase document made out by the organisation when it wants to obtain raw materials or goods from a supplier. Each purchase order has a specific number and must be signed by an authorised person. It gives full details of the items required, including any reference code, the quantity, description and price. Orders may be sent by fax if they are very urgent. Purchase documents are usually made out by the buying department for raw materials or general supplies. They may also be completed by Administration for stationery supplies from an external supplier.

▶ **Delivery note**   This document is sent with the despatched goods. It lists the quantity and type of goods being delivered – but doesn't give the price. The recipient uses the delivery note to check that all the items are complete and correct and is usually expected to sign a copy to acknowledge that the goods have been received. Delivery notes may be sent out by the sales department or by Finance.

ORGANISATIONS IN BUSINESS

In business, most goods are sold on credit. This means that the buyer pays for the goods after they have been received. You can contrast this with the way you normally buy goods. If you called into a stationery store to buy a ring binder and a pen, you would be expected to pay for the items there and then. Your college, however, will buy stationery in bulk and will then receive a bill – or invoice – from the supplier. It will probably have about a month to pay this account. This is a typical example of a **credit transaction**. The supplier does not receive the money until some time after the goods have been sold.

A **cash transaction** is when goods are paid for at the time of purchase – regardless of whether the buyer pays in cash or by cheque or uses a debit or credit card. This is because the supplier doesn't have to wait for payment.

Some businesses do not allow any type of goods or services to be provided on credit. These include small businesses, such as hairdressers, newsagents and restaurants, and many shops and supermarkets. Others – who mainly deal only with other business organisations – routinely provide their goods and services on credit. An accountant will send an invoice to a client after performing a service, and so will a solicitor. Business organisations which sell expensive goods, such as garages and furniture stores, often offer credit terms to private individuals as well as to other businesses to try to tempt them to buy now and pay later.

Finance documents

Finance is responsible for making certain that all buyers pay for the goods or services they have obtained on credit. It does this by issuing two main documents.

▶ **Invoice**   This is the official name for the 'bill' issued by finance and is sent to the buyer. It summarises all the details of the purchase and the total amount owing. It is sent after the signed delivery note has been returned.

▶ **Statement**   The statement summarises all the transactions that have taken place in a month between the buyer and seller. It will show

- the amount owing at the start of the month, if anything

- all purchases made during the month, and their value

- all payments made during the month

- the final amount owing to the seller.

Statements are normally issued at the end of each month and the buyer is expected to pay the amount due shortly after receiving the document. Some statements include a **remittance advice form** at the bottom. This is a short, tear-off slip which the customer can return with the payment.

Other documents relating to money

▶ **Petty cash** is the system used in a business to pay out small amounts of money. The word 'petty' means 'small'. For example, petty cash may be used to pay the window cleaner, magazines for reception and emergency items of stationery. The system is also used to reimburse (repay) staff who have bought items for the firm using their own money.

Petty cash documents are completed to make sure there is a record of the amounts paid and the reason for each payment. If you were asked to buy some stamps on your way to work, and want to reclaim the money you had paid, you would need two documents.

- a **receipt** for the stamps you had purchased

- a **petty cash voucher** with details of your purchase and the amount spent.

The person in charge of petty cash would check these documents, staple them together, and approve your refund.

PETTY CASH VOUCHER No: 242		Date: 10/3/04	
Name: Anna Clarke		Dept: Sales	
Purpose (attatch all receipts & invoices)	Total (inc.VAT)	VAT(A)	Net (A) (excl. VAT)
Stamps	£5.00	–	£5.00
The sum of (in words as far to the left as possible) Five pounds	£5.00	£	£5.00
Approved by: N. Wilson Date:		Allocation	
Received: Anna Clarke Date: 10/3		Amount	Account

▲ A petty cash voucher shows how much money has been spent

▶ **Cash books** are used by finance staff to record all payments in and out of the cash account. These include all cash transactions received and made by the organisation and all cash withdrawn from and paid into the bank.

Traditionally, all these entries were made in the cash books by hand. Today, however, most accounts are done using a computer and appropriate accounting software.

▶ **Receipts** are issued to customers who pay in cash. They are produced routinely by organisations such as shops and superstores. They are important if you need to return an item for any reason as they prove when you bought it and how much you paid. A handwritten receipt is provided by businesses which do not have a cash register because they rarely take large amounts of cash – such as a dentist or a doctor.

▶ **Payslips** must be issued to all employees. This is a legal requirement. Payslips are usually issued weekly or monthly – depending upon how often the employee is paid. The pay slip provides key information about current and previous earnings and tax paid. It is important to understand your pay slip so that you can check that you have received the correct amount.

Accident report forms

All accidents in the workplace must be recorded. This is a legal requirement, so all organisations have an official accident report form for this purpose. It must be completed whether the accident happens to an employee or a visitor on the premises.

The form asks for details of:

▶ the name of the person who had the accident

▶ the date and time when the accident occurred

▲ An accident book

- the place where the accident occurred
- the cause and nature of the injury (i.e. what happened and the outcome)
- the name, address and occupation of any witness or other person reporting the accident.

Details from the form are entered into an accident book which is checked by safety representatives or safety officers in the organisation.

OVER TO YOU!

1 In groups, collect at least *six* examples of common business documents. Your tutor may be able to help you with examples of compliment slips, business cards and delivery notes. If you have a Saturday job you may be willing to contribute your payslip! Your parents may have an example of an invoice they will let you borrow.

As a group, identify the type of information each document contains. You should be able to relate this, quite easily, to the main purpose of each document.

2 You are a trainee administrator at Marshall Plastics Ltd. At 9.30 am yesterday you were walking through reception in the main building, taking some files from the administration office to personnel, when you slipped and sprained your ankle. It was raining outside and the tiled floor in reception was wet and slippery. Adele Shaw, the senior administrator, was with you and summoned a company first aider, who examined your ankle and, because it had started to swell, arranged for you to go to the nearest hospital – Crayford General – for an X-ray. The hospital assured you that no bones were broken but strapped up your ankle and told you to rest for the remainder of the day. Today your ankle is much better so you have returned to work and have been asked to complete an accident report form.

At the end of this book is an Accident Report Form that you can photocopy. Use this to make a full, complete and neat record of the accident.

3 Although you will not be expected to explain all the sections in a payslip in the external examination, it is sensible to know how to check one when you are working yourself. It is also useful if you know what the headings mean.

Ask for a volunteer in your group to bring in a payslip from their part-time job and discuss the meanings of the various entries on it. Even better, arrange for several people to do this, so that you can compare the different layouts and entries. Test your ability to keep personal information confidential by *not* mentioning anyone's rate of pay or discussing the details outside your group afterwards.

4 Rashid, Kirsty, Marsha and Tom all work at Marshalls Plastics Ltd. The company manufactures plastic components for use in industry. Rashid works in the Sales department, Kirsty works in Finance, Marsha is in Buying and Tom is in the main Administration department.

Identify *three* business documents each of them will use regularly and state the purpose of each one. Your challenge is only to select any one document *once* as you do this exercise!

▼ Describe ways to be organised in order to improve work

Some people are naturally well organised. They like everything to be neat and orderly. They work in a tidy manner – putting away one thing before getting out another. They store things in the right place, so that they can always find them again. If you are like this, then you will find that you are a 'natural' for administration work. This is because administrators routinely deal with many items, including important documents and files. If you regularly lose these, or need half an hour's notice to find something you used recently, you will make life much harder for yourself. You will also have less time to concentrate on producing good work, and may not be able to do this at all because you can't find the materials you need!

This section concentrates on the positive steps you can take to develop your organisational skills at work. This is important because there are several benefits to being well organised. These include:

▶ being able to find what you put away

▶ being able to do a job correctly the first time, because you know what you are doing and have written a list of the key points to remember

▶ being able to do more in the time available, because you waste less time

▶ being able to do what you promised, so that you don't let anyone down

▶ working to time and being punctual so that you don't keep anyone waiting

▶ finding your possessions last much longer, because they are stored properly

▶ working more quickly, because what you need is close at hand and in working order.

▲ Being disorganised can cause a lot of problems

OVER TO YOU!

Check how naturally well organised you are by answering the following questions. Be truthful – even if that means you don't want to show anyone the result afterwards!

1 Your GCSE results slip was an important piece of paper. Would you:

a) find it in about five minutes

b) find it in about an hour – with luck

c) never be able to find it. You haven't seen it for months.

2 You have been invited out tonight and want to wear the new top you bought last week and wore last Saturday. This would be:

a) no problem, because it's washed and ironed and neatly folded in a drawer

b) no problem if you didn't spill anything down it on Saturday – you think it's draped over the chair in your room.

c) almost impossible even if you could find it, as it's probably lying in a heap on the floor somewhere.

3 On average, in a year, do you usually lose or forget your door keys:

a) never because they are always in your pocket or your bag

b) once or twice – normally when you've changed your jacket or bag

c) dozens of times. You don't even know where they are at this moment.

4 You agree to meet a friend outside the cinema at 7.30 pm. Would you:

a) allow plenty of time and arrive five minutes early

b) probably leave home in a rush and be a few minutes late

c) arrive sometime between 7.35 and 8.00 – depending on what else cropped up.

5 You have been working on a college project for the last two days. Does the area where you have been working look:

a) neat and tidy – all your files are stacked neatly at one side

b) a bit of a mess but only because you finished late last night

c) like a disaster zone.

6 If you had to turn out your college bag for a security check, would you:

a) be pleased to cooperate and carefully lift out your files and pencil case

b) be a bit concerned whether there was any dust, fluff or screwed-up paper in the bottom

c) cringe at the very thought, given all the stuff that's in there.

7 Your tutor asks you to take down some notes. Do you:
   a) reach for the pen and A4 lined paper you already have out on your desk
   b) scrabble in your bag, find a usable pen at the second attempt and a rather tatty piece of paper
   c) borrow some paper from a friend and put your hand up to see if your tutor has a spare pen?

Now score yourself 2 points for each A, 1 point for each B and 0 points for each C you answered.

10 – 14 means you are naturally well organised, neat and tidy. These skills will be of great benefit to you as an administrator.

6 – 9 is an average score, but you will have to improve this if you are dealing with important or valuable documents at work.

3 – 5 means you have a problem and could create chaos in an office! Read the following pages carefully and vow to change your ways.

0 – 2 may seem amusing but isn't funny for all the people who have to deal (or cope) with you. Nobody is likely to pay to put up with you, so holding down a job could prove to be a serious challenge!

Understanding instructions

You may receive instructions to do work in writing, but more often people will give you this information verbally. They may interrupt you with instructions when you are doing something else – or they may speak quickly because they are in a hurry.

To make certain that you understand what is being said:

▶ listen carefully

▶ concentrate on what is being said

▶ write down all the important details on a notepad – not on a scrap of paper which can easily get lost

▶ don't interrupt until the speaker has finished

▶ then ask about anything you do not understand or which you didn't write down properly or in full because the person was speaking too quickly.

Never be tempted to pretend to understand just to impress someone. You won't impress them later if you've done the job wrongly – or even done the wrong job!

Always ask questions at the time you are given the work. If you leave it until later then you may have problems contacting the person who gave it to you. If he or she has left the building then you may have a serious problem, especially if the job is urgent. Or they may have left instructions not to be interrupted because they are involved in a meeting or with visitors. Even if the person is available, it can be difficult remembering the details of the job some time later – which they will have to do before they can answer your question.

You can always check instructions by:

▶ asking someone (politely) to slow down if they are speaking too quickly

▶ asking someone to explain a word, expression or technical term you don't understand

▶ repeating back a verbal instruction, to check you have understood it correctly

▶ asking a more experienced person to help you to decipher bad handwriting or a term in a written document you don't understand.

There are other safety precautions you can also take when you are given a task to do.

▶ Check that you have all the information you need to enable you to do the task. Sometimes people may forget to give you information (such as a telephone or fax number) or neglect an important detail (such as how many copies of a document they want).

▶ Check that you know why the task is being done. This will help you to make sense of specific requirements, such as the deadline, the resources you can use and any procedures you have to follow.

▶ Check you clearly understand any deadlines which must be met.

▶ If the task involves finding information, make sure you know where to look for this and who you can ask for help. Otherwise, ask a colleague for assistance.

▶ If the task is one which is regularly undertaken, then you may be able to:
  – find an example to see how it was done last time
  – find out how to tackle it by looking through the files
  – be able to ask someone else who has done it before
  – be able to refer to standard procedures. You will learn more about these in Unit 4. A procedure is simply a step-by-step list of what you must do.

▶ If the task is new or complicated, arrange to check back with the person who gave you the work at certain key stages. For example, if you are asked to type and print a document and then make 50 photocopies, it is sensible to arrange for someone to double-check that your document is absolutely perfect before you make the photocopies.

▶ If the person who is giving you the job will be out of the office for the rest of the day, or must not be disturbed for some reason, find out who else you should see if you have an unexpected problem.

A simple checklist

On page 44 there was a checklist for working in a team. You wouldn't normally complete a checklist for each task you are given at work, but it helps if you can identify the *types* of key information you are likely to be given. Then you can spot more easily if one is missing!

A useful checklist for most jobs is given in the following rhyme:

I have six honest serving men, they taught me all I knew.
Their names are 'what' and 'why' and 'when' and 'how' and 'where' and 'who'.

In this case:

▶ **What** exactly must you do and what resources do you need?

▶ **Why** is the job required? This helps you to understand the task.

▶ **When** is the deadline by which work must be completed?

- **How** should you do the job, how many items are required?

- **Where** must you go to obtain your resources or information? Where must the completed work be taken?

- **Who** has given you the job? Who can you contact if you need help or information, who will receive the final finished work?

If you can't answer all these questions after you've received your instructions, it is highly likely that a key item of information is missing!

OVER TO YOU!

1 Hannah has just started work in an office and during her first week she makes some mistakes which could easily have been avoided. In each case, identify what she could have done to *prevent* the problem.

a) She typed a letter using the display she had been taught at college, whereas this was not the same as the way the firm set out its business letters. She then had to retype it.

b) Hannah received a telephone call for her boss whilst she was on the telephone and told the caller she wasn't available. Her boss was annoyed because this was an important call she had been waiting for – and the caller would be unobtainable for the rest of the day.

c) Hannah put through three external calls to Peter Jones when the callers wanted Simon Jones.

d) She used expensive presentation folders for some draft documents which were required for a meeting.

e) She didn't take an important parcel to the post because she didn't have the postcode – and it missed the deadline.

2 Petra's boss travels around the area and he often gives her jobs before he leaves each day. Sometimes he will ring her from his mobile when he is out of the office with an additional task.

a) Suggest 4 ways in which Petra can make sure that she understands the instructions she receives.

b) Suggest 1 additional arrangement Petra should make when her boss telephones her, in case she has a problem with a task later.

3 Max is given the following verbal instructions by his boss. Read these carefully and then identify:

a) the important details Max must write down

b) the vague information which Max should query

c) the information which is missing altogether and which Max must obtain before he can start the job.

'We've some important visitors coming tomorrow and I need your help. Can you start by getting together our latest catalogues and price list and a company brochure. Put these into sets with a compliment slip on each and my business card. I want each of our visitors to have their own set. Put each set in our best presentation folders with the visitor's name on it. Then make sure there's a flip chart and an OHP in the meeting room. Thanks.'

Using time efficiently

People talk about time in many different ways. They talk about 'wasting' time, 'saving' time and 'making' time. You can do many things with time, but you certainly can't make it! When people say this, they really mean that they will juggle their commitments so they have more time to do something.

If you waste time at work then you are likely to end up with outstanding jobs at the end of the day. What is more, because you can never regain the time you have wasted, you will then have to 'make time' to do those jobs tomorrow – plus any new jobs you are given.

The opposite occurs if you use time efficiently. You will find that you have more time to do your work so you can concentrate better. You may even find you have 'spare time', so you can get ahead by preparing for another busy day.

We are all guilty of wasting time, particularly if we don't like the thought of a job we must do. Time-wasting activities at work include:

▶ talking to people about things unconnected with work – such as what you did last night, your health or your holidays

▶ fiddling with unimportant things, to distract yourself from a job you should be doing but don't like or understand

▶ doing things you want to do (which may not be important) rather than things you should be doing (which may be very important)

▶ not concentrating when you are working, so you make a mess of something and have to start all over again

▶ having a messy or disordered desk or files, so that you can't find what you need to get started.

You will use time more efficiently if you:

▶ have a neat and tidy desk

▶ know where to find everything you need

▶ keep the items you regularly use close at hand and in good working order, such as stationery in your desk and your stapler full of staples and a spare supply in your desk drawer

▶ keep the information you frequently need within reach, e.g. telephone directories and internal telephone lists

▶ do the most urgent or important jobs first, when you are fresh

▶ stick to a job until it is done, even if it is difficult. Then reward yourself with a short break.

▶ think ahead – so you assemble everything you need before you start and don't have to keep running backwards and forwards.

▶ do small, outstanding jobs when you have a few moments spare, such as tidying your desk whilst you are waiting for the printer to finish.

▲ Information you need regularly should be close at hand and everything should be organised neatly

People and time – and how to cope with interruptions

One of the most difficult problems is coping with people who waste your time. These are often your colleagues who may not be as busy as you or have some interesting news they are desperate to tell you!

In an office, you may be interrupted many times when you are working. Some of these interruptions cannot be avoided, and you have to learn to cope. Others are more manageable.

Unavoidable interruptions include:

▶ the telephone ringing – especially if there is no one else around to answer it

▶ visitors appearing at reception when you are on duty

▶ your boss or another senior member of staff arriving in the office to ask you about something.

Avoidable interruptions are those occasions when a friend or colleague telephones or calls to see you for a chat. There is a tactic you can use which will not only get rid of your friend (nicely) but will also stop your boss interrupting you with less important things after you have been given a job! So:

Step 1 – when you have an important job, keep your head down! This makes it clear you are working and concentrating. It doesn't mean being bad-tempered or grumpy! Most people will leave you in peace when it is obvious you are concentrating hard.

Step 2 – if you are interrupted by a business telephone call or a visitor, you have no choice but to respond. Deal with the matter as quickly (and politely) as you can, take notes to refresh your memory later, if necessary, and return to your work.

Step 3 – if you are interrupted by a friend or colleague ringing or calling to see you then simply say 'I'm really sorry but I must finish this job in the next 10 minutes. Can we talk later?' If you are on the phone ring off. If your friend is in front of you then go back at your work. Be firm. Don't be apologetic, but stay pleasant. It is your right to choose what you do and when!

Step 4 – if your boss interrupts you, then listen carefully. The reason may be important. Otherwise you can say, 'Could I speak to you later about this? I'm trying to finish this job you gave me earlier. I should be finished in about 10 minutes.' Your boss then has to make the decision whether or not to continue to talk to you then and there – or leave you in peace to meet your deadline.

The importance of meeting deadlines

Most jobs have a deadline. The deadline is the set time by when the job must be completed. Sometimes deadlines are negotiable, on other occasions they are absolutely critical.

A deadline is negotiable when your boss asks you how long you think it will take you to do something. In this case, you are suggesting the deadline. However, the time scale must be realistic – you can't claim that you need three days to key in a two-page document! If you say it would take you all morning, your boss might ask you to drop everything else and do it immediately – or (if the job isn't urgent) he or she may be happy to agree to make the afternoon the deadline.

A deadline is critical when a job is both urgent and important, for example:

▶ an external customer has been promised something by a certain date

▶ other people are depending upon you to finish your work, because they need this before they can complete their own jobs.

In both these cases, if you miss the deadline you are either jeopardising future business for your employer or you are holding up other people.

If you have a very urgent and important job to do, then you may have to take drastic action to make sure you meet it. This can include:

▶ telling your immediate supervisor and your colleagues – so that people know not to interrupt you with unimportant matters

▶ asking your supervisor if you can work in a separate area where there is more peace and quiet. This may not be feasible in all organisations – and will depend upon the job you have been asked to do. However, it is a useful strategy if you work in a hectic and noisy office and there are spare rooms available

▶ diverting your telephone to another extension so that someone else takes your calls. Your supervisor may even agree that you can switch over your phone to Voicemail or to the answering machine

▶ arranging for someone else to deal with unexpected callers or visitors or events which you know will happen – such as someone coming to collect a parcel

▶ making sure you are well organised – so that you do the task in the most efficient way and have all the items you need close at hand.

▶ not being distracted by other jobs you may have to do. You **prioritise** when you select the task which is the most important and urgent and concentrate totally on this one. If this means that you cannot do a routine job for which you are responsible, inform your supervisor so that someone else can be asked to do it for you.

If you suddenly encounter a serious problem or make a terrible mistake, either of which will seriously affect the deadline, then you may hope that you can cover it up rather than get into trouble. However tempting this might be, it is far better to be honest. It may help you to realise that everyone has this type of problem from time to time and no one is perfect. It is how you react when problems occur that is important, not the fact that they do.

If you have problems meeting a deadline . . .

DO

- Try to solve the problem yourself, even if this means working late or missing your break or part of your lunch hour
- Tell your team leader or boss if there is absolutely no way you can solve the problem on your own
- Be positive and suggest some ways in which the problem can be solved
- Apologise and own up if you have done something silly or if you have caused the problem yourself
- Learn from the experience – so you don't repeat it!

DON'T

- Bluff and pretend everything is fine.
- Try to cover up or blame anyone else
- Sulk or lose your temper
- Be tempted to rush the job and make a mess of it.

ORGANISATIONS IN BUSINESS

It is a sad fact that, in business, no one is really very interested in your problems if you are adding to theirs! Imagine the scene. You are desperately waiting for information on some prices to go into an urgent document your boss wants to send to a customer. Finance has promised you this twice. You have now just received an email which says: 'Really sorry, we meant to look out these prices before now, but Carolyn went home with migraine yesterday and Tracey was at the dentist this morning. Will definitely get back to you later.' How sympathetic would you be about Carolyn's headache and Tracey's teeth? Probably not very, if your boss is breathing down your neck and you now have to do the apologising.

One 'trick' with deadlines is to allow more time than you think you need to make room for unforeseen problems – such as other people letting you down at the last minute. Some businesses do this all the time with external customers. They always *over-estimate* the time something will take – and then aim to give the customer a pleasant surprise. So visitors in reception are told their wait might be 15 minutes, when it will probably be 10, and customers being sent items through the post are told they will receive them in 3 or 4 days, rather than tomorrow.

This gives the business a psychological advantage, because customers expect the worst and are then pleasantly surprised. One airline has now advised their staff to use the same psychology when announcing flight delays. They argue that once people have adjusted to the fact they have to wait they accept this, but become very annoyed if they are told the wait will be extended. So, next time you are asked to specify a deadline you could ask for more time than you think you'll need – and aim to give your colleagues and customers a pleasant surprise!

1 Shahida loves using her computer and the Internet and often spends hours trying to find what she needs. Yesterday she wanted to find a graphic to put on the cover of an urgent departmental health and safety report – and it took her all afternoon. Her boss was annoyed because the graphic wasn't necessary and she still hadn't completed typing the report, which then couldn't be completed until today.

a) Would you say that Shahida uses time efficiently or inefficiently? Give a reason for your answer.

b) How should Shahida have known whether a graphic was required or not?

c) In what way did Shahida's actions affect the deadline – and why?

d) What difference would it have made if the report was wanted for an important presentation to the Managing Director yesterday rather than just for use in the department?

e) What action should Shahida have taken when she thought a graphic would be a useful addition to the cover?

2 Sajid urgently needs to finish a spreadsheet his boss needs today, even though he also wanted to clear away some files he was using earlier. All around him his colleagues seem to have finished work for the day and are laughing and chatting. Suggest 4 actions Sajid can take to help him to complete the work in time.

3 You have been asked to do several urgent jobs but you are struggling. Explain exactly what you would do in each of the following situations.

a) You have to finish photocopying an urgent document by 4 pm but at 3.45 pm the photocopier breaks down.

b) Your boss is standing over you waiting for you to print an important letter which must go in tonight's post. You suddenly notice three errors in the document on your screen.

c) It is 12.50 pm and you are meeting a friend for lunch at 1 pm. You have just finished collating and stapling some reports for a meeting which starts at 2 pm. At the last minute you see you have written 'red covers required at front and back' on your notepad – which you haven't attached.

Working tidily and efficiently

Your work area is not just the desk you use but any other parts of the office you work in. These could include the area around the franking machine in the mailroom, near the photocopier or fax machine or anywhere around the filing cabinets – or the reception desk if you greet visitors. In other words, your work area is all the physical space you need to do your job.

Working in a muddle can cause several problems.

▶ You can easily throw away something important by mistake.

▶ It can take you ages to find what you need.

▶ You may even spend longer looking for things than actually doing your job.

▶ If someone opens a window or door, half your papers can easily float off onto the floor.

- ▶ You will feel more pressurised – because you are making easy jobs hard.

- ▶ You'll probably annoy everyone else in the office!

Organising materials and equipment on your desk

At work you will have your own desk and equipment, including possibly a computer, a printer, and a telephone. Most people also have several desk accessories, such as filing trays, desk tidies and pen trays. These are useful because they remove much of the clutter.

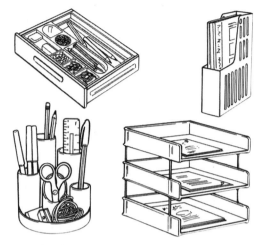

You then have to work out what to keep on top of your desk, and what to put into the desk drawers. Your desk top should be kept for items you are using all the time – and these should be arranged so that you can find anything you need quickly. Desk drawers are for personal or small items you use less frequently and for bulky items. The following tips should help you.

▲ Desk accessories can help you to be organised

- ▶ Keep papers you are not currently using in clearly labelled trays or folders. Only current papers should be on the top of your desk. The rest can be in a filing tray or in one of your drawers.

- ▶ File documents you have finished using as soon as possible. The more regularly you file, the less paper there will be on your desk!

- ▶ Position your telephone within reach, so that you can pick up the receiver with your non-writing hand.

- ▶ Have a pen and notebook within reach at your writing side.

- ▶ Put loose items, such as scissors, pens and pencils in a desk tidy at the back of your desk – so that you can't knock it over by mistake.

- ▶ Keep reference materials you use regularly – such as an internal phone list – in a small plastic magazine rack at one side.

- ▶ Keep any other small items of equipment you use regularly on top of your desk – such as your hole punch, stapler and calculator.

- ▶ Put small items you use regularly in your top drawer, such as rubber bands, floppy disks and ruler. You can buy a drawer tidy to help if necessary, so that you don't have to rummage around for anything you need. If you use drawing pins, keep them in the box unless you want to risk an accident!

- ▶ Keep a small stock of the stationery you use regularly, such as printer paper, in drawers lower down. Paper will be less likely to get crumpled or torn if you keep it in its packet or store it in a folder or a small box.

- ▶ After you've finished with something, always put it away again.

▶ Tidy up your desk every evening before you go home. Then you have a fresh start every morning!

The golden rule is to treat your desk as a workbench – not a storage area!

Keeping other areas neat and tidy

It doesn't matter whether you are photocopying, filing or just making the coffee, you should never leave a trail of debris behind you! This is a major irritant in offices, as you will quickly discover yourself if you have to work with a sloppy colleague.

It obviously helps if there is plenty of room to work in, proper storage cupboards and a table or worktop on which you can place the work you are doing. If there isn't, then it is even more important to work neatly, rather than less – as the area looks messy much more easily.

You will work effectively if you have a system:

▶ get out only what you need to do that particular job

▶ set it out neatly, in one area (see below for how to do this)

▶ use the materials you need

▶ put them all away again.

The difficulty comes when you are trying to do a job in a rush – or two jobs at once. You may find you have a natural tendency to spread things around. So if you suddenly realise you have papers all over your desk as well as on the top of two filing cabinets, on the table in the corner and a few on the floor then stop and have a clear up before you do anything else. It is also easier if you aim to finish one job before you start the next – unless you are interrupted to do something which is very urgent.

Minimising waste

If you work in a rush, don't concentrate or are simply a messy worker then you will be far more likely to waste resources – particularly paper. This means you are expensive to employ, because all these resources cost money. It also defeats any aims your employer may have to be environmentally friendly and any actions taken to support this, such as buying recycled paper and envelopes, recycling waste paper and recycling printer cartridges.

Some activities are particularly prone to waste, such as photocopying and printing out documents from a computer. In both cases, it is very easy to use far more than you really need through keying in the wrong quantity or realising – too late – that there is an error on a document and you have to start again.

Precautions you can take to minimise this type of waste are given in the table below.

▲ Is this you?

Minimising waste

Job areas and tasks	DO	DON'T
Writing a message	Think first, write next! Correct any minor mistakes rather than starting again	Use a large piece of paper for a short internal message
Keying in and printing a document	Check carefully on screen Use your spell checker but remember that this isn't perfect (see page 6) Take a trial printout and check that Use 'draft' setting whenever possible to save ink or toner	Start a large print out unless you are certain the document is perfect Take colour printouts unless you have been asked to do so.
Photocopying	Check the original is in good condition Take a test copy and check this is perfect Check if the document can be printed on both sides of the paper (i.e. back to back) as this halves the amount of paper required	Start a large print run if there is a problem on your test copy. Take more copies than you need 'just to be on the safe side'
Cutting paper	For small amounts of paper, use a trimmer rather than a guillotine Line up the paper accurately before cutting and make sure no text is being cut by mistake	Try to cut thick chunks of paper at once Assume that if the first paper in a batch is lined up correctly, the last one will be.
Stapling	Check where the staples must be positioned Use the correct type of stapler	Obscure any text Try to staple thick documents with an ordinary stapler
Telephone calls	Make notes before you make a business call – so you don't have to ring again for information you forgot	Use the office telephone for personal calls. If it's an emergency, ask for permission first
Filing	Reuse file folders by turning them 'inside out' and writing the new name on the other side of the tab	Throw away perfectly good folders and wallets which can easily be reused.
Stationery use	Store it properly so it is kept in excellent condition Reuse items you can – such as using old paper as scrap pads and reusing envelopes to send internal documents	Order more than you need and cram it into a drawer Use plastic wallets to store routine papers Use good-quality paper to draft a few rough notes for yourself

Working efficiently

In factories where people do assembly work, experts work out *exactly* how each task should be done. The aim is to minimise hand and arm movements so that the task is completed quickly and efficiently. All the materials required are within reaching distance, and those needed most often are the nearest. A conveyor belt will bring the next unit in front of the operative, who repeats the same process over and over again. There is nothing for the operative to do but to concentrate on the task in hand.

This type of analysis is less common for office work today – and can't be applied to all jobs you would have to do as an administrator. However, there are a few valuable lessons to be learned from this approach. They include:

▶ **planning a job in advance**. This means identifying all the resources you need before you start

▶ **obtaining your resources**. This is especially important if some are stored in a different area

▶ **setting out the items** you will use on a *clear* work area or desk top so that:

  – the items you need first, or most often, are nearest to you

  – you can see clearly *where* everything is

  – you can see clearly *what* everything is

  – you have taken into account whether you normally work from right to left, or left to right

▶ **having a waste bin** nearby for anything you will need to throw away

▶ **working methodically and tidily**

▶ **stacking up completed work** in a separate space or even on a different worktop to prevent confusion.

If you are interrupted or have to leave the room, note down where you were up to, so that you don't forget. If you are working in a separate office and need to leave papers out, put a note on them asking other people not to move anything. Then close the door. Locking it is even better, especially if the job is important or any of the papers are confidential.

OVER TO YOU!

1 Alana's desk is a tip. She has an L-shaped desk, with three drawers, and a computer and telephone, but the top is cluttered with papers, files and her own personal possessions!

a) Suggest where Alana should store each of the items shown in the list below. You can choose between the desktop, the top drawer and other drawers. In each case give a reason for your decision.

b) Suggest 3 ways in which Alana should change her working habits to keep her work area organised better.

c) Identify 4 benefits to her of improving her organisational skills.

Alana's Items	
Ring binder containing customer list and telephone numbers	Nail file
Spare inkjet cartridge	Box of staples
Spare comb	Mouse mat
Pens and pencils	Stapler
Printer paper	Assorted rubber bands
Letter headed paper	Calculator
Compliment slips	Internal directory showing email addresses and extension numbers
Post-It notes	Envelopes – all different sizes
Box of tissues	Scissors
Notebook	Staple remover
Bottle of fizzy water	Paper clips
Liquid paper	Hole punch
Ruler	Packet of sweets
Eraser	Floppy disk
Pencil sharpener	Six brown file folders and two envelope wallets
Telephone directory	

2 The cost of stationery at Nicola's firm has been soaring lately. The managers have asked all staff to do everything they can to minimise waste in future. Identify 6 ways in which Nicola, a junior administrator, can help to do this.

3 Collating and filing are two activities which can create total disorder in an office, mainly because of all the paper involved.

a) Work out exactly what materials and resources you would need to do each of the following tasks and then explain what you would do to ensure you worked in the most tidy and efficient way each time.

Task 1 – you have been asked to photocopy a 10-page stapled report. You have to make 20 copies of each page and collate these. They have to be stapled inside blue card covers.

Task 2 – You have been asked to make out file folders for each of 15 new staff at your company. Each one must be clearly labelled and contain a personnel record card and leave sheet. The folders must then go into a filing cabinet in alphabetical order. This also means producing a title label for each file which slides into its own plastic holder in the cabinet.

b) For task 2, suggest why it would be safer to:

i) have only the exact number of file folders, record cards and leave sheets on your desk as you work

ii) attach the title label as you put each file into the system.

Ways of improving your work

If you are conscientious and want to do well at work, you will aim to improve. Everyone improves through experience. If you do the same job several times, then you will do it better each time and your confidence will increase. Another way to improve is to watch an expert. This way you can discover excellent ways of working and short cuts you never even knew existed!

Most organisations aren't prepared to leave staff improvements to chance. They regularly review how each person is performing and then identify areas for further development. This not only helps to give all the staff new opportunities, but is essential if there is a shortage of skills in an office or if new skills are required.

Sometimes you may *know* which areas you need to improve – because you are struggling or don't know how to tackle some jobs. You may also know which new skills and abilities you want to develop. On other occasions you may be less certain. One useful method of identifying the most appropriate areas for development is to obtain feedback on the work you do at the moment.

Obtaining feedback

Feedback is the name given to all the comments that other people make to you about your work. Feedback can be formal or informal and complimentary or otherwise! If you sit down with your manager to discuss your work then this is formal feedback. If your team leader says, 'That's great. You've really got the hang of that' then that is informal feedback – but no less valuable.

Complimentary feedback – or praise for a job well done – is always marvellous to receive. It makes you feel good about yourself. Negative feedback is less easy to take. No one wants to be told they aren't very good at something – no matter how politely someone says it! Yet learning how to accept criticism which is meant to help you is another skill to develop. The key point is whether the comment is *fair*. If you know you've made a mess of something, and someone points this out, then you should be prepared to think about it even if you didn't like what you heard!

There are different ways in which you can obtain feedback at work.

▶ You can have a review meeting with your manager. This is a regular session at which your work is discussed formally (see page 130).

▶ You can talk to your team leader. This is useful if you want your team leader's opinion or views about a task you have completed or a skill you would like to learn.

▲ Informal feedback at work can be useful

- You can review *honestly* the quality of the work you are currently producing. For example, how many of your tasks do you – or someone else – have to redo? If someone has to return a job to you because it isn't acceptable, this is feedback, even if they are very understanding at the time!

- You can listen to informal comments made by other people – including your own colleagues. If, even as a joke, you hear someone say 'Well, you can give it to her if you like, but I'd think carefully if you want it this side of Christmas!' then you might like to think about the implications.

- You can ask a more experienced colleague, in confidence, for a personal opinion. If this is someone you work with regularly, he or she will know whether you have a reputation for being a hard, conscientious worker – or not!

- You can do a mental check of how much work you are completing in relation to other people. If it seems to take you twice as long to do a job as your colleagues, this should tell you something. Equally, if you seem to be always helping them, or taking on more than your fair share, so should this.

Planning to improve your performance

It is in your own interests to improve – mainly because it is probably more important for your own future than for your employer's. If you ever want to change jobs in the future or apply for promotion, you will be in a better position if you have increased your skills and improved your current abilities. Your employer will benefit only as long as you work for that particular organisation.

This is one reason why business organisations expect their employees to have a keen interest in their own development. They will therefore expect you to contribute to any discussions about what you need to improve or wish to learn.

Some people prepare for these discussions with a simple list of what they want to do – either on paper or in their head. A more organised method is to make out a **learning plan**. This is a document which identifies the targets you want to achieve. A date for achievement is usually identified for each target – to focus your mind and to give you something to aim for. Learning plans are reviewed at regular intervals to check the targets have been met.

Your own learning plan should identify:

- the skills and abilities you want to learn and improve

- the time scale over which you intend to do this

- the methods and activities you can use

- the date on which you will review the plan and your progress (or lack of it)

- the person with whom you will review it.

An example of a learning plan is shown below.

Before you complete a learning plan, it is useful to think about ways in which you can obtain the skills you want to learn. One way is to identify suitable opportunities for training – as you will see below.

Learning plan

Name: Nicola Ferro

Name of reviewer: Jill Cottam

Start date of plan: 10 September 2003

Review date: 20 January 2004

Development aim	Target date	Activity	Outcome
Improve word-processing skills	June 2004	Study for RSA Word Processing stage 1 at College	
Develop reception skills	December 2003	Work alongside reception staff one day each week	
Improve team-working skills	December 2003	Attend internal training course in November	

To be completed before the next review:

Identify any areas still outstanding. If these should have been completed by the review date, give reasons for non-achievement.

Signed .... Date ....

Opportunities for training

When you are attending a college course, it is tempting to think that all training opportunities occur away from work. This isn't true. There are three places in which you can obtain training.

▶ in your own office, whilst you are working

▶ out of your office, but somewhere else in your employer's organisation

▶ away from work, such as at college.

The best place often depends upon *what* you need to learn, as you can see in the table below.

Places where training takes place

Place	Type of training
In your own office, whilst you are working	Informal instruction such as • how to use the fax machine • how to use your computer system • how to order stationery • how to use the telephone system
Away from your own office, but elsewhere at work	Informal instruction on equipment found only in certain areas, e.g. • how to use the franking machine • how to use the switchboard Formal training related to your workplace, e.g. • how to complete certain forms • health and safety training • general computer training and security aspects
Away from the workplace, e.g. at College	Training leading to formal qualifications, e.g. • Administration – levels 1, 2 and 3 • Information technology • Specific software packages, e.g. word-processing • Key Skills awards in Use of Number, Communications and IT.

The important point is that you shouldn't sit around waiting for opportunities to be presented to you! Many informal opportunities will occur out of the blue – and it is up to you to take advantage of them. For example:

▶ your team leader asks for a volunteer to do a new job

▶ your manager is worried that a job won't be finished on time. You could offer to help!

▶ you hear about a new development. Why not suggest you are involved?

▶ you know there is a staff shortage in a certain area. You could offer to help out.

The importance of reviewing your work with a manager

In many organisations there are regular sessions when you can review your work with your manager. Your work since the last review is discussed as well as your good points and areas for development. You will be expected to contribute with your own comments and suggestions, so it is sensible to prepare for the meeting. You can do this by identifying:

▶ the type of work you know you can do well

▶ the type of work you *think* you can do well

▶ areas you know you should improve

▶ skills or abilities you don't have now but which you would like to develop in the future.

In each case, be prepared to give an example to support your views.

There are several benefits to reviewing your work in this way, which include the following.

▶ A review gives you the opportunity to talk about what you like doing and what you want to do in the future.

▲ A formal review can provide the chance to plan your future career

▶ If you are positive during the review, this tells your manager that you are interested in learning more and moving up in the future.

▶ Your manager will try to link your needs and ambitions with future needs and opportunities within the department. This benefits everyone.

▶ You will need your manager's support if you want to attend any internal or external training courses that are offered, particularly if these are during working hours and if you would need financial support.

▶ If your learning plan is agreed by your manager, you have a better chance of achieving it. However, if you fail, then you will have to provide some fairly good reasons the next time you meet!

Remember that if you have your heart set on something which your manager cannot agree to, then this needn't stop you! If you want to learn at college, for example, you can always attend evening courses in your own time. This is a useful compromise if your employer is willing to support your request but simply cannot cope if you are away from the workplace during the day. It will also demonstrate your commitment to improving your own performance.

ORGANISATIONS IN BUSINESS

Some organisations have a special name for review meetings. They may call them **appraisals** or **career discussions**. In some organisations you will have an annual or six-monthly appraisal with your **line manager**. This is the manager who is directly responsible for your work and to whom you report.

In other organisations you can discuss with your manager how often you want to talk about your career and your future.

These discussions are very valuable because managers have to think about the way the business operates – both now and in the future – and try to link the needs and ambitions of employees to the skills required by the organisation. They will then look at ways staff can improve their skills and learn new ones as this helps everyone.

Organisations which are particularly good at this can apply to be **Investors in People**. This is an award given to businesses that consistently prove that they are good at developing their staff. If you apply for a job and find out that the organisation has IIP status, you can be certain that it works hard to encourage its staff to be involved in their own self-development.

INVESTORS IN PEOPLE

1 Tanya rarely gets much direct feedback from her team leader, who works in a different office.

  a) Suggest 3 other ways in which Tanya can obtain feedback about her work.

  b) Give 2 reasons why feedback is essential if Tanya wants to improve her performance.

2 Your manager has asked you to attend a review meeting about your work. During the review meeting he wants to help you set targets and prepare a learning plan.

  a) Identify 3 benefits of having this discussion with your manager.

  b) Suggest 4 things you would do to prepare for the meeting.

  c) Suggest 2 areas for development you would like to include on your learning plan.

3 Kim works in a busy office and is keen to develop her skills. She particularly wants to improve her IT skills and would like to learn how to operate the switchboard. She is also nervous when she has to deal with customers over the telephone.

  a) Identify 1 way in which she could improve *each* of the skills she has identified.

  b) Suggest 3 ways in which Kim could take advantage of informal learning opportunities which occur in her office.

▼ Identify rights and responsibilities at work

At work your rights and responsibilities mainly relate to two important areas.

The first is **Health and Safety**. All employees have the right to work in a safe place – but also have a responsibility themselves to work safely and cooperate with their employer over health and safety matters.

The second area relates to the **terms of your employment**. You have several rights, such as the right to be paid and to be treated fairly, but again you have a number of responsibilities yourself. An employee who disregards his or her responsibilities can be disciplined and may even be dismissed.

In this section you will learn about your rights and responsibilities in both of these areas.

Working safely in an administration environment

Many people think that offices are extremely safe places and are surprised to learn that health and safety is important for administrators. This includes some administrators themselves! The reality is that you don't have to do a dangerous job to hurt yourself at work. You can be injured because you don't operate machinery or equipment safely (including your computer), because you are careless – or even because someone else is thoughtless or careless.

It is sensible, therefore, to take health and safety seriously – no matter where you work.

Hazards in an office

A hazard is anything which could cause you harm. Therefore many common objects are potential hazards – a computer, a pair of scissors, an icy path. Even a chair is a hazard if it is wobbly or isn't being used for the right purpose.

Of course, most common objects can also be used quite safely. Just because a hazard exists, doesn't mean that an accident will occur. To prevent people being injured, workplaces have to identify all the **potential hazards** and the level of **risk**. A risk is the likelihood of someone being injured because the hazard exists.

All risks can be classed as high, medium or low. The risk is always higher if:

▶ the person has no idea how to use something (you wouldn't give a toddler a sharp pair of scissors, for example)

▶ the item is being used for the wrong purpose (such as standing on a chair to open a window)

▶ the item is in a dangerous condition (such as a slippery floor or a faulty plug)

▶ the person is careless, silly or distracted.

In the workplace, risks are assessed and, if possible, eliminated. If the risk cannot be removed altogether, then steps must be taken to minimise any dangers. For example:

▶ all staff must receive training to use special equipment or machinery

▶ health and safety training must be provided so that people are aware of the dangers of silly behaviour and using items for the wrong purpose

▶ anything which is high risk must be dealt with promptly. An icy path would be covered in sand, a slippery floor should be cleaned and warning signs put up until it is dry, a faulty plug must be replaced and so on.

▲ A wet floor is a hazard which must be dealt with promptly

Identifying hazards

Office hazards can be divided into five categories:

1 **Machinery and equipment**.   Ranging from large items, such as photocopiers, to small ones, such as letter openers, hazards usually relate to the way the equipment is used, where it is placed (especially if it is portable and can easily be moved) and how it is maintained. This is particularly important for electrical equipment because the item itself must be regularly checked and so must any connections to the mains.

2 **Unsafe use of substances**.   Dangerous, highly toxic and inflammable substances must be kept in a special place, but there are still other hazardous substances in an office, such as toner, which is used in a photocopier. This must be handled *and* disposed of properly (see Unit 4, page 189). Liquid paper is another example, as this gives off fumes. Care must be taken over the handling, storage and disposal of all potentially hazardous substances.

3 **Personal conduct and unsafe behaviour**.   No matter where you work, you can thwart even the most stringent health and safety regulations by ignoring them or taking unnecessary risks. Running downstairs, carrying too many files so you can't see where you're going or trying to lift something heavy are all examples. Not only could you have an accident yourself, but you could quite easily injure someone else.

4 **Untidiness and careless working**.   As you saw in Unit 2, pages 46–47, it is quite easy to have, or cause, a nasty injury through simple carelessness or untidiness. If you leave papers scattered on a carpeted floor, someone can easily slip on them. If you use a paper knife, stapler or scissors unthinkingly then you can injure yourself. You can even cut yourself on a piece of paper!

5 **Smoking, drinking and drugs**.   Today most organisations have a 'no-smoking' policy in the workplace. They *may* provide facilities for workers to smoke – but they don't have to. All employees must abide by the rules of their workplace, which may also include a ban on alcohol during working hours. Certainly, no employee would be allowed to work if there was any likelihood of his or her performance being impaired by alcohol. Illicit drug taking is, of course, a legal offence. If you have been prescribed drugs by your doctor which could affect your ability to use machinery and equipment safely then you should notify your supervisor.

OVER TO YOU!

Study the table of potential office hazards below.

1 Decide which of the hazards under 'machinery and equipment' should be reported to your supervisor immediately.

2 Identify 4 rules for using a hazardous substance safely.

3 Working in a small group, prepare a short instruction sheet for new employees on working safely. The title is **Reducing Risks by Working Safely**. Do this by reading the hazards listed under 'Personal conduct and unsafe behaviour' and 'Untidiness and careless working' and for 7 hazards you select, list the correct action that should be taken.

Then compare your suggestions with those made by other groups to see how many different ideas you can think of altogether.

Potential hazards in an administration environment

Category	Potential hazards
Machinery and equipment	Unsafe use because user is untrained or is not concentrating Loose or broken plugs or trailing, frayed or damaged wires Overloaded power points Trying to move heavy equipment unaided Equipment placed on uneven surface or where people may fall over it or bang into it Ignoring the manufacturer's instructions about the placing and use of equipment Trying to repair faults without proper training or authorisation Unusual noise or smell coming from electrical equipment Equipment with a broken guard, e.g. a guillotine or letter opener
Unsafe use of substances such as toner, correcting fluid, etc.	Unlabelled bottles of substances Not replacing top or cap on substances or correcting fluids Breathing toxic fumes Getting toner powder on skin or in eyes Not storing or disposing of dangerous substances according to instructions
Personal conduct and unsafe behaviour	Ignoring fire alarm or disregarding instructions to use escape routes or go to assembly point Wedging open fire doors Lifting heavy, bulky or unstable loads; carrying high loads so view ahead blocked Not using protective items when instructed (e.g. rubber gloves, hard hat, protective clothing) Not reading instructions or disregarding them Using work items for a different purpose than they were intended for (e.g. a fire extinguisher to prop open a door) Running in corridors, up or down stairs or around corners Ignoring company policy on the use of computer equipment and VDUs. Obstructing doorways or passageways Placing own desk where people could injure themselves on a corner Placing broken glass in waste bin
Untidiness and careless working	Leaving filing cabinet or desk drawers open Stacking up files on a shelf Using basic items without care (scissors, paper knife, stapler) Not mopping up spills Cluttering up floor area with personal possessions or work items
Smoking, drinking and drugs	Disregarding company rules on smoking Smoking in a 'no-smoking' area Working whilst under the influence of alcohol Ignoring doctor's instructions about taking prescribed medicines which may affect ability to use machinery and equipment Taking illegal drugs or banned substances

The law on health and safety

All employees and employers have a legal responsibility to comply with the laws on health and safety. The most important law was passed in 1974 and is called the **Health and Safety at Work Act**. This Act, and many other health and safety regulations, are in place to protect everyone at work. They also place specific responsibilities on both employers and employees.

All employers must:

▶ ensure, as far as is reasonably possible, the health, safety and welfare of all staff

▶ consult an employee safety representative or the employees themselves on health and safety plans and any changes which might affect them

▶ make sure that the workplace is safe

▶ ensure that all machinery is safe and that safe ways of using it are set up and followed

▶ make sure that all articles and substances are moved, stored and used safely

▶ provide adequate welfare facilities (e.g. hot and cold water and toilet facilities)

▶ provide information, instructions, training and supervision necessary for health and safety.

All employees must:

▶ take reasonable care for their own health and safety, for example by working safely and tidily

▶ take reasonable care for the health and safety of other people who may be affected by their actions, such as their colleagues and any visitors

▶ cooperate with their employer on all health and safety matters by obeying all safety rules and instructions

▶ work safely – by using work items correctly and wearing any personal protective equipment which is provided (such as rubber gloves), in accordance with training or instructions

▶ behave responsibly and never interfere with or misuse anything which has been provided for their health, safety or welfare.

▶ take all reasonable precautions when they are working (see page 140)

▶ undertake any health and safety training that is required

▶ deal with potential hazards when it is safe to do so and reporting any hazards they cannot deal with themselves (see page 143)

▶ follow organisational procedures in the case of fire, accidents and emergencies (see page 144).

Health and Safety at Work (Display Screen Equipment) Regulations 1992

An additional regulation specifically relates to the health and safety of employees who regularly use a computer at work – which means most administrators. The regulation not only relates to your computer but also to your workstation and your working environment, i.e. your desk and work surface, your chair, other types of computer equipment, such as your mouse, keyboard, printer, etc. and the office you work in.

According to these Regulations, all employers must reduce any risks for staff who use computers as a significant part of their work. This means making sure that:

▲ Correct seating and posture are important

▶ All workstations, the working environment, furniture and computer software meet the minimum requirements of the Regulations.

- The image on your screen must be stable and the characters must be an adequate size, you must be able to adjust the brightness and contrast and tilt or swivel your screen unit.

- Your keyboard must be separate from the screen and tiltable. You should have enough space at the front to provide a 'rest area' for your hands. The surface must be matt, it should be easy to use and the symbols on the keys must be clear.

- Your work surface must be large enough for the work you do and have a low reflective finish. You must be able to arrange your equipment to suit your own needs.

- Your chair must be stable and allow you to be comfortable and move easily. The seat height must be adjustable and you should be able to change the back of the seat to give you good back support. Foot rests must be available on request.

- There should be satisfactory lighting, but glare should be kept to a minimum. Windows should have blinds or your screen or workstations be placed to avoid reflections. Noise, heat and humidity levels should enable you to work comfortably.

- Software must be suitable for the work being done, be user-friendly and appropriate to the level of knowledge of the user.

▶ All users can have breaks or changes of activity. Short, frequent breaks are better than longer, infrequent ones.

▶ An eye examination will be arranged for all users, on request, and the employer will provide special spectacles if the test shows these are needed.

▶ All users are given health and safety training and information to enable them to use the equipment safely and adjust it to meet their own needs.

ORGANISATIONS IN BUSINESS

Most people think that modern equipment is so safe that there are few or no risks attached to its use. Yet the last few years have seen a host of new injuries, such as phone neck, computer spine and mouse wrist – as well as TMI – short for text message injury!

Phone neck is caused by holding a telephone between the shoulder and ear for long periods of time. This gives you a 'crick' in your neck. The safe way to answer a telephone and continue inputting text is to use a headset. Computer spine is caused when the position of the chair back is incorrect or the VDU and keyboard is at the incorrect height so that computer users sit 'hunched' for hours at a time. Mouse wrist (or even worse 'mouse arm') is caused by using a mouse for long periods of time. It occurs because the position of the hand is unnatural as it is being constantly twisted horizontally. Finally, children as young as six are being reported with TMI – because of the hundreds of tiny repeated movements they are making by sending dozens of text messages a day.

Both mouse arm and TMI are forms of repetitive strain injury (RSI). This causes swelling and inflammation of the affected area and can be very painful. Today, many manufacturers are producing a variety of items to reduce the dangers of RSI, from ergonomic keyboards to a mouse which is held like a pen. These devices can reduce the risks of using modern equipment but the final responsibility still rests with the user.

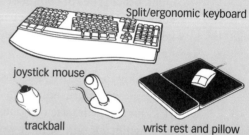
Split/ergonomic keyboard
joystick mouse
trackball
wrist rest and pillow

▲ These devices can help to make the working environment safer

OVER TO YOU!

1. Carry out a quick health check on yourself next time you are using a computer! Have you adjusted your chair to suit your own needs or can't you be bothered? Do you know how to adjust the contrast and brightness on your screen? Are your arms horizontal when you are keying in – and is the screen level with your eyes? Remember that at work you can't blame your employer if you simply can't be bothered to do anything to help yourself!

2. All computer users have a responsibility to make necessary adjustments to their equipment and workstation to suit their needs and to work sensibly. Explain what action you would take in each of the following situations.
   a) Your screen starts to flicker and gives you a headache.
   b) You are uncomfortable when you are using your computer because the document you are copying is offset to your right and you are getting neck ache.
   c) You can't see the screen properly on a sunny day because of the reflection from the window behind you.
   d) You have been working on a long document for some time and your back is starting to ache.
   e) Yesterday you changed your screen colours but now the text doesn't show up properly, so you can't read it easily.

3. Under the Health and Safety at Work Act, both employers and employees have responsibilities.
   a) Identify 3 responsibilities which apply to your employer.
   b) State 4 personal responsibilities you have when you are at work.

Risks and precautions

All employers have a legal responsibility to **assess** all the risks in their workplace at regular intervals. They do this by:

1 identifying the hazards

2 deciding who might be harmed and how this might occur

3 assessing whether the risk is, or would be, high, medium or low

4 either getting rid of the risk completely or, if this is impossible, reducing the risk to low level by taking precautions to prevent accidents.

The aim is to make every risk low level. Let's see how this works in practice.

The back stairs inside a building are steep and the flooring is concrete. They are identified as a hazard because anyone could slip and fall and be hurt badly on the hard surface. The stairs are used regularly as a short cut so the risk is classed as high – especially for visitors who are not familiar with the building.

The risk cannot be eliminated so precautions must be taken. It is decided to put non-slip floor covering on the stairs and a sturdy handrail at each side. In addition, warning notices are placed at the top and bottom that users must take extra care. Finally, all staff are told that no visitors must be allowed to use these stairs, and an additional notice is added to say this.

The risk is now low. But staff still need to take care when using the stairs – running up or down them would increase the risk of an accident.

All business organisations take a variety of precautions. For example:

▶ putting up safety signs to warn people about possible dangers

▶ allowing only trained staff to repair basic equipment faults

▶ inspecting equipment regularly. This includes all electrical equipment used in an organisation

▶ providing health and safety training to all staff

▶ issuing instructions to all staff on safe working practices (see below)

▶ appointing safety representatives who report hazards and investigate accidents

▶ having clear procedures which all staff must follow in the case of a fire, accident or emergency (see below).

However, there is a limit to what any organisation can do on its own. This is why health and safety is a joint responsibility of both employers and employees. You also have to know how to take sensible precautions yourself!

▲ Safety signs warn people about possible dangers and show the action to take

Taking precautions

We all take precautions all the time. If you take something hot out of an oven, you are wise to wear oven gloves. If you run a hot bath, you test it with your hand before you get in. These are both examples of taking precautions, to *prevent* a possible accident or injury.

At work, you should take precautions by:

▶ reading instructions carefully before you start to do something new

▶ obeying every safety sign you see

▶ walking, rather than running at work, and taking extra care if a surface is slippery or hazardous

▶ using items only for the purpose they are intended

▶ obeying all instructions and procedures you are told to follow

▶ reporting anything which you think could be a risk to someone.

Safe working practices

There is a safe – and unsafe – way of doing anything! Jon is cutting an apple. He puts it on the table and presses down with a sharp knife. Carla is doing the same thing, only she holds the apple in one hand and uses a knife. The knife is pointing towards her hand. What happens if the knife slips?

You take the same sort of risks if you:

▶ hold a stapler or paper knife like Carla

- try to move a heavy piece of equipment, such as a filing cabinet, on your own

- decide to remove some jammed paper by reaching inside a (hot) machine, such as a photocopier, without knowing how to do this correctly

- disregard the potential dangers of any electrical equipment

- stand on your chair to reach something high, rather than using a safety stool.

The list is almost endless!

There are only two steps to follow in relation to safe working practices.

1 First, find out what the safe practice is for *anything* you are about to do.

2 Do it!

▲ This is not a safe working practice!

Dealing with low-risk matters

If your employer has assessed all the hazards and taken appropriate precautions, then *all* the risks in your workplace will be classed as 'low'. For example, electrical equipment can be lethal – but is perfectly safe if it is properly insulated and earthed, positioned correctly and used according to instructions. However, the level of risk can change if:

- the equipment develops a fault or is damaged in any way

- the equipment is moved to a new location, where it is perhaps less stable or wires trail across the floor

- a new employee or trainee uses the equipment without proper training.

Your responsibility is to take care yourself and to watch for anything which can increase the risk relating to a potential hazard. In this case you should:

- take action yourself, if it is safe to do so. For example, move the equipment to a stable surface (if it isn't heavy) or change the position so ensure the wire is not trailing on the floor

- report the problem so that appropriate action can be taken by someone else.

You also have a responsibility to keep your own risks low by working safely at all times.

OVER TO YOU!

1 When a risk cannot be eliminated, warning signs must be put up. These are:

▶ red for a prohibited (forbidden) action

▶ blue for a mandatory (must do) action, and

▶ green for a safe condition.

Find at least one example of each of these coloured signs in your college – or in any other organisations you visit. In each case explain why it is that particular colour. Compare your list with others in your group to see how many different signs you have spotted altogether.

2 For each of the hazards below, identify the action you should take to remove or lessen the risk.

a) A large box of stationery is delivered at lunchtime and left in the middle of the office.

b) You notice some bare wires showing on the flex of the electric stapler.

c) The window slams closed in a gale and the glass cracks.

d) Your friend starts to move her printer when it is still plugged in.

e) You spill yoghurt on the tiled floor in your office.

f) You see smoke coming under the door of the stationery cupboard.

g) Your friend has just put a can of drink next to her keyboard.

3 There is a safe way – and an unsafe way – to do each of the following activities. Can you identify both of these? Compare your answers with other members of your group.

a) Lift a box of paper from the floor to a high shelf.

b) Open a high window.

c) Seal an envelope.

d) Throw away broken glass.

e) Move a portable electric heater.

f) File papers in a filing cabinet.

ORGANISATIONS IN BUSINESS

If you worked in a supermarket and saw a mushroom on the floor, what would you do? Ignore it, pick it up or report it immediately as being a potential hazard which could pose a high risk to a shopper and possibly cost your employer thousands of pounds in compensation?

No doubt very few people would guess that a mushroom could cause a serious problem for a major organisation, but that is what happened at Asda in Hatfield, Hertfordshire. Beverley Jackson, a nursing assistant, stepped on the vegetable and slipped. Over the months that followed she complained of increasing pain in her hip. She eventually had to give up work and, after an unsuccessful operation, was left wheelchair bound. She sued Asda for compensation.

Just before her trial was due to start in May 2003, Asda settled her claim for £550,000. Not many mushrooms work out to be so expensive to a business, but the story may persuade you to ensure that there is nothing slippery on the floor in your office in the future!

▲ Even a mushroom can be a hazard to a shopper

Reporting procedures, accidents and hazards

At work, you have a responsibility to tell someone if:

▶ you see an accident occur or you have an accident yourself

▶ you notice a potential hazard or consider that the level of risk has increased in relation to any hazard.

Accident reporting   All organisations have a system for reporting and recording accidents to comply with legal regulations. If there are more than 10 employees an accident book must be kept and all records stored for at least three years. In most cases, 'near-misses' are also logged, so that areas for improvement can be identified.

If you witness an accident or are involved in one, you will have to complete an accident report form. If the accident is serious, it will be investigated by the safety officer or a safety representative and nothing must be moved or changed until this has been done.

Hazard and risk reporting   When you first start work in an organisation you will receive basic health and safety information and training. As part of this, you will be told what you should do if you spot a potential hazard. In a small business, your responsibility will be to tell your team leader or supervisor. In a large organisation, there may be safety representatives or a safety officer who is responsible for this area.

Even if the problem seems quite trivial – like a loose carpet tile or a cracked plug – you are wise to report it promptly, so that action can be taken before the situation gets worse or someone has an accident. If there is any delay before action can be taken, a warning sign should be put up to prevent any accidents in the meantime.

Procedures for fire, accidents and emergencies

All organisations have special procedures which all employees must follow in the case of fire, accidents and emergencies. This is important, not only for legal reasons, but because a rapid and correct response is required in these situations. Wasting time by asking people what to do or dithering would increase the danger. People must know exactly what action to take to reduce the risk as much as possible.

Fire procedures

When the fire alarm sounds, all employees and visitors must follow the evacuation procedures. These are usually printed on notices around the building and are often copied onto the back of visitor's badges, so that everyone knows what to do. The usual procedure is shown below.

On hearing the fire alarm

1   Immediately leave the building by the nearest available exit.
2   **DO NOT USE THE LIFTS.**
3   If the nearest exit is inaccessible because of smoke, use the next available exit.
4   Do not return to your normal place of work or stop to collect personal belongings.
5   Close all doors behind you.
6   Report to your designated assembly point.
7   Do not return to the building *for any reason* until authorised to do so.

▲ A typical fire notice

Most organisations have trained fire wardens or fire marshals who check that all the buildings have been evacuated, provide assistance to any disabled staff or visitors who cannot use the stairs alone and liaise with the fire brigade. It is important that you cooperate with these officials at all times.

Accident procedures and first aid

When an accident occurs, the first action is to obtain assistance for the injured. The second is to notify a supervisor or safety representative.

All organisations have trained first aiders – the number will depend upon the size and type of business. A construction company, for example, will have more first aiders than an insurance office, because its employees are involved in higher-risk activities. A low-risk workplace, such as an office, should have one for each 50 employees.

▲ Do not move an injured person until the first aider is there to help

A list of first aiders is normally available in every office, together with their telephone numbers. Until the first aider arrives, no injured person should be moved, in case this can worsen the injury. Until the safety representative or safety officer arrives, nothing else at the scene should be moved. Otherwise it is more difficult to investigate the accident properly.

Emergency procedures

These are in place in case any other type of emergency occurs – such as a flood, gas leak or bomb threat. In this case, the fire alarm may be used to warn everyone to evacuate or a different method may be used to inform staff who are working in an affected area.

There are two major differences between a fire evacuation and other emergency evacuations.

1 You may be told to take your personal possessions with you. If there is a bomb threat, for example, this reduces the time needed to search the premises.

2 You may be told to leave doors open, rather than close them, to speed up access for anyone carrying out a search.

The most important point is to know the rules where you work – or study – and to follow them.

OVER TO YOU!

1 a) Explain why it is important for all organisations to have clear fire evacuation procedures.
   b) During a recent fire drill three people used the lift and one person went home instead of going to the assembly point. Identify 1 possible consequence of *each* action.
   c) Describe 2 other emergencies which could occur which would result in an evacuation of a building.

2 Describe 6 potential hazards you might find in an office.

3 a) Describe 2 precautions an employer will take to minimise accidents and 2 precautions you should take as an employee.
   b) Identify 1 reason why it is important that an accident is reported promptly and 1 reason why a potential hazard should also be reported promptly.

The legal rights of an employee

All employees have legal rights from the moment they are officially offered a job with an organisation.

The rights of employees can be grouped into three main areas.

1 **Health and safety rights.** All employees have the right to work in a healthy and safe environment – as you have already seen. This means your employer must provide you with a safe place to work and must not ask you to do anything which is hazardous and would put you in danger. (See pages 132 to 145.)

2 **Statutory employment rights.** These are the rights of every employee in Britain and are set down in many laws and regulations which have been passed by the government. All employers must abide by these.

3 **Your contractual employment rights.** These are set down in the Contract of Employment you receive from your employer. The contents of the contract will vary from one organisation to another and from one job to another, depending upon the terms and conditions of employment. Once you and your employer have signed this document, you are both legally bound to abide by it.

Health and safety rights were covered in the previous section. The following sections give you more information on your employment rights.

Your statutory employment rights

The word *statutory* means 'by law'. There are many laws which give you legal rights at work. As you continue your studies you will learn more about them. However, from the very beginning it is helpful if you know about the main rights you have. At work, your employer must:

▶ treat you fairly and not discriminate against you on grounds of race, gender or disability

▶ give you the same opportunities as your colleagues in relation to areas such as training and promotion

▶ pay you a salary which is at or above the national minimum wage for your age

▶ give you payslips which show your pay and deductions

▶ allow you a minimum of four weeks' paid holiday a year if you are a full-time employee

▶ treat you reasonably and not ask you to do anything which is against the law

▶ allow you to choose whether or not to join a trade union

▶ consult you over anything which would greatly affect your terms and conditions of employment

▶ comply with the law in all other respects in relation to your employment, i.e. your working hours, a female employee's rights to time off for antenatal care and maternity leave and so on.

▶ give you the minimum period of notice (between one and 12 weeks) if you are dismissed, depending upon how long you have worked for the organisation. The only exception is if you are dismissed for a very serious offence (see page 153).

▶ give you redundancy pay if you are dismissed because there is no work for you to do, providing you have worked for your employer for more than two years.

Laws on discrimination

A very important legal area is discrimination. Discrimination means treating someone differently. There are laws to prevent people being treated differently just because they are of a particular gender or race – or because they have a disability. Discrimination is not just unlawful when people apply for jobs. It is unlawful for employees too, such as when they apply for training, promotion, or if they are dismissed or made redundant.

There are three Acts which protect employees from discrimination at work and these are explained in the table below.

Laws relating to discrimination

The Sex Discrimination Act

This Act states that men and women must be treated the same in relation to recruitment and selection for jobs, training, promotion, the way they are treated at work and all other aspects of their employment.

The Race Relations Act

This Act states that it is unlawful for employers to discriminate against anyone on grounds of colour, race, nationality or ethnic origin.

The Disability Discrimination Act

This Act means that employers cannot treat disabled employees less favourably than able-bodied persons unless this can be justified.

Because of these Acts, most employers today have an **Equal Opportunities Policy** which states that they provide fair treatment to everyone.

Equal opportunities policies

All organisations have to comply with laws relating to discrimination. Because of this, most employers today have an **Equal Opportunities Policy** which states that they provide fair treatment to everyone. You may also see a statement in their job advertisements to say that they do not discriminate against anyone 'on grounds of colour, race, nationality, ethnic or national origin, sex, being married or disability.'

ORGANISATIONS IN BUSINESS

Discrimination laws and equal opportunities apply to other organisations as well as businesses – including schools and colleges. They also apply all over Europe – not just in Britain.

In January 2003, a former schoolgirl at Mount Lourdes convent grammar school in Northern Ireland won £6,250 compensation from her school. At 17, Margaret McCluskey was excluded from classes and forced to take her GCSEs elsewhere because she became pregnant. Although the school allowed her to return after her daughter was born, it admitted that barring her from classes at the time she was pregnant was sex discrimination.

Margaret McCluskey hasn't let this experience prevent her from getting on. After studying A-levels she then gained a place at Cambridge University and completed her studies there in June 2003.

Your contractual employment rights

It is your right to receive your terms of employment in writing after you have been employed for two months. Usually this will be in a Contract of Employment, but it could be in a letter. This is quite acceptable.

You are likely to receive two copies of the document. One is for you to keep. You will be asked to sign and return the copy to your employer as proof that you agree to these terms and conditions.

This is now a legal agreement. If either you, or your employer, fail to do what you have agreed (called **breaching** the contract in legal terms) then action can be taken.

It is worth knowing that your contract can *never* take away any of your statutory legal rights. It may, however, give you additional rights – such as the right to be paid your normal wage if you are ill and the right to take longer holidays than the statutory four weeks. It will also give you further details about how your rights are affected in certain situations. For example if you commit a serious offence you could be dismissed without notice (see page 153).

Your contract of employment *must* contain certain key items of information. These are listed in the table below.

Key items in a contract of employment

Your letter or contract must contain the following information:

- Your job title
- Your hours of work
- The place of work
- The terms and conditions of employment
- Your pay and any other benefits including sick pay and holiday pay
- The date on which your employment commenced
- The name of your employer
- Your name.

In addition, your employer must also provide you with other items of information, although this can be in a separate document:

- Details of any union agreements which affect you
- Details of your employer's grievance and appeals procedure (see page 150).

You should also be given the following information, or told where you can obtain it:

- Details about sickness benefits and sickness entitlement if you are ill
- Pension scheme details
- How much notice you must give if you want to leave your job
- Details of your employer's disciplinary rules and procedure (see page 153).

Young employees, under the age of 18, sometimes have additional statutory rights.

Today, most employees have protection from the law in relation to the hours and days they work. Under the Working Time Regulations 1998, most employees need not work more than 48 hours a week, although some occupations, such as junior doctors, are exempt. Rest breaks are also covered in these Regulations. For 16- to 18-year-olds the protection is even greater. From April 2003 it is likely that the maximum number of hours they can work is 40, with more rest breaks and no night work.

Under a different law, all employees aged 16 or 17 have the right to study or train for a qualification – usually up to NVQ level 2 – which will help them to do their job better. Employees over 18, who change their employer, have the right to complete training they have already begun and must be given reasonable time off to do this, with pay.

The process to follow when things go wrong

For the vast majority of employees, nothing goes wrong. They are issued with their contract of employment and both they and their employer abide by its contents. However, for other people, problems can occur.

▶ The organisation may not be doing well and there may be talk of **redundancies**.

▶ The organisation may want to change the terms and conditions of employment.

▶ The employee may be concerned because his or her rights are not being upheld.

Redundancy   An employee is made redundant when he or she is dismissed because there is no longer any work for them to do. Usually, employers try to find other solutions, such as transferring people to another job or asking for volunteers, but if this is not possible then compulsory redundancy may be the only option.

In this situation, the organisation must have a fair procedure and this must be discussed with the employees and with the trade union(s) at the workplace. It would not be legal for a manager to use redundancy as a method of getting rid of unpopular staff.

Staff being made redundant must be told about the payments they will receive, the proposed date on which their employment will end and their other legal rights. All staff who have worked for the organisation for more than two years are entitled to redundancy pay. The exact amount will depend upon how long they have worked there. Sometimes free counselling or retraining is also offered to help redundant employees find other work. Staff being made redundant must be allowed time off to attend training or interviews for new jobs.

Changing the terms and conditions in the contract   Most organisations will want to change the terms and conditions of employment in the contract of employment from time to time. This may be because of changes to statutory rights or to keep the business competitive and up-to-date. All employees must be notified, in writing, of any change to the terms of their contract. If the change will mean *better* conditions for the employees, it is doubtful that any of them will complain.

If the change will result in worse conditions, then employers usually try to come to an agreement with the employees, often through a trade union. If no agreement is reached and the changes go ahead, then the employee could make a complaint to an Employment Tribunal (see below).

An employee's rights are not upheld   All organisations have procedures for employees to follow if they have a complaint or problem at work. These are called **grievance procedures**. As part of the terms of your contract of employment you must be told where these are, or given a copy of them, so that you can refer to them if you have a problem.

Most minor problems are sorted out quickly and informally at work without the employee needing to use these procedures. If they are not, or if the problem gets worse or is very serious, an employee may decide that using them is the best way ahead.

Grievance procedures

These exist for employees who have a complaint about their employer. There are usually three stages:

1 The employee has an interview to talk about the problem with his or her manager. The employee can be accompanied by someone else for support – usually a colleague or trade union official.

2 If the situation is still not resolved, another interview takes place, this time with a more senior manager.

3 The final stage is an interview with an outside third party, such as ACAS – the Advisory, Conciliation and Arbitration Service, which often makes recommendations in this type of situation.

If the situation is still unresolved or the employee has been dismissed and thinks this is unfair, then he or she may have the right to take the case to an Employment Tribunal. This is an informal court which deals with employment disputes.

You should note, however, that it is rare for grievances to get to this stage. The aim of everyone at work is normally to solve the problem as quickly as possible.

OVER TO YOU!

1 Look through a local or national newspaper featuring job advertisements and find *two* examples of an Equal Opportunities statement. Compare the ones you find with those found by other members of your group and check how they differ. Remember that it doesn't matter what type of job is advertised, the policy relates to that organisation – not individual jobs.

2 Your college will have an equal opportunities policy which relates to its students, as well as its employees. You will probably have been given a copy during your induction – or in other items you were given, such as a student diary. Find out what it says and compare it with the type of statements you saw in the advertisements you obtained for question 1.

3 a) Identify 4 legal rights you have as an employee.
   b) Under what circumstances would an employee be made redundant?
   c) Identify 1 legal right of a long-term employee who is made redundant.

4 a) What is a contract of employment?
   b) Identify 5 items you would find in this document.

5 a) Identify 2 laws which protect employees from discrimination at work.
   b) An employee has a serious complaint because she thinks she is being discriminated against. Explain the process which is normally followed in this situation.

The responsibilities of an employee – and the consequences of not meeting them

You should remember that you already have responsibilities to your employer under the Health and Safety at Work Act, which you read about on page 136. In your contract of employment both these and other responsibilities are specified.

When you sign the contract you are agreeing to keep to *all* the terms and conditions which are identified in the document. This includes:

▶ working the hours stated

▶ turning up for work, unless you are ill. In this case you must comply with your employer's requirements in relation to telling them if you are absent and providing sick notes

▶ doing the work you are asked to do as part of your job

▶ complying with all other conditions specified in the contract.

▲ You must turn up for work unless you are ill

However, you also have other responsibilities to your employer which aren't explicitly stated in the contract. This is because they are considered to be so obvious they are taken for granted!

Your additional responsibilities include:

▶ behaving responsibly towards other people at work. This means respecting the needs and wishes of other people and their own commitments

▶ obeying the law yourself. This includes not discriminating against any of your colleagues and being honest

▶ working towards the objectives of the organisation. This means you work to help the business, which includes honouring your responsibilities to customers and *never* giving away confidential information

▶ taking reasonable care of your employer's property (including equipment and furniture)

▶ following all company rules and procedures

▶ being prepared to carry out reasonable instructions and requests. This might include complying with a company 'dress code' and other rules relating to personal appearance and behaviour.

▶ being reasonably competent and having the skills you claimed to possess at the interview

▶ being 'ready and willing' to do the work and acting as a 'reasonable' employee in any situation

▶ being prepared to change when the job changes, e.g. when new technology is introduced into the workplace.

These additional responsibilities mean that all employees must work in a way which enables their employers to meet their business commitments. This would be impossible if the employee was incapable of doing the work, would not carry out instructions, refused to cooperate if any changes were required and ignored all the company rules and procedures!

The consequences of not meeting these responsibilities

An employee who either ignores, or deliberately decides, not to meet his or her responsibilities causes problems for everyone. For example:

▶ an employee who ignores health and safety responsibilities can endanger other staff

▶ an employee who is dishonest and steals from the employer is committing a criminal offence and could be prosecuted

▶ an employee who discriminates against a colleague is also acting unlawfully. If the organisation did not stop this, it could itself be found guilty by an employment tribunal

▶ an employee who gives away confidential information is endangering future business which could, ultimately, lead to the organisation being less profitable and possibly having to make other staff redundant

▲ Stealing always results in dismissal

▶ an employee who simply won't (or can't) do his or her own work creates problems for everyone else who has to do more work themselves.

If the problem is minor, then the employee is likely to be reprimanded by his or her manager. If the offence is serious, then the employee will be disciplined in accordance with the **disciplinary procedures** of the organisation.

Disciplinary procedures

Disciplinary procedures are the *opposite* of grievance procedures, because this time it is the organisation which has a complaint about the employee.

Again there are usually three stages.

1 For a minor or first offence, you would be given a verbal warning. Your employer must make it clear that this is a warning – and not a friendly discussion.

2 For a more serious or repeat offence you could be given a written (or final) warning. After a final warning you would be dismissed if you repeated the offence.

3 For a very serious offence, known as **gross misconduct** you could be suspended, demoted or dismissed (sacked) without notice.

Because taking disciplinary action is very serious, all employees must know about the procedures. This is why your contract of employment tells you where to find this information. Employees should also know that disciplinary action is being taken and why – and have the opportunity to defend themselves.

However, if the disciplinary procedures are followed and an employee is sacked for a valid reason which is 'reasonable' in the circumstances, this is quite legal and the employee would have no grounds to complain about the action taken by the employer.

ORGANISATIONS IN BUSINESS

Today most organisations have specific rules and procedures that employees must follow when they use computers. The official name for these may be IT policies.

These policies are likely to state the type of Internet sites which can be accessed during working hours and the type of material which can be included in emails or sent as attachments. The aim of this is to prevent staff spending time at working booking their holiday on-line or – worse – downloading a virus onto their computer.

However, the major reason why staff are disciplined is for using emails to send pornography and tasteless jokes around the company. In 2002, Hewlett Packard, the US computer firm, sacked two members of its UK staff and suspended 150 others for alleged email abuse because they had disregarded company rules on email use.

1 All the reasons given below are legally classed as 'fair' reasons for dismissal. As a group, decide which offences are so serious they would normally result in instant dismissal and those where the employee would normally receive a warning first.

a) Stealing, either from the employer or from another employee.

b) Being drunk in the workplace.

c) Continually arriving late for work.

d) Using someone else's computer password.

e) Being absent from work for no good reason.

f) Ignoring health and safety regulations by storing boxes of stationery in front of a fire exit.

g) Taking a holiday without permission.

h) Wearing unsuitable clothes or having a scruffy appearance.

i) Sending a rude email to a colleague.

2 a) Identify 3 responsibilities you have to your employer.

b) Explain the action that would be taken if you failed to meet these responsibilities.

3 A young man is found guilty of helping himself to several CDs from his company's store cupboard. He is a hard worker and has never been in trouble before. His manager sacks him. The young man thinks this is unfair because the CDs aren't worth very much money.

What is your opinion? Discuss this as a group and then with your tutor.

4 Work in a small group to decide your answers to the following. Then compare your answers with the rest of your class.

a) Identify the consequences which could arise from each of the following employees failing to meet their responsibilities.

b) Decide what disciplinary action you think the manager should take and identify the facts (if any) he might take into account when he is deciding what to do.

   i   Two trainees set off a fire extinguisher as a joke.

   ii   An employee insults a customer over the telephone.

   iii A supervisor wants to hold a training course in an upstairs room despite the fact that one member of staff is in a wheelchair. There is no lift in the building.

   iv Two trainees start fighting in a workshop area.

   v   An employee is frequently late back from lunch and is always trying to leave early. She is also often seen chatting rather than working.

Following routine office procedures

Introduction

There are many routine tasks to do in every office. These include filing, photocopying, sending faxes and dealing with the post. These activities are carried out every day and, although they are routine, they are also very important. If they are not done correctly, there can be numerous problems. If just one document is lost in a filing system a major search will be necessary, particularly if the document is important and is needed urgently.

To prevent this type of problem, all organisations have procedures for their employees to follow when they are doing these tasks. This may sound alarming but procedures help you – and everyone else – to do many activities quickly and accurately.

In this unit you will learn the procedures you must follow for routine office tasks. You will understand the benefits of following these and be able to identify possible difficulties that can sometimes occur. You will also practise these activities and this will provide you with the skills to carry out these tasks efficiently yourself when you are at work.

Unit summary

This unit is divided into three sections:

▶ **Identify and describe procedures for carrying out office-based tasks**. In this section you will learn about the basic procedures you will meet when you are filing, photocopying, using a fax machine and dealing with the post.

▶ **Follow procedures to carry out routine office tasks**. This section gives you practical guidance on carrying out the tasks of filing, photocopying, sending faxes and processing incoming and outgoing post.

▶ **Review the experience of following procedures**. The final section helps you to identify possible difficulties in following procedures and to also identify the benefits.

Assessment

Your assessment for this unit is in three parts.

1 You will be asked to identify one procedure relating to each of the following activities and then describe the procedure by listing at least three steps in it. The activities are: paper-based filing; photocopying; sending faxes and processing post.

   You will write your answers on a special form.

2 You will prove you can follow procedures by doing 2 types of activity from the following list. You will do each of these activities on two separate occasions.

▶ If you choose **paper-based filing**, then you will have to carry out filing tasks on two occasions and, on each one, correctly file and retrieve at least six different documents or files. You will have to file at least one document in each of the following types of filing system: alphabetical, numerical system and chronological.

► If you choose **photocopying**, then on each occasion you must reproduce and assemble at least three documents correctly. You will also have to prove that you can photocopy single pages, multiple pages and make back-to-back copies.

► If you **send a fax**, then on at least one occasion the document you send must be at least three pages.

► If you **process the post**, then you will have to distribute at least six items of incoming post and dispatch at least six items of post on each occasion. You will also prepare and dispatch two parcels.

Your work will be observed by your tutor, or another qualified person, who will tell you when you have done these tasks successfully.

3 For *each* activity you have undertaken you will review the procedures you followed. You must identify:

► any difficulties you encountered when you used the procedures

► at least two benefits in using the procedures.

You will write your answers on a special form.

▼ Identifying and describing procedures

We all follow procedures every day. In fact, you will have been following procedures for many years without realising it!

Procedures are simply a set of steps that make up a task or an activity. As a child, you learned the correct procedure for crossing the road safely. As you grew up, you learned the correct procedure for many other activities so that you could do these on your own: you learned how to wash your hair yourself, how to make a hot drink, how to tie your school tie and your shoelaces – and so on.

At school and college you learnt even more procedures – how to log on to the computer system, for example. To join your college class you had to find out about the procedure to enrol. You will often hear people say 'The procedure to follow is

▲ 'Stop, look and listen' is a type of procedure

. . .' when they are explaining something to you – although you might never have realised the significance of these few words!

The steps in procedures

All procedures consist of steps to follow. If you are washing your hair, then you learn to do this by:

1 wetting your hair first with hot water (but not too hot!)

2 putting on shampoo and rubbing it in

3 rinsing your hair again with clean water.

You can, of course, add other steps if you want to shampoo it twice, or finish off with conditioner. However, it is important that you follow the steps in order. Putting shampoo on dry hair, for example, would be a disaster!

This is another reason for having a procedure. It tells you the correct order in which you should do a task. In this case, even if someone had never washed their hair before, they would be able to do it properly.

OVER TO YOU!

1 Write down, in steps, the procedure you were taught to follow to cross the road. Then check with the rest of your group. Did you all learn the same procedure or did you learn different ones?

2 Write down the procedure you actually follow, in steps, when you wash your hair. You might find it interesting to compare what you do with other people in your group!

3 As a group, try to think of at least 4 other everyday activities you undertake where you follow a procedure (even if you never think about it!). Then pick 2 of these and decide the actual steps involved.

Procedures for routine office activities

There are many procedures for routine office activities. For some activities it is very important that everyone does the task in the same way. In other cases, it is important that people know what action to take if there is a problem. The procedures are designed so that each person can work as quickly, efficiently and safely as possible.

As an example, all receptionists are taught the procedures to follow when a visitor arrives. This means that:

▶ all visitors will be greeted in the same way, no matter which receptionist is on duty

▶ no visitor is kept waiting longer than necessary

▶ each receptionist knows what action to take if there is a problem or if a visitor is abusive or threatening.

Procedures for paper-based filing

All businesses file dozens of documents every day. The type of equipment that is used was described in Unit 3. (See page 100).

There are two important aspects of filing:

1 All the documents must be stored **safely**, so they are not damaged.

2 All the documents must be filed **correctly**, so that they can be quickly retrieved.

Because many people will use a filing system, everyone has to follow the same procedure. Otherwise, documents could easily be lost or damaged.

A typical procedure for *filing* a document would be:

1 Select document for filing.

2 Punch hole in document *correctly* (see page 102)

3 Identify and remove correct file folder from filing cabinet.

4 Open file folder and insert/fasten document inside. (*Note: the top document is always the most recent.*)

5 Replace file folder in filing cabinet in its correct place.

To *retrieve* a document which was filed earlier, then the procedure may be:

1 Obtain key information on document required (i.e. name/date/reference number).

2 Extract file folder containing this document.

3 Remove document from file.

4 Replace file folder in filing cabinet.

Procedures can vary a little, especially between one organisation and another. For example:

▶ In many filing systems, you have to insert a note or record inside the file folder, to say you have removed the document, in case someone else needs it later.

▶ In others you are not allowed to remove a document from a file, you *either* have to remove the whole file (and put in a card or put a note in a special book to say you have borrowed it), *or* you have to photocopy the document which is required and then return the file to the system intact.

The reasons for these precautions is to prevent people simply removing important documents from a file and then, perhaps, losing them or forgetting to return them.

You will find further information on filing on pages 164–176. This will help you to identify other procedures related to filing.

PROCEDURES IN BUSINESS

In many organisations, files are so important that there are very strict procedures about borrowing and returning them. An obvious example is a hospital, with thousands of patient records. All the files must be carefully tracked, so none is ever lost.

Filing procedures are also likely to be different if a file contains confidential information, such as personnel records or sensitive financial documents. In this case only a few named people will be allowed access to the file.

Many organisations use computers to track files. This can be done on a computer log, either by using special software or even by creating a simple table on which the administrator records who borrowed the file and when. The advantage with using special software is that it enables you to search quickly for any missing file and tells you who borrowed it.

Another method is to give each file folder a unique barcode. Files which are borrowed are scanned through the system – just like when you buy something in a supermarket – and this automatically creates the record. When the file is returned, it is simply scanned back in again. In an organisation with thousands of files, this is much quicker than having to key in the information.

▲ Scanning a file to book it out

Procedures for photocopying

As you develop your knowledge of procedures, you will find that the *exact* procedures frequently vary, depending upon the organisation and the type of equipment being used. Photocopying is a typical example of this. If you were using a very basic machine, the procedure is different from that with a sophisticated, expensive machine – when the machine would do much of the work for you.

Most photocopiers will do several basic operations automatically. You can place the document to be copied in a document tray and it will 'feed in' automatically when you press Start. Your machine may collate a number of pages for you and perhaps staple them as well. On a more basic machine you might need to put the pages, one by one, on the document glass and collate any multi-page documents by hand.

A simple procedure to take one photocopy of a single page is shown below. Instead of a list of points, this has been shown as a flow chart. This is just a different way of showing a set of procedures.

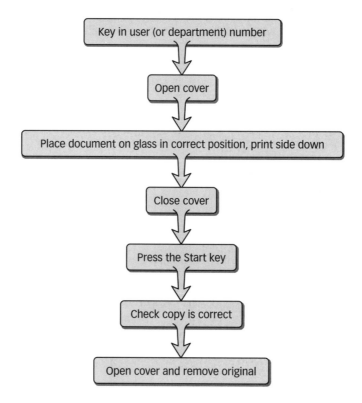

Key in user (or department) number

↓

Open cover

↓

Place document on glass in correct position, print side down

↓

Close cover

↓

Press the Start key

↓

Check copy is correct

↓

Open cover and remove original

Alternatively, when you are photocopying, you may be asked to make several copies, or to photocopy a multi-page document or to refill the paper tray. The procedures for doing this, together with other aspects of photocopying, are covered on pages 177–190.

Place single copies face down on the glass

▲ Taking a photocopy of a single page

1. You will file hand-outs and notes from your tutor almost every day at college – probably in a ring binder. You may have different binders for different subjects – or one large one with dividers. For your own system, write a simple set of procedures which states
   a) how you file new documents you are given
   b) how you retrieve a document you need to find quickly.

2. As a group, suggest 2 benefits of being given a clear set of filing procedures to follow when you start work. To help, think about what it would be like to be given no guidance at all! You may be able to identify more than two – write down as many as you can. Then keep your list safely. You will find it useful when you reach the last section of this chapter.

3. a) For the photocopying machine you are most likely to use at college, write down a list of the procedures involved to take 2 copies of a one-page document. Compare your steps with those of other people in your group. If you all use the same machine, the steps should be the same!
   b) As a group, discuss whether you would do anything different if you were making 200 copies of the document.

Procedures for sending faxes

A fax machine is simple to use and operate, especially for standard operations such as sending a fax message. There are several different types of machines, so the exact sequence may vary a little.

A basic procedure to send a fax is shown below.

1. Place the original document for faxing into the document feeder.

2. Obtain a dial tone on the machine – either by lifting the handset or pressing a button to obtain the tone.

3. Enter the fax number of the person to receive the fax on the numeric keypad on the machine. The fax machine will then take over and do the remaining sequence automatically. It will make contact with the remote fax machine, then feed through the document. As it does this, it will be scanning and transmitting the image. At the end, the fax machine will confirm to you that the fax is complete.

4. Finally remove the original document from the exit tray.

The procedure is likely to be slightly different if:

▶ you are sending a multi-page fax

▶ you are using a flatbed fax machine to fax a page from a book or magazine

▶ you have the fax number stored in memory in your machine.

▶ you want to speak to the person operating the receiving machine.

▶ your fax machine has a 'memory' for remembering messages, too, and you want to take advantage of this feature.

You can read about all these different variations on pages 191–197, which give you further information about using a fax machine. You will also find out how to do other basic operations – such as refilling the paper tray.

Procedures for processing the post

Postal procedures vary, depending upon whether you are dealing with incoming or outgoing post.

▶ **Incoming post** is all the letters and packages received by the business at the start of each working day. These have to be opened, sorted and distributed to the correct people as quickly as possible.

▶ **Outgoing post** is all the letters and packages being sent out by the business at the end of each working day. Throughout the afternoon (or all day, in some businesses) the post is prepared for dispatch so that it is ready for collection by a specific time – or for taking to the nearest post office to catch the last post of the day.

▲ Outgoing post must be ready for dispatch by a certain time each day

Large organisations have a dedicated post room and small firms have someone who is in charge of processing the post each morning. Mail for dispatch will be delivered to the post room – or to the person in charge of the post – throughout the day. There is usually a deadline for acceptance of items for each day's post, to allow enough time to prepare it properly for dispatch.

There is a range of equipment to assist with opening incoming post and preparing outgoing post. One of the most common items is a franking machine. This puts a franked image on the envelope and is a much better system for a business to use than postage stamps. Although the exact equipment will vary, depending upon the quantity of post being processed each day, you are still likely to find a franking machine being used.

On pages 197–206 you will learn about the basic procedures for preparing incoming and outgoing post and how to use some of the equipment commonly found in a post room.

1 All equipment is issued with a manual, or instruction book, which gives the basic procedures to follow. You will have received one if you have a mobile phone – which is another device, like a fax machine, that can store numbers in its memory.

Working in groups of two or three, write down the procedure you would follow on a mobile phone to:

a) call a friend, whose mobile number is stored in the phone's memory

b) call someone else, whose number is *not* stored in the phone's memory.

If necessary, use the instruction book to the phone to help you.

2 You process post yourself – every time you send a letter or receive one! Although you may use different procedures from the ones used in an office, there are still many similarities.

a) You have just picked up a letter which has been delivered to your house. Although it is addressed to you, you know it contains an article which your sister wants to read. Write a simple procedure to cover every step you would take from picking up the envelope to passing the article to your sister.

b) You want to send a letter to a friend. You have written the letter. Now write a set of procedures to cover all the steps you would take to ensure it was correctly posted.

You can write these procedures *either* as a set of numbered points *or* as a flow chart (see page 160). Why not try both, to see which you prefer? Then check your answers with your tutor.

3 At home, you probably open an envelope by sliding your thumb into the gap between the flap and the top of the envelope. This method is rarely used in an office!

a) Suggest 2 reasons why you shouldn't use this method at work.

b) suggest 2 methods which *would* be used in an office. As a clue, one is only appropriate for very small amounts of incoming post. The other is used when there are large amounts.

Discuss your ideas with your tutor.

▼ Following procedures for routine office tasks

In this section, you can learn much more about:

▶ **filing documents** properly, using different classification methods and different filing systems

▶ **photocopying documents** and related routine copying tasks

▶ **sending faxes** and dealing with basic maintenance of the machine

▶ **processing incoming and outgoing post** and the type of equipment you will find in a post room.

You will be expected to carry out only two of these operations for your assessment. However, in an office, you will be expected to carry out all of them!

For that reason, even if you concentrate *mainly* on the two types of activities you have selected for your assessment, you would be wise to find out about – and practise – all of them. You can also use this section as a quick reference guide if you need to refresh your memory before you go on work experience or start work in an organisation.

Paper-based filing

When computers became commonplace in offices, many people predicted that all documents would be stored electronically. There was much talk of the 'paperless office'. For several reasons, this has never happened. People still like to be able to read a document, take it around with them, make notes on it and, perhaps, compare the contents to that of other documents. This is much easier to do with a piece of paper than a document on screen – as you probably know!

Because paper is still very popular, and because organisations can receive and create hundreds of documents every day, all businesses need a good filing system. This way, every single piece of paper can be

▶ stored easily

▶ kept safely

▶ found quickly.

These are the three most important aspects of a good filing system.

Using a filing system

The best system in the world won't work properly unless each person uses it correctly. Most filing systems are designed to be used by several people – and this is why filing procedures exist. These specify the steps everyone must follow.

It needs only one person to ignore the procedures and things can go wrong. A missing document can take hours to find. This is both stressful and time-consuming. No one wants to spend half the morning looking for one piece of paper when they have other work to do!

When you start work, you will be told about the filing system and the procedures you have to follow. None of these will help, however, if you forget the three golden rules:

1 **File frequently**. First, because it's much easier. Second, because a huge pile of filing is overwhelming. Third, because you will often be asked for recent documents. Finding these quickly is almost impossible if you have a huge backlog.

▲ It can be very hard to find a document you need unless filing is done frequently

2 **File accurately**. This means taking your time and *concentrating*. It takes five seconds to file a document in the wrong file – and may take five hours to find it again!

3 **File neatly**. This means making sure all the papers are in good condition when you file them (see page 174), the papers are correctly aligned in the folder and the folder is both removed and replaced properly from the system. If you 'yank' out a folder by its tab, the tab will break, if you squeeze it back into a small space it will be squashed.

OVER TO YOU!

Before you read more about how to file, it is helpful to refresh your memory – or find out – about the type of equipment you are likely to find in an office and the types of folders you will use.

Look again at Unit 3, on pages 100–102 and then see if you can answer the following questions. Check your answers with your tutor.

1 What is the name of a filing system where the files are stored in large drawers in a cabinet?

2 What system is used when documents are placed in small drawers in a cabinet?

3 What is this system called?

4 Suspension files are 'pockets' which hold files. They hang down inside a cabinet drawer or along a lateral cabinet and are usually linked together. Why are these files so useful?

5 Why would you use a box file?

6 When you open the drawer of a filing cabinet, how can you tell which file is which?

7 Why is it better to fasten documents into a file folder?

8 How would you punch a document to make sure that you always correctly align it with other documents already fastened in a file?

You may file documents in a four-drawer cabinet or laterally, in a cupboard. But how would you store the mortgage documents relating to thousands of customers if you worked in a bank or building society – or the patient records of thousands of patients in a hospital? You would obviously need more than one cabinet or cupboard!

In these organisations, very sophisticated filing systems are in use. They often comprise floor-to-ceiling cupboards which slide along the floor, opening and closing to allow access. The whole system can be automated, so that keying in a file name in a computer or on a keyboard results in the correct file being extracted automatically.

Now imagine what would happen if the operators of these systems didn't bother filing regularly, accurately or neatly!

▲ A mechanised system can store thousands of documents

Classification systems

'Classification' relates to the *order* in which documents are filed. There are three main systems which you need to be able to use.

1 **Alphabetical filing**. In this case you are using the letters of the alphabet. In most systems the files are stored by **name**. In other cases the files are stored under **subject headings** or by **geographical area**.

2 **Numerical filing**. In this system the files are stored in number order. Each file has its own unique number. Because you cannot remember the number, a separate **index** is required which gives you this information.

3 **Chronological filing**. This means filing in **date order**. This is often because the date is the most important factor for these files or documents.

Alphabetical filing by name

Filing by name is often used for customer files or supplier files. You are therefore likely to find names of individuals as well as names of organisations.

It may seem a very simple matter to put a set of names into alphabetical order – everyone knows Adams comes before Turner! Problems can occur, however, when there are similar names or when an organisation has a long name, such as the Department for Work and Pensions. In this case, should you put the file under 'D', 'W' or 'P'?

To help you there are a list of rules to follow, which are shown below.

Rules for filing by name

Names of individuals

The surname *always* comes first.

Short surnames always come before long ones, e.g. Wilkins, Wilkinson

If the surnames are the same, refer to the first name or initial, e.g. Tomkins J, Tomkins P.

Initials are placed before full names, e.g. Sharpe T., Sharpe Tom

Treat all names starting Mac or Mc as 'Mac'. These *normally* come before 'M', e.g. MacDonald, McIntyre, Masters.

Ignore any apostrophes, e.g. O'Donnell as ODonnell.

Ignore d' and de' – so 'de Havilland' would be filed under 'H'

Names of organisations

Ignore the word 'The' – so 'The White Company ' would be filed under 'W'.

Change numbers to words, e.g. Four Seasons Healthcare.

If the name is identical, refer to the street or town, e.g. Marriott Hotel, Lincoln; Marriott Hotel, Manchester

Put initials before names, e.g. BT, Barnes and Watkins.

Treat Saint and St as 'Saint', e.g. St Barnabas School, Saint John's Church.

A public body, such as a local council or government office, is filed under the name or town, e.g. Inland Revenue, Irton District Council.

Sometimes a folder can be filed under more than one name. In this case, it may be **cross-referenced**. This means that, whereas the file itself is in one place, a card will be placed in any other place where people may look, to direct them to the right location. For example:

Cross-reference card

For OCR see
Oxford, Cambridge and RSA Examinations Board

Alphabetical filing by topic or subject

Many managers – and probably your tutor – prefer to file under topic headings. This is because they deal with only a few people or organisations but probably with many different topics. Using this method means that all the papers relating to one topic are kept together.

Again, this is easy to use for individual topics – you would look for Advertising under 'A' and Training under 'T'. The only rule to remember this time is that when a topic is sub-divided into different headings, all *these* must also be put into strict alphabetical order, as you can see below.

Alphabetical filing by place

Many organisations deal with customers all over the world or have branches all over the UK. They may prefer to divide their files geographically. Within each country, each customer file is then placed alphabetically. In the UK, a company with several branches is likely to have the files relating to each branch in geographical order. These may be by county first and then sub-divided into towns – or just by town. It will usually depend how many files there are.

Filing by place	
Australia	– Kookaburra Bank pty
	– Sydney Carpets
Belgium	– Brussels International Travel Service
	– Lyondell Chemical Company
Canada	– Cybermation Inc
	– Michigan Real Estate
	– Toronto Technology

1 Follow the filing rules and put the following names in the correct alphabetical order. Remember to reverse the names of all individuals so that the surname always comes first.

Filing by name

Roger Kemp
Bryant Technology
Iqbal M
St George's Society
Braintree District Council
JL Publishing

Clarendon Packaging
The Fast Company
Paul Howard
The Benefits Agency
BK Car Sales
Taylor and Watts

John McInlay
Patrick O'Reilly
2 Way Distribution
Midway Sports
Howarth K
Terry Johnson

2 The *Phone Book* is an excellent example of alphabetical filing. Names of organisations are listed in one half and names of individuals in the other. Test your ability to find names quickly by looking up five organisations you know and five people you know in your local area *Phone Book*.

3 Your friend has his own small business and has decided to set up his filing system in subject order. He has made a list of some headings and has asked you to make out the file folders for him. Write down exactly in which order you would place them in a cabinet drawer, working from the front (the first file) to the back (the last file).

Subject files

Bank – savings account, current account
Rates – business, water
Insurance – car, business, travel
Telephone – landline, mobile
Inland Revenue
Expenses – stationery, travel
Utility bills – gas, electricity
Accountant

4 You are working at the head office of a company which has several branches in the UK. Below is a list of 16 branch files, covering four counties in the north of England. Rearrange this list in the order you would sort the files ready for filing geographically.

Geographical files

Yorkshire – Sheffield, Halifax, Leeds, Harrogate
Cumbria – Kendal, Carlisle, Keswick
Cheshire – Northwich, Nantwich, Chester, Crewe
Lancashire – Wigan, Warrington, Preston, Blackpool, Blackburn

Filing by number

In some systems, each file is given a unique number. This is a better system than alphabetical if there are a large number of files, because it is simple to keep adding additional ones. If you tried to do this in an alphabetical system, then popular letters, such as B and R, become overcrowded very quickly and the whole system needs to be rearranged. This isn't necessary with a numerical system because each new file is given the next available number.

To find a file, you obviously need to know the number. This can be found by referring to a separate **index**.

An index is a way of helping you to find something quickly. There is an index in this book to help you to look up a topic quickly. A filing index helps you to look up files quickly. The index is *always* kept in alphabetical order, so you look for the name and alongside see the file number.

P	
Palmer Associates, The	8023
Parkhurst L	3504
Patterson and Walker	5981
Peters M	2938

The type of indexing system in operation can vary. If a manual system is used, you will mainly find the information is stored in a card index box or in a rotary swivel file.

▶ **Card indexes** consist of many cards which can be stored in a small plastic box or a large metal cabinet. There is one card for each individual or organisation and each is large enough to hold additional information. Guide cards are placed for each letter of the alphabet to help locate the cards easily.

▶ **Rotary files** are useful because they take up less space so can be used on a desktop. You flip the cards to find the one you want. They hold much smaller cards and there isn't room to add much additional information.

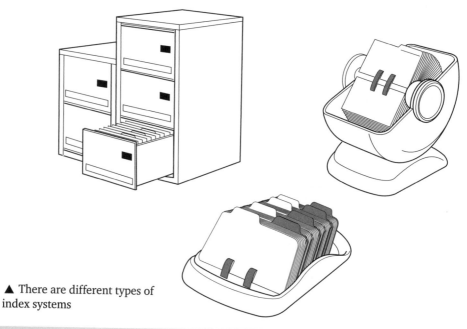

▲ There are different types of index systems

An alternative, of course, is to store the index on a computer. In this case you simply search for the file title you want and read the number.

To find any file in a numerical system, you have to follow a simple procedure:

1 Find out the exact name of the file.

2 Locate the name in the index.

3 Note down the number. (Note: *never* remove an index card from the cabinet!)

4 Find the file by looking for that number in the filing system.

The danger with filing by number is that it is very easy to misread or 'transpose' a number by turning it round – so that you write 3049 rather than 3094. You must also write clearly. If no one – including you – can tell the difference between your figures 3, 5 and 8, then you are going to create a few problems!

Filing by date

If you book a holiday through a travel agent, then when your tickets arrive they will be filed in date order of travel. Why? Because this is the most important item on the ticket. Unless you collect your ticket before the date of travel you will be unable to go on holiday! The travel agent can quickly check if any tickets are still outstanding for collection, simply by glancing at the first few tickets in the system.

In all offices, the documents *within* a file folder are stored by date. The most recent document should always be on top. There are three reasons for this:

▶ if you have a good idea when a document was produced, it is much easier to find

▶ generally more people want to refer to recent documents than older ones, so it is helpful if these are on the top

▶ people often want to read through a sequence of correspondence. Although the sequence will be in reverse in the file, it is helpful that they are in a logical order and not filed randomly in the folder.

However, this system also means work for you! If you have six documents to put into the same file, the *first* action you should take is to put them in date order.

Sometimes special files contain special documents in chronological order, perhaps in a lever arch or box file, for example:

▶ vouchers or receipts which are issued by date

▶ birth and death certificates

▶ examination results filed by date of examination.

1 Copy each of the following numbers. Make sure you write each one exactly as it is printed here. Then rearrange the numbers into numerical order.

92804	39308	59608	30829	20819
48098	20048	18920	38092	17209
67339	50298	18098	68779	72863

2 The following files have been put on your desk in alphabetical order, whereas your filing system is numerical. Change the list so that it is correct.

Abbott K	8096	Ahmed E	4738
Adams J	2779	Ainsworth L	6827
Adamson P	1089	Airey M	4729
Adcroft A	5893	Akhtar T	8409
Addison M	1488	Alderson	2973
Adelman P	7221	Allen	6046

3 You have eight documents to put into the same file. Arrange these so that they are in the correct order, with the most recent document the first (because it will be on the top).

Letter dated 9 October	Email dated 12 October
Memo dated 29 September	Letter dated 1 October
Letter dated 5 October	Memo dated 30 September
Email dated 2 October	Fax dated 4 October

Handling confidential information

If a file contains 'sensitive' or personal information, then special precautions must be taken to make sure that it remains confidential. A typical example is personnel files, which contain information about members of staff. You would be right to be upset if everyone at work knew where you lived, what your manager said to you during your last review and how much you earned – simply because your file had been left lying around for anyone to read.

The precautions you should take are listed below.

▶ Never talk about what you read in a file with other people.

▶ Don't leave confidential papers to be filed lying around on your desk.

▶ Don't leave a confidential file on your desk.

▶ Don't take confidential files into public areas, such as reception.

▶ Don't lend the file to anyone unless you have permission to do so.

▶ Make sure you always put away the file after you have used it.

▶ Always lock the cabinet and put the key in its proper place if you have been told to do this.

Using filing systems

You have already seen that there are four different systems of filing.

▶ Vertical – when files are stored in a cabinet with large drawers

▶ Lateral – when files are stored sideways in a large cabinet

▶ Horizontal – when special documents are stored in small drawers

▶ Rotary – when box files or lever arch files are stored on a rotating stand.

If you have forgotten about these, turn back to page 100 and refresh your memory!

The two you are most likely to use at work are vertical and lateral. There is one key difference:

▶ when you are using a vertical system, you will open a labelled drawer and look at files with their labels running from front to back

▶ when you are using a lateral system, you will be looking at files suspended across the cupboard, with the labels running from side to side, normally from left to right.

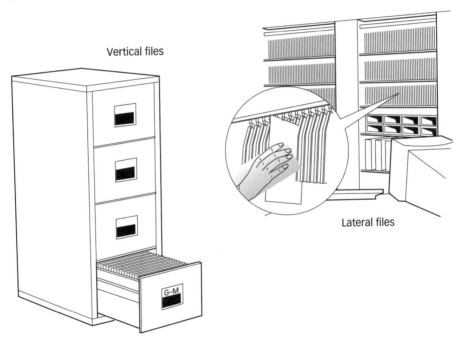

Vertical files

Lateral files

▲ Vertical and lateral filing systems are the most popular

Before you get to this stage, however, you need to know how to prepare documents for filing – and how to locate the files themselves. In this case you have certain procedures to follow.

Preparing documents for filing

Most offices have filing trays in which documents are placed for filing. Some organisations have an additional system. They put a special 'release mark' on documents which can be filed – such as a 'tick'. This means the document has been dealt with and is no longer needed. If your employer uses this system, then always query any document which doesn't have this mark.

If you have a batch of documents to file, the best procedure to follow is:

1 Mend any torn papers (with sticky tape) and remove any paper clips which could 'hook' other documents. Replace paper-clipped pages with staples.

2 Pre-sort the documents, depending upon the classification system.

   ▶ Put them in alphabetical order if you are filing by name

   ▶ Put them in alphabetical order if you are filing by subject or geographically – but be careful of sub-divisions within the system.

   ▶ If you are filing by number, look up the number in the alphabetical index and write the number on each document. Then put them into numerical order.

   ▶ If you are filing chronologically, put them into date order.

3 Put any documents which are to go into the *same* file folder in date order, with the most recent on top.

4 Punch the documents correctly (see page 102).

The documents are now ready for filing.

▶ **In a vertical system:**

1 Identify the drawer which holds the file folder for the first document you must file. You can tell this from the label on the outside (such as A – F or 1000 – 1099)

2 Open the drawer and look along the tabs or labels for the correct file.

3 Take out the file folder immediately *behind* the label.

4 Insert the document in the folder, fastening it securely, and replace the file folder in the drawer.

▶ **In a lateral system:**

1 Identify the row of files which contains the file folder for your first document. Again this will be labelled – often at one side.

2 Look along the row and read the tabs to find the file you need.

3 Take out the file folder in the slot immediately to the *right* of the label (in most systems)

4 Insert the document in the file folder, fastening it securely, and replace the file folder into its slot.

The only problem you could encounter is that you can't find a folder for the document you must file. This could be because:

▶ you haven't looked properly – so check again

▶ you transposed the number or are looking under the wrong name – again, double-check

▶ someone has borrowed the folder. In most systems this will be logged, so check the records – or ask your supervisor for help

▶ there *is* no file for this document yet. In this case, check with your supervisor or team leader if a new one must be created.

Retrieving a file

This simply means taking a file out of the system.

▶ In an alphabetical system, simply look for the name.

▶ In a numerical system, always look at the index first. The procedure to follow was given on page 171.

▶ In a chronological system, look for the correct date.

In many organisations you will have to make a record of any file you remove to lend to someone, so that other people know where it has gone. This is important in case someone else needs it urgently. Page 158 gave a basic procedure for retrieving a document and you may want to read this again.

Maintaining a safe filing system

If you have already studied Unit 3, then you will know that health and safety applies to all areas of office work, including filing. The main points to remember when you are filing include the following.

▶ Never leave open cabinet drawers (especially the bottom one) for people to fall over.

▶ Never carry so many files or folders that you can't see where you are going.

▶ Never arrange for a filing cabinet to be placed near a door or too near a desk, so that anyone entering the room or using the filing cabinet would be at risk.

▶ Always use a safety stool if you have to reach files in a tall lateral cupboard.

▲ Health and safety also applies to filing!

All filing cabinets today are designed with an anti-tilt mechanism, so that only one drawer will open at once. However, the cabinet is still much safer if heavy items are in the bottom drawer. The cabinet itself could overbalance when the top drawer is fully open if the only things in the bottom one are the staff coffee mugs!

OVER TO YOU!

1 As a group, and with your tutor, discuss what you would do if you encountered the following situations when you were filing.

a) You have written down the number of a numerical file – 60180 – and when you go to the cabinet there is no such number.

b) You are about to put a document in a file dated 23 February when you notice the top document already filed is dated 25 February.

c) Your supervisor is at lunch. She keeps her filing cabinet locked, with the key in her drawer because she stores several confidential papers. A caller, whom you haven't seen before, pops into your office and asks if he can borrow a file just for a few minutes.

d) You have to file a report but the top page is torn and the remaining pages are paper-clipped together.

e) You have a letter to file from Keith Watson. When you go to the file there are two folders with that name.

f) You have three advertisements to put into the job advertisements file. When you go to the cabinet that particular file is missing.

2 Write down the name and date of birth of everyone in your class on the whiteboard or a flip chart.

Now reorder the list *twice*. First into alphabetical order and then into chronological order – with the oldest member of the group listed *first*.

See if you can do both lists quickly *and* accurately, first time!

3 Many people are very good at preparing documents for filing but less good at finding folders or retrieving files. The reason? They don't look carefully enough or read file labels properly. This means they either can't find what they are looking for or choose the wrong file.

Test your own ability to find things quickly by looking in the index of this book. This is in subject order, but you may sometimes have to identify the key word under which you should look. See if you can find and write down accurately the page number(s) for each of the following.

Office documents	Franking machines	Learning plan
Dress codes	Telephones	Procedures for sending faxes
Voicemail	Duplexing	Customers and confidentiality

Carrying out photocopying tasks

Photocopying is a routine activity in all organisations. Many documents need copying so that they can be read by or sent to several people. For this reason, if you work in an office, you will be expected to do this job quickly and efficiently.

Photocopier facilities

There are literally hundreds of different photocopiers on the market, ranging from very small desktop machines to extremely large ones. The facilities you have available will depend upon the type of machine you are using.

▶ Some will print only black and white copies, whereas others will reproduce colour originals.

▶ Some will only print copies, others will collate as well. Collating means putting the pages of a multi-page document in the correct order.

▶ Many will staple, in a variety of different positions.

▶ Virtually all will enlarge or reduce text and graphics.

▶ Some will do automatic back-to-back copies, where both sides of the paper are used. On others this is a manual operation.

▶ Most will print out on either A4 or A3 paper, or on special mailing labels.

▶ Some will copy only from paper originals whilst others can receive copying instructions direct from a computer.

The first thing to find out is what are the main facilities on the photocopier you will be using. Every photocopier is delivered with a manual which contains detailed instructions for operators. If you are lucky, there is also a shortened version which summarises the basic instructions. These can be copied and placed in a special folder nearby, or put on the wall for quick reference.

OVER TO YOU!

Look at page 178 which shows the main items on most photocopiers.

1 Check that you understand all the explanations given. Talk to your tutor if you are unsure about any.

Photocopier facilities

1 **Hinged lid** This protects the exposure glass (2). It also often contains the document feeder (3).

2 **The exposure glass.** You can lift the lid and put originals on the glass print-side down for copying. Indicators around the side tell you exactly where to position different sizes of paper, such as A4 and A5.

3 **The document feeder.** Multi-page originals are placed in the feeder in a stack. The machine automatically feeds through each page in turn.

4 **The paper tray**. Each machine has one or more paper trays for holding blank photocopying paper. There may also be a different tray for holding special paper, such as card or labels or transparencies for overhead projectors.

5 **The output tray**. This is where most photocopies emerge.

6 **The originals tray**. This is where the original document emerges.

7 **Power on/off switch**. Photocopiers are normally left switched on all day. Some even go into automatic 'sleep mode' when no one is using them and wake up again when someone approaches them! These may be left switched on all the time. More basic machines are normally switched off at the end of the day – but only then!

8 **Finishing unit**. This is where completed sets are collated and stapled.

9 **The control panel**. On a complex machine there may be many keys on a touch screen. The most basic ones you can expect to find are:

a) Number keys – to enter the number of copies you want
b) A Start key – to start copying
c) An interrupt key – to pause copying if you want to do a quick job in the middle of a longer one
d) A Stop/clear key – to cancel an entry you have made or stop copying if there is a problem
e) Special keys or a display panel for entering instructions such as collate/back-to-back and for displaying error messages.

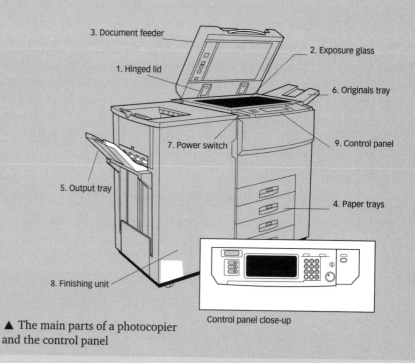

▲ The main parts of a photocopier and the control panel

2 Discuss with your tutor the exact facilities which are available on the photocopier you use. In particular, find out whether it will collate and do back-to-back copies automatically. This is important for your assessment.

Copying of an appropriate standard

Regardless of whether the photocopies you make are only for internal use, or are being sent to the most important customer you have, they should *all* be perfect and 'right first time'.

If it takes you ten attempts, you have wasted both time and paper! If you can never get them absolutely perfect, so that you always need to explain what went wrong when you hand over the copies you have made, then your lack of skills will be noted. Not only will you regularly irritate people, but you will also rarely be asked to do jobs which are important and interesting!

Ideally, you should be able to 'tick' every aspect of the checklist below, for every photocopying job that you do.

Checklist for photocopying standards

On *every* page

The paper is smooth – not crumpled, creased or torn	✓
The image (i.e. the printed section) is perfectly clear	✓
The image is positioned in the correct place on the paper	✓

For the whole document

All the pages have been copied	✓
The correct number of copies has been made	✓
All the pages are in the correct order	✓
Also, you have remembered to return the original to the person who gave it to you	✓

If you are having difficulties, then the following may help you.

▶ **The paper.** This will crumple if it misfeeds. Unless you have been trained to remedy this problem yourself, you must report it (see page 187). You must then take another copy to replace the spoiled one.

▶ **The image quality.** Your original must be clean and the image on it must be clear. If it has dirty marks then you can remove these with special photocopier correction fluid. Do wait until it is completely dry before putting the document on the glass or in the document feeder. If the glass is dirty you will need to clean that, too. (See page 188.)

Originals on coloured paper or with coloured print both create difficulties. Most photocopiers can be adjusted to cope with this, so again you may need assistance.

▶ **The alignment of the image.** This will be awry if:

– the original image is also slanted

– you haven't positioned the paper properly on the glass

– your document wasn't straight when it entered the document feeder wrongly.

Always check the original before you start. If the image on the original is slanted then you could try to correct this by adjusting the position on the glass and taking a sample copy until you get it right.

▶ **All the pages are copied**. You can avoid problems if you always start by checking that you have a 'complete set' in any multi-page document you are asked to copy. If you have, a test document is invaluable. Often these are called 'sample copies' – and many photocopiers now have a 'sample copy' key especially for this purpose, which you press after entering the total number of copies you want. You can quickly check your sample and, if this is correct, go on to make the remaining copies.

▶ **The correct number of copies**. This means *writing down* your instructions and keying in the number carefully! You can do a manual check for a few copies, but this is hardly practical if you were asked for 500!

▶ **The pages are in the right order**. This means you must put the original in the document feeder in the right order. No photocopier is capable of muddling them up for you! Again, always check the original, then check the sample copy.

▶ **You return the original**. You will be amazed how many people leave the original document on the glass or in the output tray. This is probably because they are thinking about the copies – or something else entirely! Many times, this may not be critical. A quick dash back to the photocopying room and you may find some kind person has put it on one side for you. The crisis occurs when the document was important – and has disappeared – or was strictly confidential and has been left in there for everyone to read!

OVER TO YOU!

A simple procedure to help you avoid these difficulties is given below – but some of the words are missing. Write this out yourself, completing any gaps by using the words given below.

adjustments	original document	complete
sample copy	instructions	right order
clear	key in	straight

1 Always write down the . . . . for copying a document.

2 Always check the original document first, to make sure it is . . . ., the image is . . . . and . . . . and the pages are in the . . . .

3 Make any . . . . to the original that are needed, before you start.

4 Always take a . . . . and check this carefully.

5 If it is perfect, ... the exact number required.

6 Remember to remove both the copies and the . . . . at the end.

PROCEDURES IN BUSINESS

Every business has to be careful about what their staff copy. This is because any original work – such as a book, newspaper, magazine – is protected by copyright. Copyright law means that you cannot just copy anything you want without permission. In certain circumstances, copying for personal use is allowed, such as students who are doing research or private study. Your college or local library will have the details.

Organisations which break copyright law can be fined. In 2001, the Ordnance Survey, which produces maps, won a payment of £20 million from the Automobile Association. It proved that the AA had based some of its maps on those originally created by the OS but without permission. In the same year, Marks and Spencer was involved in a complicated legal case after it had made copies of newspaper cuttings without a special licence. Although Marks and Spencer successfully defended the case, the time and cost was considerable.

Therefore, if you are ever in doubt about what you should copy, ask your supervisor for advice.

Logging the use of a photocopier

A common feature of most office photocopiers is a **user code**. This has to be keyed in before the machine will operate. It stops any unauthorised users from making photocopies. Staff may have individual user codes or – more likely – a departmental code.

The photocopier records the usage against each user code automatically. This enables the overall cost of photocopying to be checked and controlled. On a basic machine, without this facility, users may have to record the number of copies they have taken in a special 'log' which is kept next to the machine. They may have to record just the number of copies they make or, as a double-check, to record the start number showing on the 'counter' on the machine and the end number.

The disadvantage of this system is that people may forget – either deliberately or accidentally – to put an entry in the log. For this reason, most business organisations prefer to have a modern photocopier which will record this information automatically.

Date	Name	Department	Start no	End no	No of copies

▲ Typical headings in a photocopier log

Refilling the copier with paper

There is normally a spare supply of paper kept near the photocopier and the main paper store is kept in a stationery cupboard.

Photocopier paper needs to be stored carefully. It should be kept wrapped and stored flat, in a dry place. Otherwise it can jam in the machine. You need to know the right type of paper to use in your machine, especially if there are several types in your storeroom or cupboard.

Photocopier paper is delivered in large boxes, each one fastened with a plastic strap. There is a knack to opening these. You can either cut it with scissors *or* lay the box on its side and where the strap meets underneath, separate the ends by pulling the bottom strap first. Then put the box the right way up and remove one packet of paper. This contains 500 sheets.

The procedure you should follow to refill the copier is shown below.

1 Take the paper out of the packet.

2 'Square' the paper. This means making sure it is straight vertically and horizontally. The easy way to do this is to hold it firmly at each side and give it a sharp tap, two or three times, on a firm surface.

3 Open the paper tray. This may pull out, in which case you should pull it out to its furthest extent, or there may be a cover you open.

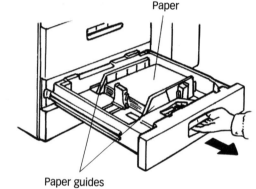

Paper

4 Put the paper into the tray against the guides. There is often an illustration in or next to the tray to show you how to do this.

5 Check that you haven't stacked the paper over the limit mark. The maximum level is clearly identified on the tray.

Paper guides

▲ Refilling the paper tray

6 Close the tray.

Following instructions for using the photocopier

In many offices, photocopying instructions are written on special forms. An example is shown below. This is sensible for several reasons.

Photocopy request form

Name _Martin Fraser_   Department _Sales_

No of originals [6]   No of copies required [4]

Special instructions (eg back-to-back, collate, staple, etc.)

Please print back-to-back, collate and staple at top left corner.

Date required _14 March_

▲ A photocopy request form

▶ The instructions can be quite different and quite detailed for each job. For example, on Monday morning:

- Natasha wants some pages from a book copied. She wants 1 copy of pages 10 – 15, 78 and 79 and 100 – 105.

- Jim wants 14 copies of a 2-page document, but wants them back-to-back.

- Sara has asked for 25 copies of a 5-page document, collated and stapled.

▶ Photocopying tasks may arrive throughout the day, and be done in batches – say mid-morning and mid-afternoon. In this case, the work to be done is normally stacked in a tray.

▶ Written instructions prevent arguments or disputes about what was required – provided, of course, that the operator has followed them correctly!

If you are following written instructions, it is important you read them carefully before you start. If you cannot read someone's handwriting, ask a colleague for assistance – don't guess!

This doesn't mean, of course, that you will *never* be given verbal instructions to do a job. If a senior manager wants an urgent job done quickly, you would not be wise to insist that a form must be completed first! In this case, listen carefully and write down what you are told to do. Then do it!

Carrying out instructions for single, multi-page and back-to-back copying

Sometimes you will be asked to copy a single page, on other occasions a document may consist of several pages. You may be asked to make sure these are back-to-back, usually to save paper.

Before you start, it is useful to check the machine to make sure that the settings from the previous user are not still in place. You can usually remove these by pressing Cancel. This gives you a fresh start as it returns the machine to its default setting.

Single originals   On many machines you can choose whether to place a single copy on the exposure glass or put it in the document feeder. Do make sure you have the print facing the right way (up or down), otherwise the result will be a blank page! You will always place an original on the glass print-side down, but this may be different if you use a document feeder.

A flimsy original or very important document is always better placed on the glass to avoid the risk of damage. If you are copying a page from a book then this *must* be put on the glass. Then close the lid as far as you can. This will give you a better copy than if you leave the lid open and will also protect your eyes from the bright ultraviolet light when the copy is made.

Assuming you are using a standard photocopier, a simple procedure to take ten photocopies of a single page could be:

1 Key in user (or department) number (or write start number in log)

2 Place document on glass correctly

3 Key in '10' on the key pad.

4 Press the Start key.

5 Remove photocopies plus the original (and enter end number in log)

Remember that you do not need to enter a number on the key pad if you want only one page as this is the default number. In this case, you just press the Start key.

Multi-page originals   You must always place multiple pages in the document feeder. Before you start, *always* check the following:

▶ that there are no staples or paper-clips holding the pages together. If there are, then these must be removed before you begin.

▶ that your original pages are in the correct order. This is easier if the document has numbered pages, if not read the bottom and top paragraphs to check.

▶ whether the original pages have print on both sides. If you just put these into the document feeder in the normal way then only one side will be copied. You have two choices. On most modern photocopiers you simply *tell* the machine that you have two-sided originals and then select whether you want one-sided or back-to-back copies. On a basic machine you would have to photocopy both sides of each two-sided page yourself.

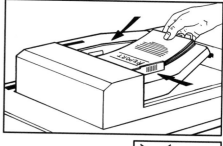

Multiple copies face up in the document feeder

▲ Copying a multi-page original

The procedure to follow for multi-page copies is shown below. It assumes that you do not have a 'sample copy' option on your machine.

1 Check the original is complete and in the right order.

2 Key in user (or department) number (or write start number in log).

3 Place document in document feeder.

4 Press the Start key to take a sample copy.

5 Check copy is clear, aligned properly and all pages are correct. If not, make adjustments and take another sample copy.

6 When the sample copy is correct, key in remaining number required then press Start.

7 Remove all copies plus original (and write end number in log).

Two other operations which are often linked to multi-page photocopying are collating and fastening. You can read about these below.

Back-to-back copying   Modern photocopiers do this automatically. In the instructions or manual you might find it listed under **duplexing**. This process saves paper.

The first step is to tell the photocopier whether your original is one-sided or two-sided. The second is to specify how you want your copies. In this case you would select 'two-sided'. You will enter this information on the control panel.

Be aware that you will now have a longer wait before you see the finished copies. This is because the machine has to 'flip' over each page being copied before it puts it into the output tray.

The first time you do this, it is sensible to do just one page – and watch what happens. As you become more experienced, it is easier to tackle multi-page back-to-back copying.

This is a harder operation if you have only a very basic machine – but not impossible. In this case, you would take a copy of the first document and then put that copy *back* into the paper tray (probably print-side down, but you would have to check) and then copy the second document. When you press Start the second time, the paper would feed back into the machine for the reverse side to be printed.

Collating and fastening

When you are photocopying multi-page documents you may be asked to:

▶ sort or **collate** the pages. This means putting them into the right order.

▶ fasten the pages – usually by **stapling**.

Some photocopiers will do both these operations automatically, others will do just one and some will do neither! You therefore need to know how to collate and fasten the pages both manually and on the machine.

Collating by machine   If your machine can collate documents, you will usually see a set of small trays at one side. If you select 'collate' on the control panel, then the machine will put the first page in each tray, then the second and so on. At the end, you simply lift the completed sets out of all the trays.

You obviously cannot collate more sets at once than you have trays. Equally, if you are collating fewer sets than there are trays, then not all the trays will be used.

However, some machines without collating trays will also collate! In this case, the collated sets are put in the output tray. Each is offset, so that you can easily separate them. You should therefore ask a colleague – or check the instruction book – about any machine before you assume it can't collate for you.

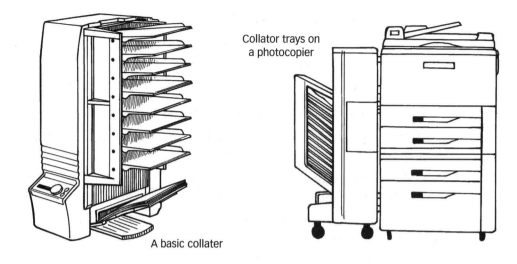

Collator trays on a photocopier

A basic collater

▲ Collator trays can be very useful

If you have no option but to collate manually then you must work carefully and methodically, preferably on a large, flat surface. As you obtain copies of page one, turn these face down and spread them out on the working surface. Then add page two, then page three and so on. You will know if you've gone wrong (e.g. by putting two of page 3 on one pile) because you will be short of a page before you have completed all the sets.

Finally, check that all the sets are complete and all the pages are in the right order. Collating many copies of a very large document by hand can be very tedious. It is much easier if you can find someone else who will help you.

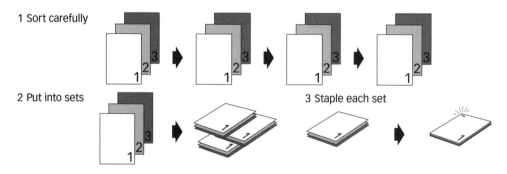

1 Sort carefully

2 Put into sets

3 Staple each set

▲ Manual collating means you have to work carefully and methodically

Fastening photocopies   You may be asked to fasten the pages of a multi-page document using paper-clips, but a more permanent and secure fastening is to staple them.

If your photocopier can staple automatically, you can select on the control panel the position of the staple(s) and the number to be used. The most usual options are at the top left (at an angle if you prefer) or down the left hand side.

If you are stapling manually, use the stapler safely and remember that the print must *never* be obscured on any page.

The following procedure should be used.

1 Put the stapler on a clear, flat surface.

2 Use a heavy-duty stapler if the document has many pages.

3 If you are stapling in the top left corner, place the staple just over a centimetre from the corner.

4 If you find it easier, don't angle the staple but line it up with the top or side edge of the paper.

5 Keep your fingers out of the way and firmly press down on the stapler.

6 Learn how to unjam a stapler *safely* – and how to refill it. If you are using an electric stapler, always unplug it before you do either of these operations.

Procedures for reporting problems

You have already learned several procedures for resolving difficulties yourself. You learned how to refill copier paper on page 182 and you learned how to solve minor problems on page 179.

On other occasions you should not attempt to resolve a problem yourself – you must report it. Often a machine problem will be indicated by a symbol on the control panel. Sometimes the machine can still be used but on other occasions it cannot.

The first thing to know is *who* to contact if you experience a problem. The name of this person – sometimes called the **key operator** – is often posted up near the machine. This person has had special training to remedy most of the problems you might experience, such as the ones listed in the table below. If the problem is serious, or cannot be remedied immediately, he or she will put a notice on the machine saying that it must not be used until it has been repaired.

Photocopier problems which must be reported

Problem	Reason	Action to take
The machine tells you to wait	It is warming up.	Wait until the 'ready' light appears.
Paper jam	There is a misfeed in the paper travelling through the machine	Copying will have stopped. Notify the person in charge of rectifying the paper jam. Never attempt to clear this yourself.
Toner low	The toner (powdered ink) is running low	Copies will start to become very faint. You may be able to finish a small job. Then notify the person who can replenish the toner.

Problem	Reason	Action to take
Copies are not stapled	The staples have run out or jammed	You can continue to copy but cannot staple automatically until the stapler cartridge has been refilled or cleared. Notify the person who can do this.
Smoke or smell of burning	This could be due to a serious electrical fault	Stop copying, switch off the machine and the power switch on the wall. Unplug the machine and immediately notify the key operator or supervisor
Unknown error message	The machine has a fault and is trying to tell you what it is!	Stop copying and notify the key operator or your supervisor

Finally, if you experience a machine problem you may not be able to complete the work you have been given on time. It is important that you notify the person who gave you this work promptly, so that alternative action can be taken if the copying is urgent – such as finding another machine which can be used.

Minimising waste

Near every photocopier you are likely to find a large wastepaper bin. Responsible organisations may have a recycling bin instead, so that spoiled papers can be sent for recycling. This does not mean that it then doesn't matter how much paper you waste! Photocopier paper is expensive, so ruining endless sheets of paper wastes money. It also wastes your time if you have to do the job all over again.

You can minimise waste in the following ways.

▶ Always checking the original before you start, repairing any torn pages, removing any dirty marks with special correction fluid and making sure all the pages are in the correct order.

▶ Checking the exposure glass is clean. Any marks on it – including blobs of correction fluid – will come out as black marks on your copy. This is why you should always make sure any correction fluid is completely dry before making a copy. If the glass is dirty then clean it with a *damp* (not wet) cloth.

▶ Never using paper which isn't meant for the job. This is highly likely to jam in the machine.

▶ Placing the original correctly and *always* taking a sample copy.

▶ Learning how to reposition the original so that you can compensate for text which is crooked or not in the centre of the page.

▶ Keying in the correct number of copies – and not taking extra copies 'just in case'.

▶ Learning how to stop the machine quickly if something goes wrong.

▶ Staying alert during printing, so that you can spot a problem quickly.

Following safety procedures

Your photocopier manual will contain specific safety procedures which should have been observed when the machine was first installed. These include:

▶ The positioning of the machine. All photocopiers must be positioned so that they have a flow of air around them. They should be on a stable surface and kept away from humidity and dust.

▶ The connections to the machine. The plug should always be put directly into the wall socket – and not into an adaptor or extension lead. The wall socket should be easy to reach, in case the machine needs unplugging quickly in an emergency.

▶ Metal objects and containers holding liquids must be kept away from the machine. If the contents fell inside, then a fire or electric shock could be the result.

The other safety procedures relate to the operator. This means you! The most important requirements are shown in the table below.

Operator safety procedures

- Never attempt to move a photocopier from its recommended position.
- Don't try to remove the plug if you have wet hands.
- Immediately turn off the power and disconnect the copier if
  - you spill anything into the machine
  - a cover is broken or damaged
  - the machine needs to be serviced or repaired
- Never disregard a notice which specifically tells you not to use the copier at the present time.
- Keep paper-clips, staples and other metallic objects away from the machine so that they cannot fall inside. Many copiers have a little tray for these.
- Use the recommended type of paper and never overfill the paper tray. Never use bent, creased or torn paper, slippery or perforated paper, metallic paper or thick art paper.
- Clean the machine and the glass with a soft damp cloth, then wipe it with a dry cloth to remove any wet areas. Never use any chemical cleaners.
- If you are asked to dispose of a used toner container, follow the instructions. *Never* incinerate them or discard them near an open flame. Wash any spilled toner powder off your hands or clothes with cold water. Store toner containers in a cool, dry place, out of direct sunlight and on a flat surface. Never attempt to reuse spent toner.
- Don't make copies with the lid open and stare at the light. Although the ultraviolet light doesn't actively damage your eyes, it won't do them any good either!
- Never open any cover on the machine or attempt to use it if a cover is damaged or broken.
- Never try to remedy a fault unless you have been trained to do so. If you have been trained to remedy simply faults, never touch parts labelled with a warning or marked 'hot surface' otherwise you could burn yourself.

▲ Don't let this be you!

OVER TO YOU!

1 Test your knowledge of photocopying by answering each of the following questions either True or False.

a) All photocopiers can collate documents.

b) All photocopiers need a good air flow around them.

c) You cannot use the document feeder if you are photocopying a book.

d) It is better to take a few extra copies, just in case.

e) The photocopier should be switched off when you have finished copying.

f) Another word for 'back-to-back' copying is duplexing.

g) If the exposure glass is dirty, your copies will be spoiled.

h) It is quite safe to put a can of drink on the machine whilst you are copying.

i) Coloured print or coloured paper originals can be difficult to copy.

j) If you are doing several copies, it is sensible to take a sample copy first, and continue only if this is correct.

2 Improve your copying skills by learning how to make simple adjustments to a poor original. Ideally, you need at least one original on coloured paper and one where the text is offset to the left or right. Your task is to end up with a clear, well-aligned copy of *both* documents. Ask your tutor to show you how to make the necessary adjustments on your machine – and then practise doing these yourself.

3 Write a simple set of procedures to cover *each* of the following photocopying tasks on your own machine.

a) Taking three copies of a single document, assuming that you are the first person to use the machine that day.

b) Refilling it with paper.

c) Taking four copies of a 10-page document and collating and stapling them.

d) Taking three copies of a 6-page document which must be photocopied back-to-back.

Check your answers with your tutor.

Sending faxes

If you have completed Unit 3, you will already know something about fax machines (see page 95) and in Unit 1 you learned to write fax messages (see page 17). If you have forgotten about this, you can turn back to these pages to refresh your memory. In this unit, you will learn the procedures to follow when you operate the machine to send a fax.

Fax machines are used to send urgent messages and information which would take too long to send by Royal Mail. For that reason, outgoing faxes should be sent promptly. Some organisations have a basket in which outgoing faxes are placed, ready for sending. Most, however, operate a 'fax on demand' service for urgent messages. This means that if someone gives you an urgent fax, you stop what you are doing and send it immediately.

To do that, of course, you need to know how to operate your own fax machine.

Standard features on a fax machine

Fax machines can vary from small models to quite large ones. Most have some standard common features and these are shown in the table on page 192. Before you read this it is useful to know the following points.

▶ Most fax machines 'feed' the original document into the machine. This is the type described in the table on page 192. On more expensive machines you may have the option of putting the original document on a flat-bed (like a photocopier). This means you can fax pages directly from a book, for example. Otherwise you would have to photocopy the page first.

▶ Some older fax machines use special coated paper to produce faxes, but most, today, use **plain paper** – such as the type you would use for printing computer copies or making photocopies.

▶ All fax machines can be used as a **standard copier** – though they are usually slower than photocopiers.

▶ Some fax machines have a **memory facility** for fax messages. This means that:

　– an outgoing message can be scanned into the memory and the machine will then return the original document before transmitting the message. This is useful if you have to return the original very quickly.

　– incoming messages are held in memory if the machine is busy. This means no messages are missed just because someone is sending a fax.

Although you will not be expected to use any memory feature during your assessment, it is useful to know this exists, in case someone refers to it!

▶ Most fax machines give the option to print a **cover sheet**. This is discussed on page 193.

▶ Most fax machines will hold commonly held **fax numbers in memory** too – just like your mobile phone. This means that you often follow a different procedure if you are sending a message to a frequently used number.

▶ All fax machines can be set to print a **confirmation report** at the end of the transmission. This tells you how long the fax took to transmit and says whether the fax was sent successfully or not.

▶ Fax machines can send message **automatically or manually**. In this first case you do not pick up the handset, but use the keypad to tell the machine what to do. You send a message manually when you set the machine to manual, pick up the handset and, after keying in the number, listen for the fax tone at the other end before you start to send your message.

▶ All fax machines have a **display panel** and a **key pad**. The display panel will tell you the current status of the machine. The key pad is for entering fax numbers.

▶ Fax machines need an air flow or they overheat, so they all have an **air vent**. This vent must never be covered or obstructed.

Common fax features

1 **Document hopper.** This holds and supports the original document so that it is straight as it feeds into the document feeder

2 **Document feeder.** This is the slot into which the original document is placed for faxing.

3 **Document guides.** These can be adjusted to match the width of the original document.

4 **Display panel.** This shows you the status of the machine. When the machine is switched off, the panel is blank.

5 **Control panel.** This has keys you press to operate the machine.

6 **Document exit and tray.** This is where your original document comes out.

7 **Output or printed document tray.** This is where an incoming fax arrives or any copies made on the machine.

8 **Telephone handset.** This is exactly the same as a handset on a normal telephone.

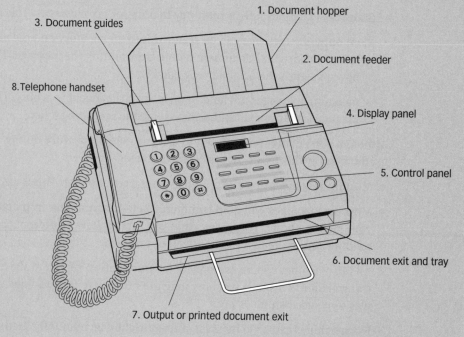

▲ The main parts of a fax machine

Preparing to send a fax

Before you start to send a fax there are certain aspects you need to consider:

- whether you know the fax number
- whether you have to send a cover page
- the quality, type and size of documents you have to send
- the number of pages you have to send.

The fax number A fax number is just like a telephone number. This isn't surprising because fax messages are transmitted using telephone lines. You may have dialled a fax number yourself by mistake in the past. You can tell because, instead of a ringing tone, you hear a series of high-pitched shrieks at the other end!

Someone may have written the number of the recipient's fax on the message you have to send. In this case you simply key that number into the machine. You may be told that the number is that of a frequent contact and is already be stored in the fax machine. If you do not know the number, then you need to refer back to the person who has given you the message to ask them.

Sending a cover page *All* fax machines automatically print a very short header at the top of each page. It will look something like this

| 15/12/04 | 16:10 | +44 161 878 3987 | ARTFUL DESIGNS | PAGE 01 |

The problem is that this type of header doesn't give very much information. A cover sheet provides far more information and most machines will produce one automatically. Cover sheets are useful because you can use the space to send a short message. An example of a cover page is shown below. This is different from the version shown on page 18, because fax cover pages often vary, depending upon the type of machine used and the preferences of the organisation.

Fax message from:

Date / Time:	15 December 2004 16:10
Name:	Artful Designs Ltd
Fax Number:	+44 161 878 3987
Message:	Attached are the designs you requested (3 pages). Please ring Colleen Price on receipt

▲ A fax cover page

The type and size of document   The documents you are sending must be clear and in black and white. If you are given a coloured original, or one on flimsy or coloured paper, then you need to photocopy it first. You should also do this if the document is particularly valuable in case it gets damaged if you feed it into the machine.

The size of the document – and the text area – is also important. The short header at the top of every fax takes up space, so if the text runs from top to bottom (or from side to side) with very small margins it is likely that part of it will be cut off. You should query any document like this with your supervisor.

The number of pages   Many faxes comprise multiple pages. It is usual to number every page in the following way: Page 1 of 3, Page 2 of 3, Page 3 of 3. This means the recipient can easily check that the complete fax has arrived. If you are sending a multiple-page fax, you also need to check that the pages are the right way up and are in the correct order.

OVER TO YOU!

1 Compare the fax machine you will use with the illustration on page 192. Find out where all the items listed are found on your machine and, if possible, watch someone send a fax message both automatically and manually.

2 Explain what you would do in each of the following situations.
   a) Your fax machine is very basic and you need to fax an illustration from a book.
   b) You have to send a cover sheet plus a copy of an invoice. The invoice is flimsy and is torn at one corner.
   c) You have an urgent fax to send but there is no fax number written on the message.
   d) You are asked to send an urgent fax message just as you were about to leave for lunch.
   e) You are asked to send a fax to a customer. One page is a copy of one of your coloured leaflets.

3 Fax machines are normally left switched on 24 hours a day, 7 days a week. Can you suggest why?

Procedures for sending a fax

You have a fax message in your hand and the fax machine is in front of you. You now have to transmit the fax. The first thing to check is how to insert your original document into the machine:

▶ whether you insert it print-side up or down (normally it is print-side down, but this can vary)

▶ which end of the document should go in first, top or bottom (normally it is 'top', but do check)

▶ whether the first page of a multi-page fax should be on the top or the bottom

▶ whether you should fan the pages of a multi-page fax before you put it in the machine, to stop them sticking together.

Once you are clear about these, you are almost ready to begin. The procedure below assumes you have been given the fax number to key in and you are sending the message *automatically*. This means that you do not have to lift the handset.

1 Make sure that the document guides are correct for the width of your document.

2 Insert the document in the document feeder. You may now receive confirmation on the display panel that the machine is ready.

3 Obtain a dial tone (if necessary on your machine), enter the fax number on the keypad and then press Start.

4 Your fax machine will now contact the other machine and transmit the message automatically.

5 When your machine 'beeps' to tell you the transmission is ended, collect your original document from the output tray.

6 Collect and check the confirmation report.

7 Return original plus confirmation report to the person who asked you to send the fax.

You can compare this procedure with sending a fax *manually* which was described on page 161.

PROCEDURES IN BUSINESS

Today most fax machines have a new facility – they can be programmed to block 'junk faxes'. They can do this by accepting only faxes from specific numbers logged in their memory, or by rejecting faxes from a blocked list of senders. Sometimes this can mean that authentic faxes are blocked, but many fax owners are prepared to take that risk. Why is this – and what are junk faxes?

Junk faxes are sent from unknown and unauthorised senders, by the thousand, to unsuspecting fax owners. They are often sent by people to advertise their products or services. They are not just irritating, they also cost money because they use the receiver's paper and ink and tie up the fax line.

There is another method of dealing with junk faxes, in addition to blocking them on the machine. Fax owners can register their number with the Fax Preference Service (FPS). If, after 28 days, junk faxes are still being received, the FPS will follow up the problem with the company concerned. It can do this through the header which is printed at the top of the junk fax. Sending junk faxes is unlawful, so the FPS can take legal action against the sender.

Routine maintenance operations

Fax machines need to be kept clean and full of paper and the printing mechanism needs replacing when necessary. The manual which is supplied with the fax machine will tell you about all these operations and the best way is to practise doing these whilst someone more experienced watches you.

Cleaning   The most basic maintenance operation is to keep the air vents clear of dust. You should do this with a small brush – never use water!

Paper   You need to check whether your machine uses special paper or plain paper and then find out where this is held in the machine. In most cases it is stored in a small paper tray or cassette which is pulled out to be refilled. Most trays will hold about half a packet (250 sheets) of A4 paper, but some machines hold much more.

Printing   All faxes need ink to print, but the type of mechanism can vary considerably. For this reason, if your faxes are only faint or a warning message is showing on the display panel, inform your supervisor.

What can go wrong?

Most fax messages are sent without any problem, but not always. If something goes wrong, the secret is not to panic! The table below shows the main reasons why you might have a problem – and what to do.

Solving fax problems

Problem	Action to take
You key in the wrong number by mistake.	Press the cancel key and start again.
Your fax cannot connect because receiver's fax is engaged.	Wait. Your fax machine will attempt the number again automatically in a few moments. If you continue to have problems, notify the person who gave you the fax to warn them there is a delay transmitting the message.
Your original document starts to crumple as it enters the machine because it was crooked.	Press Stop on the machine (you may have to do this more than once) to stop the transmission. Then lift the cover to retrieve your document. Do *not* try to tug on the document to get it back again.
The confirmation report shows a strange message or code.	It is likely the fax did not transmit successfully. Notify your supervisor and be prepared to resend the message.
The phone rings when you are sending a fax.	This simply means someone at the other end wants to talk to you! Neither of you can talk to each other during transmission, so pick up the receiver and wait for someone speak to you.
Your machine signals it is out of paper.	Ask for assistance unless you have already been shown how to replenish paper in the fax. It is important that the correct paper is used and that it is put into the machine properly.

1 Test your knowledge of fax machines and fax messages by answering each of the following questions True or False.

a) The air vents on a fax machine should never be covered.

b) There is nothing you can do if you keep getting junk faxes.

c) You should clean a fax machine with a wet cloth.

d) You know you are through to a fax machine if you hear a high-pitched screech at the other end.

e) You can speak to the person at the other end only after the transmission has ended.

f) A confirmation report is issued by the machine only if the transmission is successful.

g) A cover sheet is always sent automatically.

h) All fax machines have a handbook which tells you what to do.

i) You can look up an unknown fax number in the *Phone Book*.

j) Staples and paper-clips must be removed from a multi-page message before it is faxed.

2 Write a short procedure for someone using your fax machine and who wants to send a one page fax message manually.

3 Explain what you would do in each of the following situations.

a) You have tried for half an hour to send an urgent fax message but the line is engaged and you cannot get through.

b) The phone rings insistently when you are transmitting a fax.

c) You have been asked to fax a copy of a student's examination certificate to another college. You are worried it may get damaged in the machine.

d) You see a code you don't understand on the confirmation report.

Processing incoming and outgoing post

All organisations have procedures for dealing with incoming and outgoing post. Although these may vary a little from one organisation to another, once you have learned what to do it is usually very easy to adapt your skills if you work somewhere else.

In a very large organisation which receives and dispatches several sacks of mail each day, processing the post is a skilled job and is undertaken by specialist mailroom staff. You will learn more about this if you continue your studies to Level 2.

However, even the smallest organisation receives and dispatches post each day. In addition, in many large organisations, departmental staff must process the post for their own department and there will be procedures in place to help them do this.

Procedures for handling incoming letters

All incoming post must always be treated as urgent because it may contain important information. For that reason, the post is opened and distributed as rapidly as possible. This job is often done twice a day – after the morning delivery of mail and again, in the afternoon, after the lunchtime delivery.

Maria has started working in a local solicitor's office and she has been asked to help with the incoming mail. She has been given the following procedures to help her.

Procedure for dealing with incoming letters

1 Collect mail
2 Open all mail using letter-opener *except* items marked 'Confidential' or 'Personal'
3 Date stamp all mail
4 Check any enclosures are firmly attached
5 Sort mail into recipients
6 Put any items marked 'Urgent' on the top
7 Distribute mail to recipients
8 Retain opened envelopes for 24 hours

It is worth looking at each of these steps in more detail.

1 Collect mail   In many offices the mail is delivered to a central point and then has to be collected by the person responsible for dealing with it.

2 Open mail   Maria should open all the envelopes but *not* if they are marked as 'Confidential', 'Private' or 'Personal'. In this case she must pass the envelope to the recipient unopened. For all other mail Maria must use a letter-opening machine to open the envelopes. You can read about equipment like this below.

3 Date stamp all mail   This is done in all offices to identify the date when the letter was received. It is important in case there is a query about a letter. It may have been written several days before posting – or have been delayed in the post. The difference between the date on the document and the date of delivery would highlight this.

4 Attach enclosures firmly   Many envelopes contain several documents. Some may be valuable, such as a cheque. It is very easy for documents to become separated from each other so they must always be clipped or stapled together.

5 Sort mail into recipients   Letters are usually addressed to an individual. In Maria's case, each solicitor in the practice will receive mail. Maria has to put all the letters for each solicitor together, in a batch. To help her, in most mailrooms, there are labelled trays or baskets for each person. Maria simply puts the letters for each person in the correct basket.

6 Urgent items on top   It is normal to put any documents marked 'Urgent' at the top of each batch, so that these are the first ones to be seen and dealt with.

7 Distribute mail   Maria must now take the mail around the office and deliver it to the different solicitors. Remember that this must be done promptly. Many solicitors in the practice may be waiting for urgent documents that morning.

8 Retain opened envelopes   This is a safety precaution. It is done in case anyone queries the contents of an envelope, which would happen if an enclosure is missing. After 24 hours the envelopes will be thrown away.

Incoming mail equipment

Maria's working area is arranged so that she can deal efficiently with the mail. She has

▶ a clear working area on which she can stack and open the envelopes

▶ an electric letter-opener. This takes a tiny slice from the top of each envelope that passes through it. This minimises the danger of damaging the contents

- a container in which she places the empty envelopes for 24 hours
- a date stamp
- trays and baskets labelled with the names of different individuals.

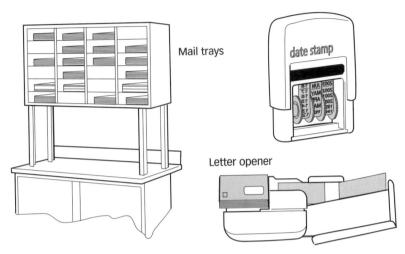

Mail trays

date stamp

Letter opener

▲ Useful equipment for dealing with mail

Procedures for handling incoming parcels

Parcels can be delivered throughout the day to an organisation. Some may be small packages and others could be quite large. A few may be urgent. For this reason, there must be a procedure for dealing with these.

- In many organisations, parcels are delivered to the recipient *unopened*. This is so there is less danger of any of the contents being lost or mislaid between delivery and receipt by an individual.
- Parcels which are labelled 'Confidential' or 'Personal' are *never* opened.
- If you receive a very heavy parcel, don't attempt to lift and deliver it on your own. You will need help.
- If you are instructed to open a parcel, then you will often be asked to check the contents against a delivery note. Do this carefully and methodically, ticking every item as you go.
- If you are asked to sign for a parcel which is being delivered then remember that you are now responsible for making sure it reaches the recipient! You will be asked to sign only if:
  - the parcel is important or urgent
  - the parcel contains a delivery of ordered items. In this case, you cannot keep the delivery person waiting whilst you check it, so you should make a note on the document you sign that you have received the item but haven't yet checked it.

Dealing with problems

There may be procedures to guide you if you encounter a problem but on other occasions you will be expected to use your common sense.

Problems can be caused because of errors by the sender, the Royal Mail or because of staff absences. If someone is away from the office for a few hours then it is usual to deliver the mail as normal. If someone will be in hospital for the next month the situation is very different!

You can see how to solve most of the problems you may encounter by going through the table below.

Solving incoming mail problems

Problem	Action
No name on envelope or name unreadable	Read the contents to see if these give you a guide. For example, you may know who deals with all job applications or all invoices. If not, ask a colleague for guidance. *Never* guess who to give it to!
Item delivered to wrong organisation or address	These should be marked 'delivered in error' or 'not known at this address' and reposted. This costs nothing.
Damaged or torn document	Repair this with sticky tape and attach a Post-It note saying that it was torn on delivery.
Recipient absent from the office	If you know a recipient is on holiday for two weeks – or ill – then it is no use putting mail on the desk. Ask your supervisor who should receive this person's mail until he or she returns.

Carelessness causes further problems. It is very easy to lose concentration and put a letter in the wrong basket – or to pick up a batch of mail for different people without clearly differentiating the start and finish of each individual pile. In this case, you will put letters for one person on another person's desk.

Although members of staff will quickly realise that some items are for someone else, this does not mean that they will send them on immediately. On a busy day, they may simply put these items in their out-tray for re-delivery – which will cause a day's delay. It can be even worse if the person who has received the item by mistake is away for a day or two. The document then simply sits in their in-tray or on their desk – whilst the real recipient still anxiously awaits its arrival.

There are two ways to prevent this.

1 If you deliver post to several people in one journey, so are carrying batches for different individuals, 'offset' these in your hand, so you can clearly see where each pile starts and ends.

2 Double-check, as you distribute mail, to make sure that all the items are for that particular person.

▲ Offset mail for delivery

1 As a group, find out how the mail is collected and distributed by the staff who work in your college office by talking to one of the administrators. Then write a simple set of procedures that you would follow if you were working there.

2 Explain what you would do in each of the following situations. Then compare your ideas with other members of your group.

a) You open an envelope containing a job application form. It is addressed to Mr Patel. There are two Mr Patels in the firm – Hussein Patel works in Purchasing and Sajid Patel works in Personnel.

b) You open an envelope which contains a remittance advice slip. This states a cheque is enclosed for £350 but there is no cheque in the envelope.

c) You distributed the mail an hour ago when you receive a telephone call from one of the managers. She says that she was expecting an urgent letter this morning and saw an envelope from this firm lying on your desk at 8.30 am, ready to be opened. It was addressed to her but there is nothing from this firm in her pile of mail.

d) One morning, as you deliver mail to a manager, you notice that the last two days of mail is lying on her desk untouched.

3 In Maria's firm, she is told that she must date stamp only letters, invoices and other general documents that arrive. She must *not* date stamp any legal documents. The date must always be positioned so that it doesn't obscure any text on a document.

As a group, write a simple set of procedures for anyone who is doing this job.

Procedures for processing outgoing mail

All day long, in all organisations, documents are being prepared which must be dispatched by post that night. They must be processed by the time the post is collected or by the deadline for taking it to the nearest post office.

Maria has been given the job of preparing the outgoing mail. The procedure she must follow when she is dealing with standard documents is shown below.

Procedure for processing outgoing post

1 Check enclosures
2 Insert mail into appropriate size of envelope
3 Address envelope, if required
4 Seal mail
5 Weigh mail
6 Frank mail
7 Dispatch franked mail in special pack.

A further explanation of each step is given below.

1 Check enclosures Many envelopes must contain several items. For example, a letter may have more than one page or may have a brochure attached. Alternatively, brochures and leaflets may be dispatched with a compliment slip attached. It is important that all the correct items are placed in the envelope together.

2 Insert mail Brochures or catalogues should never be folded so the envelope chosen for these items must be large enough. Letters are normally folded three times and inserted in a DL size envelope – but a multi-page document may need a larger size. You can check envelope sizes and how to fold documents properly by looking back to page 105.

3 Address envelope This may not always be required. Sometimes a label will have been produced with a letter or the envelope itself will have been typed. Alternatively, window envelopes may be used, where the address shows through a transparent covering. Sometimes you may need to write a label for a large envelope or for a parcel. In this case make sure you use a water-resistant pen (such as a biro) and write very clearly. Then follow all the rules in the table opposite.

4 Seal envelope Today most envelopes are self-seal. Always check a window envelope, before you seal it, to check that every line of the address is showing clearly. If you are sealing a much larger envelope, such as a jiffy bag, then it is better to fold over the flap first, then staple it together. Finally cover the staples on both sides with packaging tape. This is stronger and wider than sellotape. *Never* lick an envelope. This is unhygienic and you are also in grave danger of cutting your tongue! (For sealing parcels, see page 204.)

5 Weigh mail The weight of an item affects the cost of posting it. You can send only items under 60 grams for the price of a standard first or second class stamp. You might want to remember this yourself! If you are sending some useful information to a friend in a 10-page print out, and just put an ordinary stamp on it, your friend will have to pay the postage owing plus a surcharge – which is currently 80p! For this reason, most items of mail are weighed on special postage scales (see page 205).

6 Frank mail Most organisations prefer to frank outgoing mail rather than use stamps. They do this by putting all the envelopes through a franking machine which prints the postage on each one. Franking machines are explained in more detail on page 205.

7 Dispatch mail Franked mail cannot be put in an ordinary post box like stamped mail. Instead it is usually put in a special pack and handed over the counter at the post office. Larger organisations can arrange to have their mail collected by Royal Mail.

▲ Franked mail can only go in specially marked post boxes

Addressing an envelope

Rules to follow

- Start writing on the envelope halfway down and one-third of the way across, so that the address will be in a central position

- Start each line vertically under the previous line.

- The first line should be the name and title of the addressee (e.g. Mr J Brown).

- If you are writing to a business person, write the job title on the next line (e.g. Sales Manager) and then, below this, the name of the organisation.

- Start a new line for each line of the address

- Always write the name of the town in CAPITALS

- *Never* use abbreviations, such as Rd for Road or St for Street. However, there are some allowable abbreviations for long county names, e.g. Glos for Gloucestershire.

- The postcode must be the last item and preferably written on a separate line. It must not contain *any* punctuation or be underlined.

- If you are addressing an envelope to go abroad, put *both* the city (or town) *and* the country name in capitals. Don't be surprised if the address is in a strange order – in some countries the town is shown before the street or the number of the house after the street name.

- Write any special mailing instructions in capitals at the top left, e.g. airmail or urgent.

- If the item must be marked PERSONAL (or Private and Confidential) then this is written two lines *above* the name line.

- If you are sending a package or parcel you must put the sender's name (i.e. your organisation) and address on the reverse side.

Procedures for preparing and dispatching parcels

To do this task properly you need:

▶ a clear space to work on

▶ the correct packaging materials to protect the item

▶ appropriate containers, such as a jiffy bag or box

▶ sellotape, packaging tape and appropriate sticky labels.

A wide range of packaging materials and containers are available. Jiffy bags are excellent for items which will fit in an envelope and need padded protection, such as a floppy disk or a very large document. They are available in a wide range of sizes, from very small to very large. Cardboard-backed envelopes are available for items such as certificates and photographs. These are clearly marked 'Do not bend' on the front.

However, you cannot use a jiffy bag or a cardboard-backed envelope to send very large or fragile items through the post. In this case you should use packaging material such as bubble wrap or polystyrene shapes. Some organisations use the paper waste from the office shredder as a cheap alternative.

The first step is to protect the item being posted. If you are using bubble wrap you can wrap it around the item and sellotape it.

Next put the item in its container – usually a box – and fill any spare spaces with polystyrene shapes or paper waste from the shredder. Alternatively, you can tear up old newspaper into long strips. The aim is to fill all the space so that the item cannot bump about inside.

▲ Bubble wrap can help to protect fragile items

Fasten the box and seal it, using strong, wide packaging tape. You can start off with sellotape, if you find this easier, but do cover it with packaging tape. Check that all joints, corners and other vulnerable points are protected – you can put packaging tape over these, too, if you want.

Finally, write *two* address labels. The first is to the recipient. Stick this on the box. Then write another address label headed *Sender* with the name and address of the person sending the parcel. Stick this on the side of the box.

If the item is fragile you might want to finish the parcel by putting a 'fragile' sticker on the top and sides and labelling the box 'this way up' with an arrow.

The parcel is then ready for weighing on special parcel scales. You can read about these – and how to frank parcels – on the next page.

PROCEDURES IN BUSINESS

All business organisations have procedures so that outgoing mail will be processed in time for it to be dispatched the same day. In the same way, the Royal Mail has procedures for processing all the post it receives to meet its targets for delivery. It aims to deliver 92 per cent of first class mail the next day. As it deals with an average of 82 million letters a day, this is no easy matter. Sometimes items of post are delivered late, sometimes they are delivered to the wrong address by mistake. Sometimes the fault is due to the Royal Mail, at other times it is because the address isn't correct.

Poorly addressed mail is currently costing the Royal Mail £10 million a year. This money is needed to pay for the Return Letter Centre in Belfast where 300 staff are employed. In 2001, they coped with 72 million misaddressed items of mail and even managed to find the correct recipient for a letter addressed to 'H, daughter of the new bishop, somewhere in the Midlands beginning with B.' Other recipients weren't so lucky. If the recipient can't be located, the item is returned to the sender. This is possible only if the sender's name is included somewhere on or in the package. Otherwise, most items are destroyed after three months.

Outgoing mail equipment

Several items of equipment can be used to prepare mail for dispatch. The range and type available will depend upon the quantity of post handled each day. Maria's firm of solicitors will not have the same range of equipment that you would find in a large bank or mail order company, for obvious reasons.

The items you are most likely to see are the following.

Postage scales Most mailrooms today have electronic scales which automatically calculate the correct postage charge. You simply put the item centrally on the scales and the correct charge is shown on the display. If you are weighing a special item or something to be sent abroad, then there are keys on the scales which you press to denote this – and the charge is adjusted accordingly.

Electronic scales will normally take only envelopes or small packets. Large parcels need to be weighed on larger scales which just give the weight – not the charge. You then have to read off the charge on a postage rate chart. Until you are used to doing this, it is sensible to ask a more experienced colleague to check that you have read the chart correctly.

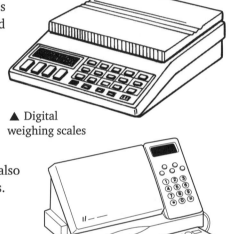

▲ Digital weighing scales

Franking machines Franking machines put a printed impression on each envelope. They also print labels for sticking onto parcels and packages. They can process a large number of envelopes or labels very quickly and the printed impression can also include an advert, logo or slogan as well as a return address for undelivered mail.

The type and size of machine can vary considerably but the basic procedure is the same.

▲ A franking machine and franked label

1 Check all the envelopes are the right way up and facing in the right direction. (Otherwise some will be franked on the bottom or on the wrong side!)

2 With some franking machines, if you are franking different sizes of envelopes, all the small ones must be at the top.

3 Check that the postage is set correctly for first or second class post.

4 Check that the date is correct (this changes automatically on most machines).

5 Press the Start key.

6 Collect the franked envelopes from the receiving tray.

If you want to frank a label to fix on a parcel or very bulky envelope, then you would normally set this option on the machine before you start. The label is printed on special tape which is held inside the machine.

Most organisations routinely send all items by second class post, because this is cheaper. Any items which are to go by first class post must be specially marked by the sender, using a marker stamp which identifies this category of post.

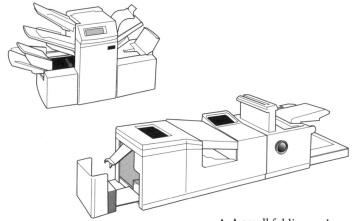

Folding and inserting machines These machines automatically put a number of enclosures into an envelope. They operate much like a collator. The separate items are each put on a paper tray and the envelopes are stacked at the other side. The machines feed the items towards the envelope, fold them, insert them and seal the envelopes automatically. These machines are invaluable in any organisation which regularly sends out mailshots to its customers.

▲ A small folding and inserting machine

Miscellaneous equipment This can include marker stamps, to indicate whether an item should be treated as 'urgent' or 'fragile' or sent by 'first class' or 'second class' post; scissors, string holders and trolleys for moving around large batches of post.

▲ A mail trolley can carry up to 60 kg of mail

OVER TO YOU!

1 Read the instructions for wrapping a parcel on page 204. Then convert these to a set of simple procedures which could be given to someone who is wrapping and dispatching a fragile parcel for the first time.

2 a) Write three envelopes, one for each of the following addressees. Ask your tutor to check them for neatness and accuracy.
   i. Mr K Holland, 16 Denbigh Drive, Chelmsford CM2 6FB
   ii. Mrs P O'Donoghue, Sales Manager, Juniper & Cox Ltd, Watling Street, Nuneaton, Warwickshire CV10 8DM
   iii. Mr P Platt, 15 Cedar Drive, Newmarket, Ontario, L3Y 6Y4, Canada

   b) See if you can find all the mistakes Maria made when she typed an envelope. You should be able to find at least 10.

   > To:
   > John Kelly, Distribution manager
   > Simpson Supplies
   > Cross St
   > PUDSEY
   > Leeds
   > LS28 4ky.

3 Try to visit the mailroom at your college and identify the equipment that is used. In particular, check the difference between the scales used to weigh envelopes and those used to weigh parcels. Then see how the charge is calculated on the postage chart. Finally, watch the franking machine being used to produce both envelopes *and* labels for parcels.

▼ Reviewing the experience of following procedures

Hopefully you have found the procedures in this unit useful in helping you to carry out many of the practical activities you have undertaken. That's what procedures are all about. They are written by people who are experienced with an activity, to help anyone who isn't. You will find them in all kinds of manuals at home – from how to operate your cooker to how to use the remote control on your television.

There are several benefits to having procedures – which is why they are so popular! However, this doesn't mean that there are never any difficulties.

For the final part of your assessment for this unit, you have to identify two benefits and any difficulties you experienced when you were carrying out your tasks. The following section will help to give you ideas – although you should obviously select only those which actually applied to you.

Benefits of procedures

These can include the following.

▶ They help you to **carry out a new task more quickly** because you don't have to work out for yourself what to do and when to do it.

▶ They enable you to **meet the requirements of your job** properly. This is because you can refer to procedures at any time to remind yourself how to do anything you are asked to do.

▶ They help you to **organise the work** before you start, because you can see what you have to do in advance.

▶ They help you, and other team members, to **work efficiently**.

▶ They enable all team members to do the task **in the same way**.

▶ They enable you to **check your progress** as you go. At each stage you can check that you are following the procedure. This helps you to monitor your progress and the overall quality of your work.

▶ They enable you to **check your own role and responsibilities**. You know which steps you can do yourself and the type of problems you must refer to someone else.

Possible difficulties you may meet

Sometimes you may have no problems at all. Other times life isn't so simple. Even when there are procedures in place, the following types of difficulties can be met.

▶ **The procedure is unclear or difficult to follow**. Many people who buy equipment – from mobile phones to DVD players – struggle to follow some of the instructions in the manual they are given. If the procedure is poorly written then this creates a problem, because you often have to guess what you are supposed to do.

▶ **Other people don't know about the procedure**. If a few people are 'doing their own thing' because they don't know the procedure exists, then this causes difficulties. Filing is an obvious example. If you are following the procedure for filing alphabetically and someone else isn't, then a lost document will affect you all – not just the person who actually filed it.

▶ **The procedure may break down altogether**. This can happen if it is out-of-date, inaccurate or is simply ignored by a large number of people. For example, you may have a procedure to log on to your computer system at college. If the computer system was changed, then the procedure would have to be changed, otherwise it wouldn't work. Similarly, if a new fax machine was installed, the procedures to operate that particular machine could easily be different. That is why, throughout this unit, you have been asked to check the *suggested* procedures included in this book against your own equipment. A procedure also breaks down if everyone ignores it – which they are apt to do if it doesn't work or if they all think there is a better way of doing things. For that reason, all procedures need reviewing regularly to check that they are appropriate, up-to-date and that they really work.

▲ Procedures must be up-to-date and easy to follow

OVER TO YOU!

For each of the following situations, identify 2 benefits and 1 difficulty each person experienced. Then compare your ideas with other members of your group.

1 Maria has been processing the incoming and outgoing mail at her workplace for two weeks now. She rarely looks at the actual procedures any more because she knows them so well. She thinks they are useful because she quickly learned what to do and, when she is on holiday, she knows that whoever stands in for her will deal with the mail in the same way. She has, however, told her manager that the procedures for using the franking machine must be changed before she goes away because they were written for the old machine. The new one can automatically weigh envelopes as well as frank them, so the procedure to follow is now different.

2 Shahida wants the old photocopier in the office next door to be replaced. Because many people use it, she designed clear procedures so everyone could work more efficiently. She arranged for stocks of paper to be constantly available to prevent delays. If a paper jam occurs, everyone knows exactly who to tell so that it can be cleared quickly. All users are also supposed to record the number of copies they take in the photocopier log, but everyone is ignoring this – they argue they haven't time. Shahida cannot check what they do all day so she now wants a machine that logs usage automatically.

3 Jack is fed up. He is responsible for keeping all the customer files in order for his boss. The files are colour coded by country, so that they are easy to follow. This suits Jack because he likes to be well organised. He can also check quickly that all the files are in the right sections. What annoys him is that people keep borrowing files when he is away from his desk. Last week he fell out with a colleague who said he didn't know that there was a procedure for booking out files. Jack wants his team leader to run a training session so that all his colleagues know what to do if they need to borrow a customer file.

Message Form ☐ URGENT ☐ NON-URGENT

TO: _____ DEPT: _____

DATE: _____ TIME: _____

CALLER'S NAME _____

ORGANISATION _____

TEL No: _____ EXT No: _____

☐ Telephoned   ☐ Please return call

☐ Returned your call ☐ Please arrange appointment

☐ Called to see you   ☐ Left a message

Message:

_____
_____
_____
_____
_____
_____
_____
_____
_____
_____
_____
_____
_____
_____
_____
_____
_____
_____
_____
_____
_____
_____

Taken by: _____

FAX MESSAGE SHEET

TO: _____

FAX No: _____

FOR THE ATTENTION OF: _____

FROM: _____

DATE: _____

SUBJECT: _____

No OF PAGES (including this page): _____

**Freeman
Electronics**

Middleway Industrial Park
REDBRIDGE
Berks
RD3 9PS

Tel: +44 118-390289
Fax: +44 118-398200
email: admin@freemanelec.com

Message:

Signature of sender: _____

Royton Estate Agency

CUSTOMER ENQUIRY FORM

Name _____

Address _____

_____ Postcode _____

Tel No (home) _____ (work) _____ (mobile) _____

Property to sell: Yes/No*

First time buyer: Yes/No*

Maximum price: £ _____

Area/location (please specify) _____

_____

_____

_____

_____

_____

_____

_____

_____

_____

_____

Type of property: Detached: Yes/No*   Semi-detached: Yes/No*   Terrace: Yes/No*   Bungalow: Yes/No*

Other requirements (please specify) _____

_____

_____

_____

_____

_____

_____

_____

_____

_____

_____

_____

_____

_____

Staff name logging enquiry (please print) _____

Staff signature _____ Date _____

* delete as necessary

Kenmere Recruitment Ltd

CLIENT REGISTRATION FORM

Title (Mr/Mrs/Ms/Miss) _____ First name _____

Surname _____ Email address _____

Address _____

_____ Postcode _____

Tel no (home) _____ (mobile) _____

Job status: Employed*/Currently out of work*

If employed, state current job title _____

Salary _____ Length of experience (years) _____

Brief description of current responsibilities _____

_____

_____

_____

_____

_____

_____

_____

Job search status: Actively looking*/Open to offers*

Current qualifications: _____

_____

_____

_____

Job type required: Permanent*/Temporary*

Any other relevant information: _____

_____

_____

_____

_____

Client signature: _____ Date: _____

FOR OFFICIAL USE ONLY

Qualifications checked by: _____ Date: _____

Client ref no: _____ Logged on system: _____

* delete as necessary

Marshalls Plastics Ltd

ACCIDENT REPORT FORM

This form must be completed in all cases of accident or injury to an employee and passed to the Safety Officer immediately.

Name of person who was injured _____

Date of birth _____ Job title _____

Date of accident _____ Time of accident _____

Place where the accident occurred _____
_____
_____

Activity being undertaken at the time the accident occurred _____
_____
_____

Describe how the injury occurred _____
_____
_____
_____
_____
_____

Details of injury _____
_____
_____
_____
_____
_____

Was first-aid treatment given: Yes/No*

Was injured person taken to hospital: Yes/No*

If yes, please state name of hospital _____

Please state name and job title of any witnesses to the accident:
_____
_____
_____
_____

Signature of person reporting accident: _____ Date _____

* Please delete as appropriate

Index

A

ACAS 150
Accident report forms 110, 212
Accident reporting 143
Activity checklist (and teams) 43, 44
Address labels 107
Address, styles of 56, 68, 69
Administration activities in business 92–131
– and equipment 94–104
Allocated tasks (carrying out) 45
Alphabetical filing 166–168
Answering machines 15
Apostrophe 19, 20
Appointment cards 107
Appraisals 131
Assisting team members 51

B

Body language 75
Bullying 61
Business cards 107
Business documents (preparing) 1
Business letters
– key facts 22
– understanding 21
– writing 24
Business organisations 82–91
– activities of 89
– administration activities in 92, 93
– departmental functions and activities 90
– describing 82
– documents used in 106–111
– equipment used by administrators 94–104
– in the private sector 82–85
– in the public sector 87, 88
– objectives of 85, 86
– roles and responsibilities in 89
– working in 85, 88

C

Calculators 101
Capital letters 6, 7
Card indexes 170
Career discussions 131
Cash and credit transactions 109
Cash books 110

Checklist
– for team work 44
– for other work 115
Client registration form 211
Collating 185
Comma 25, 26
Communication
– and customers 64, 68, 70, 71, 73, 74
– and teams 50, 52, 54, 56
Communication methods 55
Computers, printers and software 98, 99
Confidentiality
– and customers 71
– and filing 172
– and teams 47
Conflict (and teams) 59
Contract of employment 147
Contractual employment rights 148
Cooperation (and teams) 49
Copyright 181
Customer enquiry form 210
Customers
– and asking questions 75
– and body language 75
– and confidentiality 72
– and personal presentation 66
– and presenting positive image 64, 66
– clarity of information to 71, 75
– communications with 70
– effective communications 73
– effective customer service 65
– greeting and addressing 68, 69
– information (obtaining or providing) 75
– internal and external 64, 65
– organisational image 68
– problems (coping with) 77
– prompt service 69
– understanding each other 74

D

Deadlines – importance of 119, 120
Delivery note 108
Departmental functions and activities 90
Disability Discrimination Act 147
Disciplinary procedures 153
Discrimination 61, 147
Display Screen Equipment Regulations 137
Dress codes 67

Duplexing *see* Photocopying, back-to-back
    copying

E

Emails 106
– key facts 2
– preparing 3
– understanding 2
Emergency procedures 145
Employment Tribunal 149, 150
English – using English correctly 6, 10, 14, 19,
    25, 31
Envelopes 104, 105, 203
Equal Opportunities Policies 147

F

Fax cover (or message) sheet 17, 106, 193, 209
Fax machines 95
– features of 191, 192
– maintenance operations 195
Fax messages
– key facts 17
– preparing 18
– understanding 17
Faxes
– and problems 196
– preparations before sending 193
– procedures 161, 194
– sending 191
Feedback (on your work) 127
Filing 164–176
– and confidentiality 172
– by date 171
– by name 166, 167
– by number 170
– by place 168
– by topic or subject 167
– classification systems 166–171
– indexes 170
– maintaining safe systems 175
– preparing documents for 173
– procedures 158
– retrieving documents 175
– using a filing system 164, 173
Filing equipment 100, 101
Finding and extracting information 32
Fire procedures 144
First aid 144
Flexibility 53
Flip charts 103
Folding and inserting machines 206
Following routine office procedures 155
Forms

– completing 29
– key facts 29
– understanding 29
Franking machines 100, 205

G

Government departments 87
Grievance procedures 61, 149, 150
Guillotines 101

H

Harassment 61
Health and safety 132–145
– accident procedures and first aid 144
– and filing 175
– and photocopying 189
– and teamwork 46
– and the law 136, 137
– Display Screen Equipment Regulations 137
– emergency procedures 145
– fire procedures 144
– hazards in an office 133–135
– Health and Safety at Work Act 136
– low-risk matters 141
– repetitive strain injury 138
– reporting procedures, accidents and hazards
    143
– risks and precautions 139, 140
– safe working practices 140
Hole punches 102

I

Identifying and describing procedures 156
Improving your work (ways of) 127, 128
Indexes (filing) 170
Information to customers 71
Instructions
– and using photocopiers 182, 183
– for tasks 46
– understanding 114
Interruptions (coping with) 118
Invoice 109

J

Junk faxes 195

L

Language and tone
– and team communications 56
– with customers 70

Leaflets 106
Learning plan 128, 129
Legal responsibilities of an employee 151–153
Legal rights of an employee 146–148
Letterheaded paper 23, 106
Letters *see* Business letters
Limited liability 84
Listening skills 73
Local authorities 87

M

Mail *see* Post
Mail documents 106
Memos
– key facts 8
– preparing 9
– understanding 8
Messages
– blank form 209
– key facts 13
– preparing 13
– understanding 12

O

Objectives of businesses 85
Office documents 106
Office hazards 133–135
Order or purchase orders 108
Organisational skills (and improving work) 112–131
Organising own materials and equipment 122
Overhead projectors 103

P

Paper and envelopes 104, 105, 203
Paper-based filing *see* Filing
Paragraphs 10
Partnerships 83
Payslips 110
Personal presentation 66
Petty cash 109
Photocopiers 94
Photocopying 177–190
– and copyright 181
– and minimising waste 188
– and safety 189
– back-to-back copying 185
– collating and fastening 185, 186
– following instructions 182, 183
– logging use of 181
– multi-page originals 184
– photocopier facilities 177

– procedures 160
– refilling paper 182
– reporting problems 187
– single originals 184
– standards 179, 180
– tasks 177
Positive image – to customers 64, 66
Post
– addressing an envelope 203
– dealing with problems 199, 200
– incoming and outgoing 197–206
– incoming letters 197, 198
– incoming mail equipment 198
– incoming procedures 199
– outgoing mail equipment 205
– preparing and dispatching parcels 203
– processing outgoing mail 201, 202
Postage scales 205
Preparing for work in business organisations 81
Prioritising – and teamwork 53
Private limited companies 84
Private sector organisations 82
Problems with customers 74, 77
Procedures
– benefits of 207
– difficulties with 207, 208
– following routine office procedures 155, 163
– for fire, accidents and emergencies 144
– for handling incoming letters 197
– for handling incoming parcels 199
– for paper-based filing 158, 164–176
– for photocopying 160, 177–190
– for preparing and dispatching parcels 203
– for processing outgoing mail 201, 202
– for processing the post 162, 197–206
– for reporting grievances 61
– for reporting team conflicts 59
– for routine office activities 157
– for sending faxes 161, 191–197
– identifying and describing 156
– reviewing the experience of 207
– steps in 157
Processing the post (procedures for) 162
Pronouns 14
Public corporations 87
Public limited companies 84
Purchase and sales documents 108

R

Race Relations Act 147
Receipts 110
Redundancy 149
Reporting accidents and hazards 143

Requisitions 108
Reviewing own contribution to team 62
Reviewing team activities 62
Reviewing the experience of following
    procedures 207, 208
Reviewing work with a manager 130, 131
Rights and responsibilities at work 132–154
– problems if these are not met 149, 151
Risks and precautions at work 139, 141
Roles and responsibilities in business 89
Rotary files 170
Rotary trimmers 101, 102

S

Safety *see* Health and Safety
Service to customers 65, 69
Sex Discrimination Act 147
Software 98
Sole traders 83
Spellcheckers 6
Staplers and stapling 102, 186
Statement 109
Statutory employment rights 146
Switchboard 96

T

Teams and teamwork 40
– asking for help 49
– assisting other members 51
– carrying out allocated tasks 45
– communicating information 50, 54
– communication methods 55
– communication styles 56
– conflict, reporting procedures 59
– instructions for tasks 46
– prioritising 53
– qualities of team members 58, 59

– reporting back 49
– responsibilities to your team 43
– reviewing own contribution 62
– reviewing team activities 62
– safety issues 46
– security and confidentiality issues 47
– sharing information 52
– sharing resources 52
– working relationships 58
– working with others 49
Telephones 96, 97
Tidy and efficient working 121, 123, 125
Time
– coping with interruptions 118
– using it efficiently 117
Tone of communications
– in teams 56
– with customers 70
Training opportunities 129

U

Unlimited liability 83

V

Voicemail 15

W

Waste (minimising) 123, 124, 188
Working arrangements (and teams) 43
Working efficiently 125
Working in the private sector 85
Working with others to complete tasks 49
Working relationships (maintaining) 58
Working safely 46, 140
Working tidily and efficiently 121, 123
Working Time Regulations 149